# SANDY

### IN MY OWN WORDS

# KELLY

# SANDY
## IN MY OWN WORDS
# KELLY

THE O'BRIEN PRESS
DUBLIN

For my grandson, Frank Juhan: I hope that my story stays with you always and that one day you will share it with your own family and remember me and our family. I love you, Frank. Thank you for shining a bright light on my every day.

First published 2023 by
The O'Brien Press Ltd,
12 Terenure Road East, Rathgar,
Dublin 6, D06 HD27, Ireland.
Tel: +353 1 4923333; Fax: +353 1 4922777
E-mail: books@obrien.ie
Website: obrien.ie
The O'Brien Press is a member of Publishing Ireland.

ISBN: 978-1-78849-436-6

Editing, design and layout © The O'Brien Press 2023
Cover and text design by Emma Byrne
Front cover photograph © Colin Gillen
Back cover quotations from Johnny Cash and Willie Nelson are from *Kelly's Heroes* sleeve notes (1994)

8 7 6 5 4 3 2 1
27 26 25 24 23

Printed in the UK by Clays Ltd, St Ives plc.
The paper in this book is produced using pulp from managed forests.

Published in

# Contents

# FOREWORD

I've had the privilege of knowing Sandy Kelly since 1982. At the time, a musician and songwriter I rate highly, Dick Keating, asked me if my record company, Crashed Records, would work with a group called The Duskeys to record and release a song written by Sally Keating, his wife. The song was 'Here Today, Gone Tomorrow'. I'm eternally grateful to Dick for making that suggestion. We entered the song in the Irish National Song Contest, which was held on 14 March 1982, and it won: the Duskeys – Sandy, her sister, Barbara, and cousins would be going to Harrogate to represent Ireland in the Eurovision Song Contest. I've been a big fan of Eurovision since the early days of the contest and was more than happy to lend a hand and put the mighty promotions department at Crashed Records to work promoting the Duskeys.

The first step was the famous RTÉ Eurovision song promotion video, which is sent to all Eurovision TV stations to promote the country's national song. Producer/director Ian McGarry was in charge and the location for filming was Dublin Zoo, but I'll let Sandy tell you all about that.

Next we had to record the album. We booked the Lombard Studios on Lombard Street in Dublin, which later became Westland Studios, and also booked the legendary engineer Fred Meijer. Then the hard work began. I remember sitting in the control room while Sandy laid down her vocal on one of her solos – 'Our Love is Slippin' Away' – and thinking to myself, 'That voice is superb.' As The Duskeys were booked out for performances all around Ireland following their success at the National Song Contest, we were in a hurry to get enough recordings done to complete an album to take to Harrogate in time for Eurovision. As a result, a lot of the recordings were completed through the night.

The Eurovision Song Contest took place, hosted by the BBC, on 24 April 1982. It was a splendid event full of glitter and glitz, although we were all worried because Sandy's baby Barbara was ill. Sandy spent a lot of time on the telephone (no mobiles in those days) to the hospital. It was very difficult for Sandy but, ever the professional, she delivered a tremendous performance with The Duskeys. However, it was not to be their year: 'Here Today, Gone Tomorrow' came eleventh when the final votes were counted. The winner, representing Germany, was Nicole, singing the Ralf Siegel and Bernd Meinunger song 'Ein Bißchen Frieden (A Little Peace)', which became a runaway success.

We worked with The Duskeys on a number of singles as they performed around Ireland, the UK and Europe, then Sandy went solo and took on a new manager. Although we were no longer working together, I always admired her work and loved that voice.

A few years later, in 1988, I went to work for K-tel in Ireland and had the opportunity to record some Irish artists. I got in touch with Kieran Cavanagh, a friend and colleague, who was Sandy's manager at the time, and told him I wanted Sandy to record four Patsy Cline songs for me – I'd been a fan of Patsy since Maisie McDaniel introduced me to the music of Patsy Cline and Hank Williams as a fourteen-year-old – and I loved Sandy's voice and how she interpreted and performed every song with emotion.

But when I explained my plan, to my horror, she was having none of it. She felt the songs didn't suit her. I had already engaged Frank McNamara, musical director of *The Late Late Show*, to arrange and produce the songs, so this was a big disappointment. After a long meeting with Sandy where she tried to get me to consider other songs, we agreed not to fall out, but she was steadfast: she would not record the Patsy Cline songs. I said I would look for another singer but I didn't have anyone else in mind, as I hadn't expected Sandy to turn down the chance to record these great songs.

About two hours later, I got a knock on the door. It was Sandy. She said she would record the Patsy Cline songs if it was the only way she could get signed. So we went into the studio (Sandy says she was brought in 'screaming and shouting') and recorded 'Crazy', 'Sweet Dreams', 'I Fall to Pieces' and 'Faded Love'. Very late one night I was in the studio while Sandy was doing her vocal on 'Sweet Dreams' and she said from the studio floor, 'I can feel that woman [Patsy] like an angel on my shoulder, while I'm singing this song.'

When we released 'Crazy' the critics loved it. Sandy's voice was exactly right, the public showed their support and the record flew up the charts. Every radio show played the song and Sandy was a media success, becoming the new Patsy Cline! One day, during a break in recording, Sandy and Frank McNamara went into the studio and recorded what I think is the simplest and most emotional version of 'The Wind Beneath My Wings', just Frank on piano and Sandy on vocal.

The following Christmas we released a K-tel TV-advertised album with Sandy's 'I Need To Be In Love'. It was a big hit, with lots of sales and radio plays. After a lifetime on the road and several versions of Sandy Kelly, this new Sandy Kelly was an overnight success!

We went on to record some more great songs in Nashville at Bradley's Barn with producer Harold Bradley, a gentleman and a friend, who played guitar on many great artists' albums, including Johnny Cash, Willie Nelson and the legendary Patsy Cline herself. Sandy recorded duets with Johnny Cash ('Woodcarver'), Glen Campbell ('As We Danced (To the World's Greatest Song)') and Willie Nelson ('Crazy' and 'Everytime You Need a Friend'). 'Everytime You Need a Friend' was written by Ben Peters (a song I brought back from Nashville) and became the theme song for Sandy's television series. Sandy was produced by the same Ian McGarry of Eurovision fame and many great RTÉ television productions, and a very dear friend to myself and Sandy. On one of our trips to Nashville, Ian and Kieran Cavanagh were travelling with us to produce a documentary for RTÉ about Sandy called *The Showman's Daughter*. On the drive into Nashville, our taxi driver was impressed with Sandy, this Irish singer coming to record an album, and he sang us some of his own compositions. Everyone in Nashville is a songwriter or singer! We really enjoyed that moment.

The rest is history: Sandy was the star and presenter of two 13-part TV series with RTÉ. The series welcomed a star-studded list of international artists as Sandy's guests and provided RTÉ with Sunday night prime-time viewing. The show also contained a weekly tribute to Patsy Cline in which Sandy would sing one of Patsy's songs. As the title of her album puts it, *The Voice of Sandy Kelly, the Songs of Patsy Cline* has been the cornerstone of Sandy's wonderfully successful career.

Through all the different directions her career has taken, the drive, positivity and (most of all) the special voice that Sandy possesses have guaranteed her place in the annals of country music worldwide.

Here we are forty years later, best friends and confidants, always available to one another, still recording together and wondering 'How did that happen?' Recently, I was with Sandy recording in Nashville, with her son, Willie, and John Carter Cash producing, and I wanted Sandy to do a particular song. I couldn't get her to record that song either, so the battle continues even now. I know it will happen some day and, who knows, it may be another big hit!

Shay Hennessy
Crashed Records

# INTRODUCTION

Shannon Airport, August 2019. I settle into my seat on board an American Airlines flight to Nashville, the home of country music and the Ryman Auditorium, the mother church of country music. A wave of nostalgia fills my heart as I prepare myself physically and mentally for my return visit to a place that always welcomed me with open arms and helped me realise some of my hopes and dreams over many years. I am returning to Nashville with my son, Willie, to go to Cash Cabin, Johnny Cash's personal recording studio on the Cash estate in Hendersonville, Tennessee, where Johnny made some of those wonderful last recordings. It has been many years since I recorded an album myself, between this and that – I'll be explaining 'this and that' to you in my story. It was Willie who convinced me to go back to Nashville to record and also to document my life's story in a book.

As we leave Ireland, I am full of anxiety and sadness, thinking back on all that has changed since I last made this journey. Weighing heavily on me is the loss of members of my family who joined me previously, especially my sister, Barbara, who travelled with me many times to Nashville. Also, I am very aware that some of the wonderful people I befriended and worked with in Nashville are no longer there. On all previous trips there had been a familiar smiling face in the arrivals hall to meet me: George Hamilton IV, Harold Bradley, Frank Oakley (Willie Nelson's assistant), or someone from the Cash family.

When I get that very rare opportunity to actually sit down for a long period of time, unless I drink a glass of wine or watch a movie, I'm forced to think about things that mostly I'd rather push to the back of my mind. Today, though, I've brought a pen and notebook and I'll try to write it down. For one thing, just to get it out of my head; and for another, my son Willie is sitting right beside me and this is a project he and John Carter Cash planned together. Maybe Willie is right: if I revisit the ghosts of Nashville and make some new music, my heart will be lighter. Losing people that you love so dearly, family or friend, is a pain like no other. I will try, as I have always done, to channel that into the songs. My life has been a roller coaster of events, some great, some bad and some I never wanted to talk about.

It's a strange thing, but maybe it's how everyone is: I've always measured my life and achievements by where it all began and my thoughts frequently bring me back to that little girl who was mischievous, always in trouble, in second-hand clothes and shoes, lovingly cocooned by her family in a travelling show, all singing, dancing, magic and more. When I put my foot on the stage at Eurovision, won the Country Music Gold Star, sang 'Crazy', looked into Johnny Cash's eyes when singing 'Woodcarver', introduced the first guest on my RTÉ TV series *Sandy*, I was still that little girl from my grandfather's show. Johnny Cash once said that I had humility, honestly the biggest compliment he could have given me. I never strove to be in show business or to be a recording artist; that's just the course that was already laid out for me and, in the end, it's the course I followed. It's what I'd been trained to do from the day I was born into Dusky Dan's Variety Show. Although long gone, my travelling-show family are always with me on my musical journey: flashbacks, their enormous sense of humour and fun, and my grandfather's words of advice. I'm never alone on the stage; my heavenly choir are always out there with me, with a warm feeling of support and love.

Over the years as a performer, it almost felt like someone had reached into my cot, lifted me out and placed me centre stage in front of a micro-phone and a spotlight. As weird as that sounds, that's exactly how it felt and that's what I'm still doing – stage, microphone, spotlight, audience. There've been times when I've loved the stage and times when I've resented it. I've loved working with amazingly talented and kind people, the loyal fans who have always supported me, my friends. I've resented the times that I had to leave my home and family, times when I was hurting or had a sick child or a bereavement. But I still put on my happy face and did what I've always done. I don't believe that I have ever gone on stage and brought my personal troubles with me. I've never made excuses, just got on with connecting to my audience. They paid good money, as my granddad Dusky Dan would have said. I can tell you truly, no matter how I've felt stepping onto that stage, I've always felt better when I stepped off. We Duskys are made of tough stock and that's why I'm still here to tell my story.

# 1

# THE SHOWMAN'S
# DAUGHTER

One of my earliest memories is of being cosy and warm, and through the bars of my cot I see my mother and father, Babs and Frank, sound asleep in their bed. If I reach out far enough I can touch them. But then, if I reached out far enough I could touch almost everything, for this was our wagon, small but adequate, homely and built from scratch by my father with his own bare hands. I knew from a very early age that my father could do anything, always my hero. When I think back, I feel very lucky to have had such a wonderful and magical childhood, filled with laughter, colour, excitement, mystery. I surely must have been the luckiest girl in the whole world. If there was ever anything missing in this fairy-tale world of mine, well, then I'd just imagine it. Imagination is one thing

I most definitely possessed in large quantities, sometimes too much.

Dad made sure when building our home that we would be as comfortable as we could possibly be. A small space with a double bed built at the back and running the width of the caravan, it was not very big at all but it did the job and, although basic, to me it was beautiful and served as my play area during the day. My cot was beside Mum and Dad's bed and beside me was a tiny kitchen area, all just one room. My dad knew open plan before anyone. When I say 'kitchen area', I mean a basin and a press. A little Primus stove, much like a camping stove, sat in the middle of the floor and would provide heat and also be used to cook small meals. We used it until we could afford a gas ring, which was a huge luxury. For light, an oil lamp hung from the ceiling and provided a warm glow. Even after all these years, it is a lovely memory for me of happy times.

So here I was, Philomena Bridget Marion Ellis, the newest member of Dusky Dan's Travelling Variety Show, born into a dynasty of musicians, singers, actors, magicians, Ireland's Hollywood stars of the day. Rolling into your town or village to present to you a beautiful and colourful programme for at least the next seven nights and longer, if you wanted. To alert people to this wondrous attraction, my dad and I would visit a week in advance, with posters and paste in hand, to advertise our imminent arrival. Dad would put up the posters anywhere he could and would ask shopkeepers to display them in their windows in return for complimentary tickets to the show. As my grandfather Dusky Dan had been returning to these places year after year, our family had made many friends along the way and people always welcomed the show back.

My days were packed with fun things to do. Dad usually made breakfast, such as it was, the extent of that meal depending largely on how much money had been taken on the door the night before by my grandfather, which he then distributed amongst the family. At that time, the Dusky family show consisted of my parents and me, Dad's brothers Pat (the youngest) and Jack (who was married to May), Dad's sister Lizzie (who was married to Simon) plus my grandparents, Dan and Maggie. I had several other uncles and aunts but they weren't 'on the show' at that time. After breakfast I would go on my travels from caravan to caravan, wanting to know what was going on everywhere. Wagon doors wide open, the women would be busy hanging out washing and doing other chores. The men always seemed to be busy repairing something, with their head under a bonnet or legs sticking out from under a truck, repairing stage curtains or backdrops with a large needle in hand – there was always something torn or broken. One of my favourite chores was helping Dad paint scenes on backdrops for the plays and sketches, huge canvases with an array of colours and scenes. Creating even one scene took quite some time. For the play *The Wild Colonial Boy*, the scene was an Australian bush landscape. Dad would draw and paint the main part and it was my job to paint in the big spaces. That could be desert sand, the sky, the sea and so on. We would spend hours on it, with Dad telling stories and funny jokes all the while. It was never very funny, though, when I'd get back to our wagon to Mum, covered in paint, and she'd have the task of cleaning me up in readiness for the show. That's right: I was also part of the programme. Quite a big part, in fact. At three years of age, I was singing, tap-dancing, taking part in plays and also assisting Uncle Jack with his magic tricks. If you'd asked me back then, I'd have convinced you that I was the star attraction. In fact, my grandmother Maggie O'Dea was the real star of the show, with her stunning voice, delivering the most heartfelt ballads. 'Teddy O'Neill' stands out in my mind as one of the great favourites. To this day, people still talk about her voice. Everyone on the show had to take part in the programme and so it was very much expected that all of Dan and Maggie's children would marry other show people who could perform and add to the cast. Granddad had very strict rules about this. All of Dad's family were good looking and talented, so it's no surprise that, during performances, they attracted a lot of attention and not always from other show people.

Growing up, I often heard the story of how my parents had met. Dusky Dan's show rolled into a village called Ballintogher, County Sligo in 1951. Great excitement moved through the community as the caravans circled around Mel Lane's field, which also housed the community ball alley. Mel, the local butcher, had a great fascination for the show. A cheery and colourful character himself, he was also one of Baby Fallon's best friends. Baby, known as Babs, lived with her mother in a semi-detached cottage on the edge of the village, not more than a stone's throw from where the Dusky brothers were busy putting up the tent for the show that night. Babs was busy making plans with Mel to attend the show. Mel, of course, had two complimentary tickets for each night in return for the use of his field. They were sure to get the best seats in the house and that they did, sitting right up front. Babs cut a fine figure, with shoulder-length brown wavy hair and in her finest attire.

Beside Mel in the packed-out tent, Babs listened to the excited chatter of neighbours while they waited for the dark-red velvet curtains to part. Smoke filled the air as men drew on their cigarettes and pipes. The women smoked too. Dusky Dan stood to attention, brown leather bag over his shoulder, collecting the admission fee and carefully counting people as they filed through. Every man, woman and child was greeted with a great big smile and a joke, all helping to set the right atmosphere for the night. There was much movement and organising going on backstage in a very confined area in the wings, it being the opening night at this 'tober', a name given by show people to fields and the like where we set up the 'fit-up'. All the props, scenes, costumes and musical instruments had to be at the ready, for once the show started there was no stopping, except for a short interval to sell raffle tickets. Prizes galore to be won, and if you were lucky enough you could be going home with a brand-new set of sherry glasses. Suddenly, the lights dimmed and you could hear a pin drop. Then a loud drum roll, the curtains rolled back, and the whole cast in full costume launched into 'There's no business like show business, like no business I know …'

Cheering and clapping, feet stomping, as everyone tried to keep time with two accordions, a guitar, a homemade upright bass and drums, then it was straight into 'Happy days are here again, the skies above are clear again …'

With everyone raising the roof, the tone was set for the night.

Babs and Mel hung onto every scene, song and emotion that came before them. It didn't take long for Frank Ellis to notice Babs, who looked like a movie star and not a lick of make-up on her, a big contrast to the ladies on the stage. And when Frank gave her the old glad eye, she didn't disapprove. Babs was a popular nineteen-year-old, known for her sense of humour and her independence.

Frank's older brother, Jack, played accordion, sang, acted in sketches and plays, as well as being 'The World's Greatest Hypnotist and Magician'. Frank played drums, sang, was the comedian and acted in the sketches and plays – all that same night. Everyone fell under the spell of the entertainers. There was much to talk about: where exactly did that Wild Colonial Boy come from? How in the world did Maggie O'Dea learn to yodel like that?

Where did they get those sparkly shoes? Who will enter the talent show tomorrow night? Wouldn't you love to know how the hypnotist put the chicken to sleep? And on and on.

Some of the younger ones hung around to smoke and chat, including Babs and Mel. The craic was mighty and all were in high spirits. As the lights glimmered from the caravan windows and the women set about making supper, the men were putting away the props and instruments for the night. You'd imagine that would be enough, but Dusky Dan was a tough taskmaster and money had to be made. It was well known that Jack could fix clocks and watches, which was no easy task; Frank was an excellent mechanic, and both experimented with various inventions. Jack was forever receiving books and props for new magic tricks to invent and practise. Frank, covered in grease and oil, would be dissecting engines and cars to come up with an original version of what the family humorously called a 'Frank Special', and over the years there were many of them.

Show finished for the night, all packed away, Jack and Frank relaxed and chatted with the locals. Frank already knew Mel and so it was easy to get an introduction to Babs. The pair found it easy to talk. Both had a great sense of humour and a colourful personality, and their laughter rang out till the wee small hours. For sure, Babs secured a front seat at the show every night that week.

Babs' mother was not a bit happy, noticing that her daughter was spending far too much time with the 'show crowd'. After all, there was plenty of work to be done at home, with no man about the house. Frank Fallon, Babs' dad, like a lot of men at the time, had gone to the building sites in England to find work and, after returning home on only a couple of occasions, had abandoned the family. Bee Fallon was now a 'deserted wife'. Babs' only other sibling, a brother, Seamus, was ten years her junior. The Fallon household was run in military fashion. Bee became increasingly bitter and hard-natured. A hard-working, good-living, God-fearing woman, her purpose in life was to keep her tiny house spotless. She turned out her children in clothes mostly altered or made by herself, all hand-stitched or knitted sitting by the fire. Her nights were filled with these rituals, her days busy with cooking and tending her flowerbeds and vegetable garden. She worked hard and expected no less from her daughter, who carried out a lot of the chores. Babs, having lived her life so far finding ways around Bee's rules and regulations, was determined not to miss one night at the show, keeping her comb and hair clips well hidden under a loose stone in the wall of Jimmy Sommer's field next door to Bee's cottage. Night after night, Mel and Babs sat in their front-row seats and laughed and cried at all the different productions and after each show, Babs met with Frank.

The week was coming to an end, though, and as usual, the show would be moving on. That last night was very sad and difficult as Frank had to say goodbye, telling Babs that they might not see each other for at least another year. Back then, it must have sounded like an eternity, as they would have little or no communication and Babs wouldn't know where the show was. She was heartbroken, but they said their goodbyes. You can imagine how happy Bee Fallon was to see the back of Dusky Dan's show. She must have thought all would be back to normal and her daughter could rid herself of any daft notions. It was bad enough being a deserted wife, but to have her daughter mixing with the show crowd would disgrace the family alto-gether. After all, she was one of the Cartronhugh Lynches, small farmers and proud of it. There were standards to be kept.

The next morning, Babs made her usual daily visit to the creamery. It was just across the road from Mel Lane's field and next door to Gilmartin's shop. The farmers were arriving with a click-clack of donkeys' hooves and churns of milk clanging off each other against the sound of machinery in the creamery and smoke bellowing out of a chimney, a hive of activity. Babs' morning ritual was to wait, bucket and shovel in hand, until the creamery closed up at lunchtime, when she would pick out the best cinders from the coal that had fired the machinery, for the fire at home that night. Across at Mel Lane's field, the tent came down, the wagons lined up and the show slowly made its way up through Ballintogher and on to the next place. Compared to the glamour of the stage show, Babs couldn't help but think how mundane her life was. Later that evening, Mel came to visit. They got to talking about how much they were going to miss the show that night. Then Babs, the eyes popping out of her head with excitement, said 'I've an idea. Sure they're only over in Ballinagar, the next parish. It would only take about an hour to walk it and a lot less to cycle.' She convinced Mel to bring his bike and carry her on the crossbar. Before her mother could bat an eyelid, herself and Mel were flying up the village to catch the opening of the show that evening. For weeks to come and as long as the show was within cycling distance, Mel and Babs went as many nights as they could. Bee was getting increasingly annoyed and worried, for she had thought surely once the show left Ballintogher, that would be the end of it. She had underestimated Frank and Bab's love for each other, and was shocked and dismayed when her daughter announced that Frank had asked her to marry him and she had said yes.

'Over my dead body will you marry that fella and go away with the show crowd, travelling the roads of Ireland, living in a caravan, you'll disgrace the whole family.' Her face red with rage, veins sticking out on her neck, she banged the kitchen table with her fist and said, 'Let there not be one more word about it and that fella is not to darken my door.' From Bee's point of view, not only was her daughter marrying well beneath her status, but also who would do all her work around the house if she left? There was nothing good about any of this, as far as Bee was concerned. Babs was devastated, running to the back door, making her way to the back fields where she could cry. Bee shouted after her, 'You're not of age, you'll go nowhere.' And she was right. So Babs waited just over a year, till the following June when she turned twenty-one, free to marry whom she liked, and eloped with Frank. They got married in Ballinagar parish church with two witnesses. Her mother was furious, but eventually realised that nothing could be done, so she cooked them a wedding breakfast. After all, she wouldn't give the village the satisfaction of being able to say she hadn't known that her only daughter was getting married.

It was an awkward and frosty reception for Frank, to say the least, and I recall that Bee's frosty attitude to my dad lasted all her life. When you consider that she lived to the age of 106, that was a long time. She was often heard to say, 'I hope that fella dies roaring.'

Wedding breakfast over, Babs gathered her few things and set off with Frank for a life on the road. It would be a huge change for her for; as small as the Fallon household was, at least it was warm and they had regular meals, as much as her mother could afford, and of course they had their own vegetable patch, with potatoes, carrots, parsnips, cabbage and spring onions, or scallions as they were called, and fresh hen and duck eggs every morning. There wouldn't be any of that where she was going. Bee was heartbroken as she and little Seamus stood by the gate to wave goodbye, not knowing when she'd see Babs again.

The newly-weds arrived back to the show just in time to be ready for that night's performance. It was all wonderfully romantic and happy. Babs helped Frank prepare for the opening numbers and followed him out to watch the show. Not as a member of the audience, this time, but as Mrs Frank Ellis Dusky. Dusky Dan and Maggie and the rest of the family were delighted for them. Dan immediately got chatting to Babs about what she could do and how best to incorporate her into the programme. Certainly, Dan thought her good looks would enhance the chorus line. Babs was very unsure of ever being brave enough to get up on a stage, never mind be part of the show. It was a great surprise to her that, after just a few months, she was singing a solo, had joined the chorus, taken small parts in sketches and plays and was even learning to play the clarinet. (It was essential that everyone play an instrument, as part of the programme.) And so Frank and Babs were welcomed as husband and wife into the Dusky family show. Frank built a wagon for them and I can only imagine how strange it must have been for my mum to live in a wagon and move from town to town, meeting new people all the time. She would certainly have loved the company of Frank's brothers and sisters and the great stories and laughter they all shared.

Although I'm sure it wasn't an easy life on the road, I know she was really happy in those early years and loved every moment spent with Frank. They did everything together. My dad couldn't have been happier. He'd married the love of his life and they made themselves a nice cosy home. I suppose, for my father, life wasn't that different, but for my mum it was a complete contrast to her life before. The biggest change was that she'd gone from gathering cinders at the creamery, gathering wood, feeding chickens, ducks and turkeys, to wearing sequins and performing on stage.

Two years later, Babs was just a few weeks away from giving birth. The show was making its way towards Sligo, so that Frank and Babs could go to Sligo General Hospital for the birth. On 27 February 1954, Babs went into labour. She later told me that it was such a long and difficult labour she thought she would die, and at one stage the pain was so bad, she didn't care if she did. Eventually, after many hours and my father outside walking up and down the car park at his wits' end, I was born. Congratulations, Mrs Ellis, you have a fine baby girl! Frank and Babs were delighted. 'We'll call her Philomena, after the saint I was praying to, Bridget after my mother, and Marion for the Marian year.' My mother added, to everyone's amusement, that when she looked into the cot all she could see was eyes and ears. My mother brought me to stay with Granny Bee in Ballintogher until she recovered and I was a lot stronger, while my father returned to the show. When Bee looked at me, lifting me from my makeshift cot, it was the first time anyone had seen a tender and loving side to her. It was like all her guards were down and she was filled with joy and love. Her first grandchild, she'd make sure I was brought up right, with none of that show stuff. Bee Fallon's granddaughter would be a respectable, well-mannered Catholic girl, if she had anything to say about it.

After a week or so, back to the show we went. I'd say my mother was glad to get away from the nagging. Granny always meant well, but she had a very tough way of getting her message across. Dan was happy his company of players was expanding and who knew what great talents this addition would bring when the time was right. Frank and Babs had never known such happiness, and from what I've heard, it was a delight to see how Frank would take care of their new baby and just how good he was at it, better than Babs even. I suppose, though, he was used to helping with his brothers and sisters growing up. Every day he'd bring me out to the tent with him and put me lying on a blanket beside him as he took care of his work. I've heard it said that children are like sponges for soaking up stuff around them. If that's the case, I got a very early education in life on the show. The sounds, the colours, the music. Our wagon was parked as close to the tent as possible, and, lying in the cot Dad made for me, I could hear the show every night until I'd fall asleep. Because this lifestyle was what I was born into, it was the most natural thing in the world for me. However, Granny Bee was convinced that I'd die of neglect, cold or hunger, saying every time she saw me that I was thinner. Mum and Dad just laughed, paying her as little heed as possible.

Though quite eerily, Granny's concerns were justified. I don't remember much about my brother Francis' arrival, as I was only three years old and busy working on the show, but I remember him as my adorable baby brother. Everyone was in love with him and he was a joyful baby, always happy. Mum had him in a Moses basket and she would brush his blond hair to the top of his head every day and twist it round her finger to make a long sausage-like curl along his head. His basket was on a stand in the middle of the floor of our little caravan. I recall an awful panic one day, hearing Mum shouting, 'Francis, Francis!' Dad came flying out the door with Francis' basket and all under his arm. The caravan had somehow caught fire. I don't remember how, but thankfully Francis was fine and they managed to save the wagon.

The show always seemed to pick up guys along the way to help with the work setting up the tent and suchlike. They would generally be young lads who wanted to travel Ireland and liked the idea of being with a show. At this time, we had a young lad who helped us out and who was enthusiastic but maybe not the most talented. When Francis was five months old, Mum and Dad decided to visit Granny in Ballintogher and brought me along. Francis had a bit of a cough, so this young lad offered to mind him in our caravan until we got back that night.

It was raining hard and, for some reason, he decided to take Francis in his blanket to visit one of the other wagons. Well, of course Francis got wet and over the next few days developed a really bad chest infection. All I can remember is a slippery, mucky embankment to reach our wagon as a result of the heavy rainfall. Dad went to fetch a doctor, who didn't seem to be in that big of a hurry to come out. Dad was furious and Mum distraught. Eventually the doctor arrived. It was obvious, my parents said later, that he had no respect for us and treated us like we counted for nothing. Francis was really chesty and you could hear his every breath. The doctor examined him, then closed up his bag and told Mum and Dad to keep Francis comfortable and warm and to give him plenty of fluids to keep him hydrated. There really was nothing else he could suggest that might help.

Francis got worse through the night and was finding it hard to breathe. Dad, although a very quiet man, when pushed, was like a lion in protecting his family. He got into his car, went back to the doctor's house and pleaded with him to do something to help his son, but to no avail. His reply to Dad was, 'There is no point in me going back to see your son. I can't help him.' My father, full of anger, fear and pain, returned to my mother and Francis in our wagon. They sat up with him, as did some others in the family. As the hours passed, so did Francis' life and the next day he took his final breath, aged five months. Dad was heartbroken, but tried to stay strong for Mum, who was inconsolable as she held Francis in her arms.

My only other memory of Francis is travelling back to Ballintogher with Mum and Dad in the front of our car. I was sitting in the back seat and beside me was a white box. I kept asking Mum and Dad, 'Why did you put my brother into a box?' Christ, it must have been an agonising journey back home to Granny Bee's. Francis was laid to rest with Granny's family, the Lynches, in the graveyard in Kilross, just opposite where Granny Bee went to school and also where she would be buried. In all the years after Francis' death, we never passed Kilross graveyard without my mum crying.

# 2

# MY MAGICAL CHILDHOOD ON THE SHOW

A t three years of age, I was fondly referred to as 'The Elf' by my family because of my small, round face, big eyes and rather large pixie-like ears. Often, I'd hear someone calling out 'Did anyone see The Elf?' or 'The Elf is on next.' They meant well and thought it was cute, but it wasn't at all cute to me. After all, I saw myself like Shirley Temple or Judy Garland, a star in the making surely, not the creature they referred to. My days were so full of excitement, anticipation, things to do, tricks to learn with Uncle Jack the magician, scenery to paint with my dad, songs and scripts to learn, how would I ever get it all done? Always moving, new places to discover and more interesting people to meet. That was the best thing about having your home on wheels: we were always on the move and I loved that. With my granddad Dan's help, I had perfected a lovely Shirley Temple song-and-dance routine to delight the audience:

*'On the good ship Lollipop, it's a sweet trip to the candy shop.'*

I put every ounce of my being into that routine, believing I might even be better than Shirley Temple. One of my favourite songs to sing was 'Sailor', which was very popular at the time. The audience was sure to join in on every chorus, cocooning me in a warm musical feeling. It's a feeling I can still conjure up on the stage today with the right song. I can still hear my granddad Dusky Dan's voice in my head saying, 'Invite the audience to sing with you, they do love to hear themselves sing along.'

Of course, any child parts in a play or in sketches were also my job, even being carried on when only a baby, if that was needed. It has always amused me over the years when I'm asked in an interview why and when I decided to take up show business. The truth is I never had that choice to make; it was made for me from the day I was born. You know what, though? I wouldn't change a single moment of it. In a very short time, I learned all about the stage. Performance, preparation, delivery, and how to get the audience's attention.

We moved from village to village, townland to townland, in small, brightly painted wooden wagons made by the Dusky brothers themselves and towed by very old beaten-up cars, also always painted in a bright array of colours. 'Dusky Dan's Variety Show'. One by one, the wagons would be placed around where the tent was pitched, Dan and Maggie's wagon always in pride of place, wherever that was in a mucky field. I usually travelled in the wagon, peeping out as we went along at a slow but steady pace. I could see the whole world from that little window and so I built a picture of how 'real people' lived. Children and their parents would walk behind cattle, hitting the ground with a stick and calling 'Hup, hup, hup, come on now'. We would just roll slowly behind. The cattle seemed to know exactly which gap to go through, and I'd think how clever that was. Watching farmers and their families working the fields, children playing in their school yards, smoke rising out of chimneys, I figured that they must just stay in one place and thought what a terribly boring life they must have. Passing through towns and villages, shopkeepers busy about their business, housewives with their shopping bags. All the while, though, they took time to stop and look at us as we rolled in. Wagons all in place in the new tober, Dad and his brothers, with a little help from a few of the local young lads, set up the tent, or the booth as they called it in more recent years, when they could afford to buy wooden sides, again painted in vibrant colours. It was quite a vision, to me anyway. We were certainly different.

Once settled, booth up, stage in place and curtains hung, it was time to eat. The menu didn't vary that much, except that we always ate better when the show did well. So I was never sure what was coming on my plate. I ate a lot of what my mother called 'goodie' and, believe me when I tell you, it sounds a lot better than it tasted. It consisted of bread, a little milk and sugar, all in a mug filled with hot water, stirred and eaten with a spoon. As I got older, I realised that on those nights the show hadn't done well, we existed on what we could afford. Dusky Dan was a fair and good business-man. If families couldn't afford to pay admission to the show in money, we accepted food. On those occasions, we ate well. Fresh vegetables, eggs and once even a live chicken, which, as I recall, went missing soon after. I've often wondered if that chicken wandered off or if someone on the show had a chicken dinner I didn't know about. I missed that chicken for the longest time.

Myself and my mother would go down to the village before show time to look around. If we had any money, she'd buy a few essentials: milk, bread, butter, sugar, etc. Most people were really friendly – most people! I always knew I was different from them. I didn't understand why or how. Maybe it was the way they looked at me, or how uncomfortable they were to speak with us. In my mind's eye, I remember being on stage as a child, looking down at a sea of smiling faces and clapping hands, but off stage, people just looked at me. My mother made as good an effort as she could to dress me for stage, even stuffing second-hand shoes that were too big for me full of paper, because it was all she had. Checked pants and a jumper, or a little floral dress and white socks were my outfits. Except when I was Uncle Jack's magic assistant. Then I wore a turban and what my dad called 'gilly gilly trousers'. In cream satin with elastic around the ankles, they made me look like Aladdin's baby sister. My dad hand-sewed my costume especially for me (he sewed a lot). Once, when everyone decided to go swimming and I didn't have a swimsuit, Dad made me one out of an old white cotton shirt. Dad would swim with me on his back. I looked a picture in my new swimsuit, going into the water, but unfortunately, I came out of the water without it. The stitching had all come undone and my new swimsuit was floating away in the distance. Did I forget to say that, although Dad sewed a lot, he wasn't really that skilful?

I knew all Uncle Jack's tricks. He would put me into a wooden box and secure it with a chain and padlock, which would be inspected by a member of the audience. Then, a few magic words, accompanied by a dramatic drum roll from my dad (who was the drummer), the magic box would be opened and I would have disappeared and my cousin would be in my place. The audience applauded with amazement, as I crawled my way under the backdrop behind the box and off the stage. Then it was time for me to carry on and hold a chicken while Uncle Jack hypnotised it, before hypnotising some members of the audience too. It was always funny, because once he hypnotised them, he could make them do really silly things in front of the whole room. Something I'm sure they'd be reminded of for some time to come. They'd make their way through the crowd trying to sell newspapers, some men even being made to get down on one knee to propose marriage to another random member of the audience. When they were once more awakened, the crowd would be in roars of laughter, leaving the bewildered participants wondering what had just happened. I never tired of seeing how silly adults could be!

The highlight of the magic was the Electric Chair, which was terrifying. It was another stunning presentation Jack had received from America and had constructed himself. A big wooden high-backed chair and a frame attached with a metal helmet. Jack would sit in the chair with the helmet on his head, gripping tightly, until his knuckles lost all colour. A surge of electricity that presented itself like a bolt of lightning appeared to pass from one side of the frame, through the helmet and out the other side. Every night you could hear the audience gasp with terror.

As a finale to the magic show, I was invited back out on stage. With my teeth chattering and legs like jelly, I had to stand beside Jack while he sat in the electric chair. I held a small bulb in my left hand as he reached for my right and, as soon as he grasped my hand, the bulb lit up. I never figured out how he did that! I was terrified every night holding that bulb. Shoulders up around my ears and eyes closed throughout, I couldn't wait to get off that stage – alive.

The kind and right thing would have been to tell me how that trick was done, to relieve my fear. But that never happened, because I'd previously been caught out doing my worst. You see, being quite the entrepreneur from an early age, I thought it would be a good idea to run down after all the tricks, sit beside certain people in the audience, especially if they looked rich, and offer to tell them how the tricks were done for a few pence or any gift they might want to give me. It was a thriving business: I'd get money, sweets, once even a tube of red lipstick. It was all going great until I got caught. You can imagine the trouble I was in, but I was constantly getting in trouble for my moneymaking ideas.

Made up as a young boy for one of the plays, *The Wild Colonial Boy*, in the first scene I was kidnapped. In tan trousers, check shirt and a cowboy hat as the curtains were drawn, I sat in front of the backdrop of a horse corral on a dimly lit stage, whittling away at a piece of wood. A lonesome cowboy song played in the background, then came a loud noise and a gang of bandits dragged me kicking and screaming from the stage. You could feel the tension in the whole room, as people wondered what would become of this young boy. The actors had the audience in the palm of their hands. That is, until I'd run around, as quick as I could, and make my way into the audience to let a willing customer know exactly what was about to happen to that kidnapped boy in the play. At a fair price of money, sweets or whatever they could part with.

I got away with that for a while, until an actor/author called Dennis Franks joined our show's entourage for a while. Now Dennis Franks was well known as being very professional and serious about his craft. Very distinguished and well dressed, he struck an impressive no-nonsense figure. For some reason, I have a memory of him tapping the side of our caravan. I was still in bed and when I pulled back my little curtain, there he was in full dress riding gear sitting on a huge white horse and tapping my window with a riding crop. 'Time to get up, come on, we have work to do.' Terrified, I got dressed and rushed out, thinking I'd woken up to Heathcliff from Wuthering Heights. He dismounted and, inviting me to walk along, he said, 'Now, little Miss Philomena. Repeat after me: How Now Brown Cow.' So I did, although for the life of me I couldn't think why we were talking about a brown cow and me not even having had breakfast. 'No, no, no,' he said. 'That won't do at all. You must open your mouth and roll your tongue to pronounce the words correctly. The audience must understand every single word. Again, repeat after me, How Now Brown Cow ...' After I'd finished repeating that line for what seemed like forever, I didn't even want my breakfast and could hardly move my jaws.

Anyway, that's how my business venture regarding *The Wild Colonial Boy* came to an end. One night, while I was bargaining with a member of the audience, Dennis Franks grabbed me by the back of the collar and dragged me outside. In a raised voice, his face full of anger, he told me that under no circumstances was I ever to leave the stage to take up residence amongst the paying audience. Members of the company should never mix with the audience until after the performance and certainly not just after you've been kidnapped. Well, that was it: another of my enterprises gone by the wayside. I'd have to dust myself down and think of a new one. It was fine and well for Mr Franks, but did he not realise the only means I had of getting or buying sweets or any other treats was my little ventures on the side? After all, it seemed only fair as I didn't get any payment for my work or performances on the show.

At last, with Dennis Franks gone, life went back to normal, my family busy with performances at night and fixing clocks, cars and tractors during the day for local paying customers. With everyone busy, I had time to come up with a few more moneymaking ideas. Ingenious ones, or so I thought. One of the local shopkeepers had given me an old but very large book of wallpaper samples: good strong paper with lots of lovely patterns and colours. I decided that each sample page would be perfect for kids to use to cover schoolbooks. Kids came to the show every evening so it was perfect: the customers would be coming to me. I set up a little spot just outside the entrance to the field, positioned perfectly to catch my customers on their way into the show, but out of sight of any of the family. With everyone busy and distracted in getting ready for the evening's performance, I sat on the ditch with my sample book, offering a page of choice at a very good price to cover your schoolbooks. To my amazement, not one page was sold. People just smiled, or maybe it was a giggle as they filed past me and my sample book. My excitement turned very quickly to disappointment, so I turned my attention to preparing for that night's show and put my thinking hat back on the following day, after I'd had a chance to lick my wounds.

It took me a few weeks to recover and find excitement in anticipation of a new venture. It was a very hot summer and I'd noticed that it was especially hot during the show with the audience all squeezed in together under the canvas of the booth. 'That's it!' I thought. They needed paper fans, like the ones I saw in one of the films Dad showed sometimes after the show. My granddad always had newspapers, so I went to his wagon and asked for any old newspapers he had. He handed me a few without asking what I wanted them for. I set about carefully tearing out each page, then folding and pleating it neatly to make a fan. I made up a bunch of them for the show that evening and, thank God, it was sweltering hot. The plan was that I would crawl under the stage from the back, making my way to the front, as I often did to look at the people in the audience. Just before the interval, fans in hand, I made my move. I parted the curtains that ran across the bottom of the stage like a little skirt. Peeping out, waving a fan to attract the attention of anyone in the front row, in a loud whisper I called out, 'Fans for sale, fans for sale'. They roared laughing, thinking it was part of the entertainment. My grandfather came around to see what all the commotion was. When he saw me and my paper fans, I knew I was in trouble, again. To everyone's amusement, he grabbed me by the hand, ushering me out and back behind the stage for my telling-off.

Looking back, though, my mum and dad were the most wonderful, fun parents, always laughing and joking. They were so happy, at least during these early years. When I think back, I'm filled with joy and pride that although my parents had only each other and the show and little else, they created a life and home for me that was loving and magical.

❧ When the show would arrive at a new place and all the wagons were carefully parked around the booth as always, the Dusky brothers and sisters would busy themselves, the women cooking, the men organising the booth for that night's show. I would have a wee scouting expedition around the immediate area to see what mischief I could get up to or, more important, what treasures I could get from kind well-to-do locals. I'd discovered that the Irish in America were always sending home parcels full of all kinds of grand things. My usual routine on these expeditions would be to pick out the finest-looking houses and knock on the door. Now, imagine in your mind's eye: I was only about six or seven years old. The door would open and most times it was the woman of the house who would answer. I'd give my well-rehearsed introduction: 'Hello, I'm Philomena from the show. We just got here and I was wondering do you have any clothes or toys you don't need? I would be willing to sing and dance for you in return for anything you might part with.' Well, let me tell you, as soon as I said that, I'd be brought into the kitchen and with all the family summoned to see my performance, I'd hop up on the table and do my whole routine. Sure they didn't need to go to the show at all, having already seen the star attraction. I'd get tea, cake, sweets and even clothes and the odd toy.

Two occasions stand out in my mind. On one, I got the most beautiful gold sequined cape. I'd never ever seen anything so incredibly beautiful; it sparkled and shone. I looked exactly like the movie stars in my dad's films. My audience would be star-struck. My mum was suspicious, though, as to where and how I'd come by such a gorgeous object. I told her that a lovely lady had dropped it off and, lucky for me, I was the one she'd given it to. That seemed to go over okay. Another time, I knocked on the door of a fine big house and the payment for my song-and-dance routine was a lovely porcelain-faced doll dressed in a bright yellow silk dress and bonnet. My eyes nearly popped straight out of my head when I saw her. The kind lady told me it was a very special doll that had come all the way from America. I thought to myself, I knew it, I just knew it, there was some great stuff in them parcels from America and here I was, proud as punch, bringing home one of the very best of them for my singing and dancing. I should have known things were going too well that day.

As I approached our wagon, my new prized possession carefully cradled in my arms, I could see my mother, hands on hips, glaring at me. I could feel myself welling up, as I desperately tried to come up with a good story, as there was no hiding that bright yellow satin dress. Too late, there she was, my mother, towering over me: 'Well, what's it this time?' I tried to explain that a lovely lady had come running out with the doll and had made me take it. Mum made me bring her back to the house and knock on the door. The kind lady of the house appeared again, this time looking a little confused. She looked down at me with my precious cargo in my arms. My mum said to her, 'I hope my little one here hasn't been a nuisance.' Thankfully, the lady assured her that had not been the case and that, in fact, I had been a joy and entertained them royally. So I was somewhere beyond happy when my mother allowed me to keep the doll. All things considered, this whole matter had been a godsend because now that my mother knew the whole story, well part of it anyway, I would no longer need to hide my beautifully attired doll behind the wheel of our wagon, which was my usual hiding place for any of my treasures.

Daily, weekly and monthly routines continued on the show. Some of the family would pull up in their wagons to join the show as others would hitch up and leave, according to who was talking to whom at the time. I don't ever recall any rows between any of the men on the show but, as I remember, there seemed to be quite a few disagreements between the women and when one of the wives said it was time to leave, the men had little choice but to hitch up the wagon and move on, most times not even knowing where they were going. They never seemed to stay away long, though.

I had a full knowledge at this stage of the programme; after all, I was eight years old. The show would open with full cast on stage, to a medley of uplifting songs, to get the audience in the right mood for the rest of the show, followed immediately by a funny sketch, and we had many of them. Then, one by one, the different artists would present music, song and dance, everyone playing an instrument. This would lead up to Uncle

Jack presenting his magic and hypnotism, with me as his assistant. He was just wonderful: a tall good-looking man, with huge charisma. When he spoke as the magician and hypnotist, he had a commanding voice, much like Richard Burton. His voice could transport you deep into the world of magic and the unknown. Then there was the interval, when all the girls from the show would move around the tent selling tickets for the all-important raffle at the end of the performance. Tickets in hand, the audience settled down as the lights dimmed and the appropriate music was playing in the background for whatever dramatic production would follow and bring the audience on a theatrical journey never before experienced. A different play featured every night, anything from the already mentioned *The Wild Colonial Boy* to *Noreen Brown* to *Frankenstein*. That one used to terrify me. My father, Frank, would fill his boots with paper to make him taller and wear clothes too small to make him look bigger (like when the Incredible Hulk bursts through his shirt and trousers), and with stitches all over his face and arms. The first night I watched it, my mother couldn't get me to go back to our wagon to go to bed, I was so traumatised.

My grandfather, quite craftily, would invite someone from the local parish to play a character in some of the dramas. Well he knew that this would bring in a huge local crowd to see one of their own either rise to the occasion or make a complete fool of themselves. Either would work. There was the talent competition every night, which built up to the semi-final on the second-last night of the show and the final on the last night. The booth would be heaving with people to see who would be lucky enough to bring home Dusky Dan's much-coveted silver trophy. Sometime in the last few years, I came across someone who'd won this cup. I had remembered it as being huge, but it was actually quite small.

I hinted that I would love to have this memento from my family's show, but there was no parting with it: the cup had been hard won and it would stay in pride of place on the mantelpiece where it had stood for more than sixty years, all polished and shined.

I was well schooled by my mother, though I often attended the local national school for the duration of the show's stay. It wasn't nice attending so many different schools for such short periods of time. I'd walk in a total stranger, and though I was always made welcome, I was different. I was from the 'show crowd', lived in a caravan and didn't really belong anywhere. I still don't. I've never had that feeling of belonging. I have memories and attachments to places and people, but never that sense of being from somewhere, or belonging. To the other children at the various schools, I suppose I was just a novelty and to overcome the awkwardness of this, I would go straight into my entertaining mode, with my little routines. Which always worked as a great distraction for me and made it easy to befriend people. These are traits I have carried with me through my whole life, still useful, often helping me out of awkward or uncomfortable situations and, in my line of work, there have been many of those.

# 3

# DUSKY DAN & MAGGIE BRENNAN

**M**y granddad Daniel Hanna was born in Belfast, a Protestant, who served in France in the British Army during the Second World War and later worked at the Harland and Wolff shipyard. At night, he worked in local venues and small theatres as an entertainer, as 'Dusky Dan', specialising in song, dance and comedy. At thirty-five years of age, with a wife and family, he still dreamt of one day seeing his name up in lights. He was always well spoken and dapper, with a charming personality and the charisma of Clark Gable. He could pretty much talk his way out of anything and was particularly popular with the ladies.

On this day, as he would often do, he walked through St George's Market, a vibrant redbrick Victorian marketplace, full of stalls and people bartering over everything you might want to purchase. Suddenly he could hear the most magnificent voice, 'the voice of an angel', or, if not an angel, surely a star in the making. He quickly made his way towards this magical sound, and there she was: Maggie Brennan, sixteen years old, of slight build, in a floral dress and her long hair braided into plaits and pinned up each side of her head. She was singing her heart out, standing by her mother's bric-a-brac stall to attract customers.

Immediately smitten, he stood and listened. Waiting his chance, Dan casually went over and started chatting to Maggie. Over the next number of weeks, he would make sure to visit the market to hear Maggie and chat. Maggie was always happy to see him and loved the attention she received from him and what he had to say. He persuaded her that, being in show business himself, with his help, experience and contacts and her wonderful voice, they could really hit the big time. 'Just think of it, Maggie: I can see it now, I'd book us into some of the best venues and theatres, north and south, England, Scotland. We'd be stars with our names up in lights – oh Maggie, what do you think?'

Sitting here now writing this, I try to imagine what it must have been like for them in 1923 trying to organise something like that, the challenges, the hurt and shame endured by their families. Not only was Dan married with a family, but he was also almost twenty years Maggie's senior, and she was a Catholic. The sectarianism in Northern Ireland would have prevented them being a couple, even if nothing else had.

They eloped across the border in 1924. Dan bought a small caravan and they started their life as a couple, and set about putting their musical act together. No doubt Maggie dreamt of singing, beautiful dresses, spotlights, stages and captivated audiences. Life was very hard, a small horse-drawn caravan barely big enough to sleep or eat in, the only light being an oil lamp, travelling from county to county, picking up what work they could. Seven children arrived – Danny, Phyllis, Jack, Frank, Rita, Tommy and Liz – with little space between them; the eighth, Pat, came a few years later. Any chance Dan got he was in the local pub after the show, charming the locals with his colourful stories from the road. As the family grew, so did the cast. Dan and Maggie taught the children their craft.

One story I was told was about a family they met along the way. Finding it hard to manage to look after and feed all the children, Dan asked this family if they'd keep the oldest two, Danny and Phyllis, and look after them until they came back around that way again. It sounds crazy today, but this wasn't an unusual practice for show people back then. At least the children would be warm, fed and get schooling. I can't imagine the tears and pain of leaving two of your children behind and how awful it must have been for Danny and Phyllis. Over time, they settled into the family, in spite of it being a totally different experience for them living in a house, never moving, not being part of the family show. I can identify with that part of it myself.

When the show returned to the town many months later, Dan and Maggie went to reunite with Danny and Phyllis. However, on seeing them, the children ran back into the house, crying and afraid. The woman told Dan and Maggie to leave, that their children were now part of her family. Over the next number of weeks, Maggie and Dan tried to get their children back but without success. On the last occasion, when they went back, the family had moved, leaving no trace and taking Maggie's children with them.

I'm certain this traumatic event was the beginning of the end of Maggie's mental stability. Life had dealt her some painful blows and huge disappointments, but this must have crushed her. Many years later, and sadly after Maggie's death, Phyllis found a way to connect with her father, brothers and sisters. I remember her well, a lovely warm woman, married with a family herself. Very much a Dusky in looks and voice. I remember as a child it was such a happy reunion, Phyllis delighted to be reunited with her family but also sharing some devastating news. The older brother, Danny, had been taken ill with TB at a young age and died. Maybe it was a good thing that Maggie never knew.

Once, some time after Phyllis had connected with the family, I asked my mum and dad how come Granny and Granddad hadn't gone to the gardaí. I was told that whatever threat was made against them, it frightened them enough not to. Those were different times and, in fact, Phyllis said that she had a good life and that the family were very kind to them.

But as everyone in show business knows, 'the show must go on' and so it did. Maggie O'Dea (formally Brennan), Dusky Dan and a full cast brought their show to every corner of Ireland they could reach.

### Dusky Dan's Variety Show

*Dusky Dan – Producer & Actor*

*Jack Dusky – Actor, Magician, Vocalist, Master Accordionist*

*Frank Dusky – Comedian, Actor, Singer, Drummer*

*Rita Dusky – Actress, Singer, 'the voice of an angel'*

*Tommy Dusky – Actor, Singer, Accordionist*

*Liz Dusky – Actress, Singer, Accordionist*

*Pat Dusky – Actor, Incredible guitarist, Incredible singer*

*Drama! Variety! Comedy, Magic, and Music all under one roof. A show not to be missed … Come along and enjoy the show!*

Oh yes, the show must go on. How many times in my life have I heard that, and at what cost!

Little by little, Maggie changed. Not only did she never see her name up in bright lights anywhere, she spent her life in a caravan, travelling the roads of Ireland, mother and wife by day and singing sensation Maggie O'Dea by night. She became resentful of her once great love, Dan, and laid blame on him for all that had happened. They grew further and further apart. He was still the ultimate showman, always keeping the sunny side out, while always still reassuring Maggie that things would get better. But her mind would not let her rest. Dad told me that she would rush out of her wagon at any hour of the day or night, insisting she had to go, but when asked where to, she didn't know. The pain of it! It's a wound you cannot see for it's all in your head.

My father told me with tears in his eyes that one minute she'd be the cheery, funny, loving mother they knew so well and the next like someone they'd never met. The children were much older now and living in their own hand-made wagons. One night, Maggie had one of her episodes. While Dan was holding court in the local pub, Maggie went to bed and lay in wait with a knife under her pillow. When Dan returned, Maggie flew at him, wielding the knife. He might not have been sober when he left the pub, but he was now. He managed to save himself and secure the knife, calming Maggie, while calling the lads for help. Early the next morning, it was decided that they could no longer give Maggie the help she needed. In despair, Dan sent for the local doctor, who admitted her to a mental institution for examination and possible treatment. My father told me that when the show moved on to the next townland, he cycled back to the hospital to see his mother. He was shocked to see her restrained and agitated, and immediately got her released and brought her back home. He often wondered if he had done the right thing and that maybe if he'd left her there, she would have received the help that might have saved her.

Over the years, Maggie's suffering, her periods of depression and strange behaviour continued, as did her resentment towards Dan. One night during the show, while Dan was on stage to a full house and in the middle of his comedy routine, Maggie stood at the back of the tent, filled her lungs to capacity and as loud as she could and with great conviction, gave the best rendition of 'Teddy O'Neill' that you could ever hope to hear. Of course, every head in the audience turned around to hear and poor Dan was left standing on the stage. He'd lost his audience to Maggie O'Dea. Maggie was delighted with herself and slept well that night. I know, though, in my heart and soul that Dan and Maggie truly loved each other and their children, but those were hard times. As I know myself, hard times and challenges in life strain even the best relationships.

In 1957, the show pulled into Callan in County Kilkenny to rest up for a month or so. During this time Maggie became unwell and was admitted to the local hospital. I vaguely remember my father saying it was something to do with her heart, but she recovered and was soon due back home. We were told she was in such good spirits, in fact, she was singing and dancing around her bed with one of the nurses the night before she was due to leave. Sadly, she passed away later that night. As you can imagine, a huge sadness overcame the family that day and the sense of loss and grief was immeasurable. The local people were kind and supportive during those difficult days. Maggie O'Dea was laid to rest in the little graveyard in Callan. With heavy hearts, Dusky Dan's Variety

Show carried on performing and touring, returning to places where Maggie's voice would have captured the hearts of everyone who heard her sing. She was a huge loss to us all.

Her own family in Belfast, the Brennans, didn't know where she was or even that she had passed away. Many years later – 1991, I think – I was performing a concert in Belfast's Ulster Hall. As would often happen, some cards and notes came back to my dressing room for me. I noticed one, a letter from a family called Brennan, saying that they were my grandmother Maggie's family and that they would like to meet me. I was hesitantly optimistic, as since I had gained fame, I seemed to have accumulated relatives everywhere. However, I met this family after the concert and they told me some stories about Maggie and gave me some lovely photographs. I was beyond thrilled. I was able to let them know that Maggie had passed away many years ago and where she was laid to rest.

I visit my grandmother's grave any time I am in Kilkenny and have always felt sad at the thought of her in her solitary grave far from all her family. I wish that her life could have been easier and happier and that at least some of her musical dreams could have come true. Honestly, I have always felt a connection with Belfast any time I've played a concert there because of her. I give my performances everything I can, always doing it in her memory and hoping that, in some way, it allows part of her dream to come true, through me. It has always been emotional and uplifting at the same time.

Granddad continued touring with the family for many years after Maggie died and then eventually married a woman called Kathleen, who he'd spotted in the audience one night. He still had the charm and chat to attract the ladies. Dusky Dan retired from the show and settled down with

Kathleen in Ballymote, County Sligo, only about nine kilometres from where Granny Bee was situated in Ballintogher.

They lived in a UK army house provided for him because he had served in the British Army and his health had been affected from his time serving in France. I have lovely memories of that house in Camross, Ballymote and stayed there sometimes. Granddad and Katie always had nice things to eat (I especially loved the packets of pea soup). At one point, Mum, Dad and my sister, Barbara, who was aged around three at the time, lived there for a short while in our small caravan in the garden of the house, although I don't know what the circumstances of that were. With Dan now retired, the family were left to carry on the touring themselves, which wasn't without its challenges. For some of this time I was living in Ballintogher with Granny Bee and going to school there.

I'd sometimes spend a weekend in Ballymote, either in our wagon or with Granddad and Katie. I loved that because I got sixpence every Sunday and would walk into Ballymote to go to the cinema with some of the neighbours' kids, the Cawleys. I'd have enough money for the picture and a bag of sherbet. There wasn't a young girl anywhere happier than me, chatting, laughing and skipping down that road on those Sundays.

My grandfather and Katie later moved into Sligo to another ex-soldier's house, where they happily lived out the rest of their lives. We would often visit and I enjoyed our time together because I loved my grandfather. The years had rolled on and I was now singing with The Fairways Showband and due to release my very first record, 'Come Back, Billy Joe'. My grandfather couldn't have been prouder when I visited with that news. Granddad told me to order eight singles, one for him and one for each of the family. That was to be the last time I got to chat with him, my wonderful granddad

Dusky Dan. A few days later, I got a message from Katie to say he had taken a bad turn. I drove straight to the house and spent his last two nights with him, taking turns with Katie to sit by his bedside.

Thankfully, I was with him when he took his last breath. Dusky Dan died peacefully in his own bed, aged eighty-seven. I was devastated. I'd lost one of the people I most loved and admired. He had always been there with support, advice, help and anything else I might need. Two women who lived close by came to lay him out and, although I'd never experienced such a ritual before, I insisted on helping them to wash, prepare and dress my granddad for his final journey. This was the last act of kindness I could bestow on him. It broke my heart when my record was released and played on the radio shortly afterwards – Granddad had never got to hear it.

# 4

# GOODBYE TO THE SHOW

When I was aged almost nine, one day my whole world suddenly came crashing down around me. My magical life on the show was about to come to a very abrupt end. My mother and father brought me into the wagon and sat me down to tell me that the authorities had got on to them to say that I would have to enter mainstream education on a full-time basis. I couldn't understand it, as I was going to school about three times a month and anyway, my mother was giving me a great education – what more could I possibly need? My protest went unheard and before I knew it, I was retired from the stage and brought to live with Granny Bee in order to attend Ballintogher National School full-time. I was completely heart-broken. The show was the only life I knew. As I'm writing about it now, I can still feel the same sense of loneliness and abandonment as I watched the tail lights of Mum and Dad's car fade away. I had no idea when I would see them again, nor where they would be.

Granny Bee was a very regimental, no-nonsense sort. There would be no crying or feeling sorry for myself. Almost immediately, she set about getting me ready to attend school and at last she would have the chance to knock the 'show-craic' out of me, to make me a respectable church- and school-going girl. I knew from the beginning that this was not going to be anything like the life I was used to.

Straight away the tin bath was put in front of the fire, filled with hot water from a big pot on the range, then out came a cloth and a big bar of carbolic soap (I can still smell that soap!). She scrubbed me to within an inch of my life and got me dressed for bed. I spent a long, lonely night and wept for Mum, Dad and my baby sister, Barbara. I tried to console myself with the notion that since I was one of the star attractions on the show, they would have to come back to get me. I'd be severely missed. That was wishful thinking on my part and it was several months before I saw my family again. In fairness to me, though, over time I adapted quite well to being the 'real person' Granny wanted me to be, considering I'd had no previous training. I managed in a few different ways to generate a small audience for myself here and there, much to Granny Bee's dismay; she couldn't knock the show out of me completely. She'd say, 'Sure it's like a disease. You've some of that bad blood in you.'

I'll never forget my first day at Ballintogher school. The school had been built in the 1800s, two classrooms, both heated with log-burning stoves. My granny had resized one of my cousin's dresses for me, with a cardigan, white ankle socks and shoes. My hair parted to the side and held back with clips, I looked like a little angel. I walked up the village, schoolbag in hand, and up the steep hill from Mrs Treston's shop. No one went with me, so I had to introduce myself. It was a bright, sunny morning and, as I approached the school, I could hear all the children chattering in the field next to the school. I could see some sitting on the ground in a circle around a really pretty lady in a bright floral dress. They were all listening to her as she told a story and asked questions. She beckoned me to come over to join them and I did, kind of sheepishly. This was to be my teacher, Miss Philomena Dowling, and these were to be my classmates. We sat and talked as Miss Dowling introduced herself and the pupils to me and me to them. Introductions over with, we all went inside. It was a big-enough classroom, spotlessly clean, two children to each wooden desk, which had two inkwells and faced the teacher and blackboard. I didn't realise that day how lucky I was to be seated beside Margaret Craig, who would become a dear and lifelong friend. We had a connection straight away. Miss Dowling asked me to stand and tell everyone about myself. Shoulders back and head up, I proudly told them about my family and my time on the show. Immediately I knew I wasn't like the other children. I'd had a much different upbringing and I certainly was no shrinking violet, but, all in all, my first day went really well. I had a new friend in Margaret, and Miss Dowling, though strict, was lovely. I rushed back to Granny's to share all of my news about my first day at school. Granny was very proud, although she didn't show it.

Living in Granny's cottage with me were Bridgie and Teresa, the two daughters of one of Granny's brothers, Willie. Their two sisters, Mary and Margaret, lived with Aunty Sissy, Granny's sister next door. Their mother had died when they were very young and they came to live with Granny and Sissy while their father, Willie, went to England to work. The two sisters living with Sissy had a much easier life than poor Bridgie and Teresa. Granny Bee was very strict on them and they certainly lived every day in military fashion. I think I got the softer side of her, because I was always so tiny and pale, and she was afraid I'd get sick. On a daily basis, I was given cod liver oil to build me up. I hated the stuff, but a spoonful would be shoved into my mouth every morning.

There were many aspects to my new life and I embraced them as best I could. I was good at school as my mother had taught me well and anything I fell short on, my good friend Margaret Craig would help with. Miss Dowling, to my great surprise, was also a brilliant music teacher and when she discovered that I could sing, took a great interest in my voice. She trained me how to sing properly and to use my diaphragm. I would be kept in most days for an hour after school to practise. I really didn't appreciate it at the time, but what Miss Dowling taught me back then still stands to me today. I would never have gotten through eight shows a week, week after week, in *Patsy Cline – The Musical* or all the rehearsing and recording for my RTÉ series *Sandy*. I've done a lot of singing these past sixty years and I only remember a handful of occasions when I had a problem with my voice, all because Miss Dowling taught me how to use it properly. She would enter me in the Feis Shligigh and Feis Ceoil in Sligo and most of the time I won, thanks to her.

Miss Dowling even brought me to an audition for RTÉ Television's *Seoirse agus Beartlaí*, which I got. She took me to Dublin in her Volkswagen Beetle and left me with a woman she knew who ran a B&B. I was only eleven years old and when it came time for me to sleep in my own room, I was absolutely terrified. Cowering under the blankets, eventually I got up to find the lady and she let me sleep with her in her bed, which is hilarious to think of now. You see, I'd never slept in a room on my own before, not ever. I was glad to see the morning light, and I got dressed and waited for Miss Dowling to collect me and bring me to the RTÉ studios. I was beyond excited and nervous sitting in the RTÉ canteen and seeing so many people I recognised from the television. I had my autograph book at the ready and plucked up the courage to ask for a few signatures. Everyone was happy with my performance and we made our way back to Sligo.

I will forever be grateful to Miss Dowling for everything I learned from her and the wonderful encouragement she gave me. I adored her and we stayed in touch. She was invited to take part in a programme about me for RTÉ television in the early 1990s. I was very saddened when, not long after, at a relatively young age, Miss Dowling passed away. I won't ever forget the huge debt of gratitude I owe her.

Granny decided that I'd done enough of the singing lark, and to fit in locally, she signed me up for Irish dancing, which really wasn't my thing at all. Every Saturday, I had to cycle eight kilometres to Dromahair to Michael Gillespie's dancing school. I was a very good dancer, in my head at least; the problem was getting that confidence to my feet. Very soon, Granny and Mum were bringing me to the feis to compete, Granny no doubt thinking she'd make a real person out of me yet. But my mum and I had different plans. Mum would distract Granny Bee and I'd sneak off to enter the singing competitions. At the end of each feis, I had a handful of medals going home. Granny Bee told everyone she met in Ballintogher that I'd won them all for the dancing. She even made me a sash belt and sewed all my medals onto it. Poor Granny went to her grave thinking I was a champion dancer. My mother got a great kick out of that.

I settled in well in Ballintogher and learned, as my mother had as a young girl, how to navigate around Granny Bee's strict rules. In fact, it amused me to come up with new ideas, much as I had on the show. Granny Bee was devoted to her berry and flower garden. She grew gooseberries, blackcurrants and redcurrants. We would be sent, basket in hand, to collect the berries when ripe, and bring them along with eggs to Gilmartin's shop, to trade against the bill she ran up in her shopping book. She would send me to get whatever she needed and put it in the book on tick, and then hand in my basket of merchandise to trade against it. Isn't it such a quaint idea when you think of it? As delicious as those berries looked, I would never get away with eating even one of them. Granny had them counted, even while they were still growing on the trees, and they were strictly out of bounds for us. The eggs were also very important and not one of them could be wasted. One of the chickens used to peck her egg once she'd laid it and break it, so it was my job to stalk her till she'd go into the shed to lay the egg. I'd watch her and, as soon as the egg popped out, I had to grab it quick. Well, that chicken was so stubborn, she would lie in the nest, covering as much of herself as possible by pulling pieces of hay over her body with her beak while I sat in the dark watching her until eventually, she had to give in and lay the egg.

The flowers, on the other hand, could be a possibility for me. One day when Granny was visiting Sissy next door, I sneaked into Granny Bee's prized garden and discreetly picked a flower from here and there in the hope that spreading my collection out would make their disappearance less obvious. My beautiful flowers in hand, I set off to visit one of my favourite people, Mrs Jim Moran, who owned Moran's pub on the main street. In I went and hopped up on a stool at the bar where Mrs Jim was cleaning glasses. I asked her if she'd like to buy my lovely bunch of flowers to display in her bar. She smiled at me and said, 'Would you like a bar of chocolate, a sixpence piece or a bottle of Britvic orange as payment?' I thought it over and we agreed on the sixpence. I decided it would be easier to hide with no explanation needed when I got home. I thanked Mrs Jim and left, but as I got closer to home, the fear started to come over me. What if Granny knew? What if she was waiting on me? There was nothing else for it, so I opened the small garden gate and proceeded up the path and into the kitchen. There was Granny standing beside the range, frying Donnelly's sausages in the pan and boiling a pot of potatoes. When the sausages were done, she'd add a mug of Bisto gravy and some onions, and the smell was marvellous. All was well and my little expedition had gone unnoticed, this time at least!

My days in Ballintogher were busy with chores for Granny, including collecting the cinders from the creamery for the fire as my mother had done, and carrying buckets of water from the pump up the village. Once a week I'd have to accompany my cousin Mary, Sissy's daughter, to the chapel, to dust and clean. I loved that because I could go anywhere in the church that I wanted, even the sacristy, which had always seemed so mysterious to me. Full of ornate robes, candles and all kinds of wonders. On one occasion, I found a bottle of sacramental wine. Curiosity got the better of me, as I'd often seen the priest drinking it on the altar during mass. As quick as I could, I pulled out the cork and took a few sips. It wasn't too bad, red in colour and very sweet. I'd never really tasted anything like it before, except maybe the sherry I'd stolen from Granny the Christmas previous. My inspection over, it was time to dust the windowsills. They were quite high, but I'd hop up and, as I dusted each one, I would sing at the top of my voice. The sound in an empty church is just glorious. I'd sing to my heart's content, because when I'd get home there'd be no singing.

Cousin Mary, or Big Mary as she was called, also cleaned a large and ancient but beautiful house at the top of the village. Old Mrs Maguire lived there with her many cats, too many to count. On occasion, I used to help Mary clean the house and see to the old lady. I'd never, even in my wildest dreams, seen a house so full of beautiful things. It was like a manor house, but long and narrow, so there was no hall; you went from one room to the other. I would enter by the kitchen, where the range was always on, and so immediately felt warm and welcomed. The cats were everywhere: on top of cupboards, on tables, on chairs. A little creepy, perhaps. Most times I was there, Mrs Maguire would be in bed. She had a terrible shaking in her head and hands and it also affected her voice. I now realise, of course, that she had Parkinson's. From the kitchen, you went through the long, dark dining room and it led into a long, dark sitting room. Over the fireplace there was a really large, scary picture of a fox eating a chicken. The fox seemed to be glaring at me with hungry eyes. I never spent much time in that room but had to pass though it to climb the stairs to Mrs Maguire's bedroom. I was a little scared of her, but it seemed she was fond of me. Sometimes she gave me pocket money and one time a beautiful Victorian Christmas decoration. It was a circle of trumpet-blowing angels, attached to a circle of little candles, and when you'd light the candles, the angels would spin around. I loved it, I really wish I still had it, but I don't remember what happened to it.

# 5

# LIFE IN BALLINTOGHER

In a very short time, I got to know everyone in Ballintogher. If my memory serves me right, almost everyone welcomed me to the village, but a few certainly treated me differently. I hadn't fully grasped that, because of my father's occupation and my background, I really wouldn't be like others. I would on occasion hear whispered quietly, 'That's the showman's daughter' or 'She's a showman's daughter.' This got me thinking. I knew my mum and dad kept their private papers in a tin box in the trunk in Granny's room, the one she'd brought all the way back from America after my mum was born there. That trunk was completely off limits to anyone, except Granny Bee. But of course my curiosity got the better of me one day, and when I was sure she was out, I had a very quick but careful look. Mostly Bee's best bed and table linens, a few pieces of jewellery and the tin box containing the papers belonging to Mum and Dad. In it was an official piece of paper that said 'Birth Cert – Philomena Bridget Marion Ellis'. On this document it also said, 'Father's Occupation – Showman'. Right there and then, I knew who I was and I've been so proud of it ever since. So what if the odd person didn't accept me for who I am? It has never made me feel like a victim, but rather an achiever.

Most days, Granny would cycle over to her father, Tom Lynch's house. Although in his late nineties, he was still very active, but she liked to go over to clean the house and cook dinner for him and her brother Tom, who also lived there. The Lynch side of our family, Granny Bee's side, were, in her words, 'Respectable, good-living people'. This little white cottage out in the countryside was where she and her sister Sissy and their three brothers, Tom, Dan and Willie, were reared. I loved that wee house. It had three rooms. As you opened the half-door you entered the kitchen, which was in the middle of the house. To your right was a small bedroom with two beds; Great-granddad and Tom shared that room. On the other side of the kitchen was a small, pretty sitting room. A neat round table sat in the middle with two chairs, and a sideboard housed the family's best china, cutlery and glassware, used only on very special occasions. One such occasion was when it was their turn to have the 'station'. That was when the priest would come to say mass in the house and all the neighbours would attend and the cottage would be on show. We'd have been disgraced if the house wasn't spick and span, walls whitewashed inside and out, curtains and all table coverings washed. There would be fresh sliced ham, lettuce, tomatoes and scallions, accompanied by home-baked soda bread and freshly brewed tea, which would be served in a cup with a saucer, even if extra tea sets had to be borrowed for the day. That would be followed by home-baked apple tart and cream, and there would have to be a selection of pipe tobacco and cigarettes displayed throughout the house. But the most important aspect of the day would come when mass was said. The house and family blessed, the food eaten and the priest gone home, out would come the whiskey, sherry and porter. The drinking, singing and dancing would go on well into the wee small hours.

Great-granddad Tom's house was small, but cosy. There was a large open fireplace in the kitchen, which had crooks with big hooks to hold the cast-iron pot, pans and kettle over the coals. It was the centre of life in the home, heating the house, cooking the food and boiling the water for cleaning, washing us and any clothes that needed to be freshened up. There was a square stone laid each side of the grate to hold the heavy pots and pans. On the mantelpiece was an old clock that loudly tick-tocked day and night, sometimes sending you off to sleep if you sat in front of the fire. Also on the mantelpiece was a candle on each side, always at the ready in case the electricity went. There were a few old wooden chairs and milking stools on the stone floor around the kitchen. There was also a little hole in the stone floor where Great-granddad would pour in milk for the cat. The wooden kitchen table was beside a small but deep window, which had a pretty lace curtain.

Placed on the windowsill was the most precious thing in the house, the radio. Brown, wooden and shiny, it was guarded as if it was the family jewels; only Granny or Great-granddad were allowed to touch it. Many a Sunday was spent around the fire after lunch, listening to football. On other days, the radio would be switched on only for the Angelus and six o'clock news and a bit of céilí music after that. On certain nights of the week, a few ramblers would call in, local men, friends of the family. Great-granddad Tom would have a few bottles of stout warming in the ashes under the grate for the visitors. There was great excitement when we all gathered round to listen to the dramatic commentary as Cassius Clay fought Sonny Liston. It was the World Heavyweight Championship, 25 February 1964, just before my tenth birthday. Great-granddad Tom was delighted when Cassius Clay won the fight in the seventh round. When another tray of drinks went around to celebrate, even Granny Bee had a glass of sherry for the night that was in it. Quite often, and definitely on that night, I would do some Irish dancing, singing and play a few tunes on the tin whistle. There wasn't much Granny Bee could do to stop that, as my audience for the night clapped along. It would be quite late these nights when we'd start the walk back to Ballintogher. It was a long walk on a pitch-black road. I'd hear and see all sorts of spooky things from the fields and hedges.

Great-granddad Tom was always kind to me. Gilmartin's, like most shops back then, had a travelling shop and when it would call, he'd buy me a treat and I'd make it last all day. Another treat was when he'd let me hop on the back of the donkey and cart and go with him for spins. I was heartbroken when, aged ninety-nine years and counting down the days to his hundredth birthday and a cheque from the President, he went to kick the cat out of a bag of flour in the bottom of the dresser, fell on the stone floor and broke his hip. He was confined to his bed and died not too long after. I missed him and my visits over to the cottage very much. When I think of him, I think of the beautiful cherry tree in the front garden, which was planted by his dear wife, Mary, who passed away at a young age. Tom worked for the railroad and ran his small farm. Granny Bee, as the oldest girl, washed, fed and clothed her siblings. The little white cottage lies derelict now and there's no trace of the cherry tree. I've always regretted not buying it for my own family to enjoy. Ah well, we all have regrets of one kind or another.

Not all my memories of time spent in Ballintogher are good ones. Whenever anyone in the parish died, I dreaded the instruction from Granny Bee, 'Will you go to the shop, buy a mass card and run up to Father Gill's house to get it signed.' Going to Father Gill's house by yourself was a scary thing and to be avoided, if possible, because he was a very tall man, with a big red face, most of the time full of rage about something. I remember he was a regular visitor at Moran's pub, which could explain the red face. He was strict about the church and the school. I was on the balcony at mass one morning when he saw a woman in trousers coming up for communion. He roared at her to get out. He wouldn't allow women to wear trousers in church, and we had to cover our heads with black lace mantillas or hats.

That wasn't the worst of it. Some days I'd have to walk several miles on an errand of some kind for Granny Bee. I was always on the lookout for Father Gill driving his car. Even if I was walking with friends, he'd pull up beside me us and tell them to walk on as he needed to speak with me. In those days, the priest was the boss, so they did as they were told. I would never be cheeky, but when he'd offer me a lift, I'd have a list of excuses as to why I couldn't take it. He'd make me promise not to miss confession, which was as terrifying as the car. I always timed my entry into the confessional when it was busy and lots of people were waiting after me. I could get in, confess my sins, do my penance and leave. I'd be sitting there in the dark confessional, waiting for the little wooden hatch to open, revealing a metal ornamental grille with the priest sitting on the other side. Well, I'd say I'd said a bad word, or stolen flowers from Granny's garden and sold them for sixpence. I decided not to mention drinking some of the sacred wine; I figured I'd work that out with the man above directly. Father Gill would give me my penance, usually three Hail Marys, three Our Fathers and an Act of Contrition. But then the

Me, aged three, in 1957. I performed on stage every night as part of Dusky Dan's show.

Aged four, assisiting the magician (aka Uncle Jack).

(L–r): My grandmother Maggie Brennan, Dusky Dan, Uncle Pat as a child, Aunty Rita, Uncle Tommy, Frank (my dad), Aunt Liz and Uncle Jack.

My grandmother Maggie Brennan (who sang as Maggie O'Dea), with Frank (my dad) and Uncle Jack.

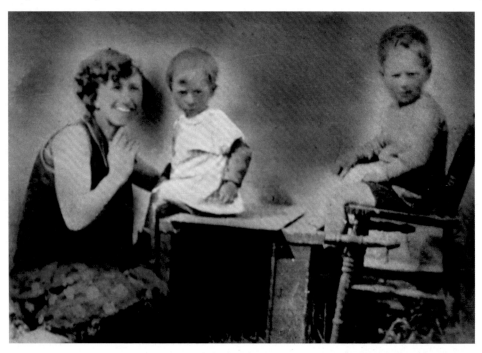

*Above* (back l–r): Uncle Tommy and my dad Frank; (front l–r) Aunty May, Uncle Jack and my mum Babs.

*Right:* My dad Frank singing on the show.

*Below*: My dad and Uncle Jack performing a typical drama on the show.

My mother, Babs, in 1954.

Dad and my sister Barbara in Granny Bee's garden, in 1964.

With my family the day I won the Maisie McDaniel Cup at the 1966 Carney Feis. Back (l–r): Mum, Dusky Dan, Aunty Liz, me, Dad; front (l–r): cousin Maggie, my sister Barbara and cousins Martin and Larry.

*Above left*: Me, aged sixteen, with The Jaguars, the resident band at The Golden Garter, Manchester, in 1970. *Above right*: Publicity shot for The Fairways in 1974.

The Fairways band in 1974: (l–r) Tom Kelly, me, Mike Kelly, Gary Street, Tommy McDonagh and Murrough O'Brien.

*Above*: With Granny Bee outside St Theresa's Church in Ballintogher, County Sligo, on my wedding day in 1977.

*Left*: Me and Mike leaving our wedding reception at the Forest Park Hotel to go on our honeymoon.

*Above left:* Winning the 1982 National Song Contest with The Duskeys.
*Above right*: Spending some precious time at home with my children in 1982.
(L–r) Willie, Barbara and me.

(L–r): My sister Barbara and me in a 1977 publicity shot for The Fairways.

grilling would start. He'd ask me in a very quiet but stern voice why I hadn't come up to the house to visit him as I'd promised and why I wouldn't accept a lift. I'd promise him that absolutely I'd be up to visit soon. I'd have said anything to get out of that church.

But there was no avoiding him if someone died. I'd have to go to the house and get the mass card signed. On the last occasion I went, mass card in hand, he opened the door and ushered me into the sitting room, which was small and dark. He took the card to sign it. In my anxiety, I chattered away with some nonsense. And then it happened as I'd always feared it would. He stood behind me and, in a soft creepy voice, started telling me how to relax, then placed his hands on my hipbones. I didn't have a clue what he was thinking of doing, but I knew instantly that it wouldn't be good. I grabbed the card, made for the front door and took off down the road like an Olympic sprinter. That was the last time I ever got a mass card signed and I avoided Father Gill like the plague. When he was moved to a different parish, a calm was restored to my life in Ballintogher.

I wasn't at all shy about visiting people or stopping for a chat about the events of the day. That could be the handsome new teacher who had come to the school to teach us, Seamus McCormack. He was young and energetic, with lots of modern ideas about doing plays and learning music. So, quite a bit of time would be spent rehearsing for a play or a concert in the village hall, and it was great fun. I also spent a lot of time either running errands to Gilmartin's shop for Granny or playing with the Gilmartin children. There were seven of them with their mum, Annie, and father, James, a really nice welcoming family. Sadly, James passed away at a young age, leaving Mrs Gilmartin to run the family shop and rear the children. She did a wonderful job of both. I would hang out with the eldest daughter, Marian.

She was a class ahead of me at school and was due to go away to secondary school. We spent many a day sitting on Hannon's wall, dreaming and planning out our lives. Marian ended up having a hugely successful career as a politician, Marian Harkin. Me, well, as you know, I went back to show business. All these years later, we have remained good friends. Gilmartin's shop, to think of it now, instils a warm glow in my heart. The fun playing games in the store shed, the lovely treats we'd get in the kitchen, the spins in the back of the travelling shop. Every week I'd go down just to see what new delight would be in the shop window and the highlight of my year would be excitedly waiting for the window to be decorated for Christmas. When I'd see the tinsel and lights, chocolates, biscuits and small toys on display, for me it was the start of my Christmas.

Earlier I was telling you about my first day at Ballintogher National School and how lucky I was to be seated next to Margaret Craig. Margaret, a very quiet, polite girl, pretty and with the most beautiful long blonde hair, brought so much joy to my life. I'd never really had a friend like that, a sister really. Craigs' house was a lovely old-style house. I loved it there and many times was invited to stay a night or two, which was always a delight. I loved Mrs Craig's cooking. On a Friday, the Craig family could eat meat, because they were Church of Ireland. But Mrs Craig wouldn't let me have meat because I was Catholic. Instead, I'd get a fried egg with my dinner. Also, she'd polish my shoes on a Saturday night for mass on a Sunday. She was such a kind-hearted lady. Margaret and I slept in the spare bedroom and we'd chat and giggle into the wee small hours, by the light of a candle on the bedside locker. The family used an oil lamp at night in the kitchen, which was so cosy with the heat from the range, which seemed to be on all the time.

One very dark night, Margaret had been visiting me at Granny's and I asked Granny if I could walk Margaret back down Craig's Lane and stay the night, which she allowed. To be honest, we wanted to get down the lane quick, because for a joke I'd agreed to meet a young fella from Ballygawley, which was about three miles (five kilometres) away. I never really thought he'd take it seriously and walk over. Anyway, Margaret and I ran up the village to the lane, when we heard two boys chatting in the distance but coming from the Ballygawley direction. Then I spotted him, his trademark white socks like beacons coming at me. I said, 'Oh my God, Margaret, it's him and he's brought a friend!' I was terrified. I'd never met up with a boy before – I was too young. With fright, we both burst out laughing and then legged it up the lane like rockets. But they saw us and called out. We kept running with the two boys in hot pursuit. About halfway up the lane, they caught up with us. The two boys were gearing up for a big chat, when Margaret spotted a flashlight coming along the lane from her house. Margaret said, 'Sacred Heart, it's me father.' And it was. Her dad, George, called out, 'Is that you, Margaret?' In that instant, I pushed one of the guys into the hedge and Margaret pushed the other. 'Yes, Dad', Margaret said. 'It's me and Phil.' Off we went, leaving the boys lying in the hedge. When we got into the bed, we were sore from laughing. Mrs Craig shouted down to the room, 'In the name of God, girls, what are ye laughing at? Put out that candle and go to sleep.' The laughing went on long after the candle was blown out.

I loved those times in the Craigs' home. On a sunny day we'd sit out the front, Anna, Margaret and I, reading Anna's *Spotlight* magazine, daydreaming about all the showband stars of the day. Anna would wind up her record player and we'd sit and listen to Joe Dolan, Anna's favourite.

Oh, just thinking back on it, lazy summer days lying on the grass, listening to the music and fantasising about what great things lay ahead of us in life!

I very rarely visit Ballintogher now, and it makes me sad to think back. Today the village stands very proud, with prettily painted buildings and flowers planted everywhere. Craigs' lane has been transformed into a magical nature walk with a fairy hotel. Granny Bee's cottage now belongs to a family who use it as a holiday home, not a sign of Granny's treasured berry trees or her precious flowers. Ballintogher is a beautiful place that once was home to me and my family. I can honestly say that my time there was the closest I came to belonging anywhere. I still love to visit Moran's pub but it makes me a little sad to think back. Today the village stands proud with quaintly painted buildings, Craigs' Lane has been transformed into a magical nature trail including a fairy hotel. Margaret Henry née (Craig) and I must take that walk again one day.

# 6

# MY SISTER BARBARA – THE EARLY YEARS

I remember when I first saw my sister, Barbara. I was eight, and we were out travelling with the show, moving towards Sligo so that Mum, who was nearing the delivery date for her baby, could go to Sligo General Hospital to give birth, as she had done with Francis and me. We were putting on the show in Mohill, County Leitrim, when Mum went into labour earlier than expected. There was a small hospital housed in an old but quaint building, Mohill District Hospital. I waited with Uncle Jack and Aunt May for news, while my dad waited at the hospital. Oh God, the excitement was nearly too much and the waiting seemed to go on forever. This time I was praying hard that, be it a boy or a girl, our new baby would stay with us and not be taken away by the angels, like Francis. I needed some company.

Finally, the news came. Dad arrived into Jack's wagon, lit up like a Christmas tree. I had a baby sister: Barbara Ann Patricia was safely delivered, weighing in at 6 lb 2 oz and, according to my father, she was just beautiful. I could hardly contain myself. And then, as if the day couldn't possibly be any better, Dad said, 'Put on your coat and I'll bring you to meet your sister.' Up we went to the hospital and I waited in the corridor as Dad went to get Barbara. There she was, tiny little face and hands, all wrapped up in a blanket. I peeped in. Dad was right: she was beautiful, just perfect, like a little doll. I couldn't have been happier. I didn't see Mum – in fact, they had made an exception in letting Dad bring me in at all. Just before it was time to leave and before handing Barbara back to the nurse, Dad gently placed her into my arms, and looking at her, I knew I'd have a friend for life.

It must have been wonderful for Mum and Dad to have another child and I'm sure they were happy too to have a beautiful baby, as I was just weird with my pixie ears, eyes and nose. Anyway, my new sister, Mum and I moved to Ballintogher to stay a while with Granny Bee, so that Mum could rest, while Dad continued on with the show. Barbara became the focus of my everyday life. Each new thing she learned to do became the highlight of every day. Because of the pain of losing my brother, I think our parents loved her in a very special way, but I wasn't at all put out because I loved her so much too. Every single thing she needed or wanted we tried to get for her, even if it meant going without ourselves.

I remember one occasion really well. We were moving the show to another village, Mum and Dad as usual travelling in the car, towing our wagon, with Barbara, then aged three, and me on the bed looking out the window. Barbara spotted an inflatable Donald Duck character in a shop window and started screaming and crying and by God, even then she could

70

stir up a racket. She wanted Donald Duck and she wanted it right now. Finally, I managed to get Dad to stop and when I explained what had happened, would you believe it, he and Mum put whatever change they had together and went back to get Donald Duck for the newest member of our family.

Barbara was loved, adored and probably a little spoiled by us all. As a small child she was pretty and dainty, with long, blonde curly hair and almond-shaped eyes. My dad, especially, never seemed to let her out of his arms, and that love and bond was there right up until Dad passed away in 2013. He loved her during her good, happy times and supported her and loved her on her darkest days. Because I had to grow up so young, I was very independent – Dad trusted that I'd be okay – but he always worried about Barbara and looked out for her more, as did I.

In 1968, Mum and Dad decided to apply to Sligo County Council for a house. Dad got a job in Gilmore's garage in Ballymote and I had finished in Ballintogher National School and would now go to Colaiste Muire in Ballymote. Our Sundays were spent visiting houses on the list that was provided to us. As this would be the first time we'd lived in a house as a family, it was a big deal to us, so you can imagine our excitement. The list wasn't that long and, to our dismay, the houses were all in the middle of nowhere. Old, dirty and some uninhabitable, they hadn't been lived in for years or cleaned out after former occupants.

It was heartbreaking to see Mum and Dad's excitement fade to disappointment with each house. They were told there was nothing else available. We went to see a semi-detached house near Ballymote, as Dad could drop us to school on his way to work and then we could walk home. It hadn't been lived in for several years. The first thing that greeted us was the awful smell. Everything was dark: the inside doors all painted black and the walls a reddish colour. One bedroom, a kitchen and a living room downstairs, with just two bedrooms upstairs. The small kitchen was filthy and opened out into a dark, dreary living room. A small hallway, but no bathroom. There was a mattress on the bed upstairs kind of folded over and I swear it was moving. Unfortunately, we got way too close before we discovered it was riddled with fleas. We all legged it down the stairs, Granny Bee and all, out the front door into the garden. Well, the itching and scratching started and I can tell you without a word of exaggeration we were doing Riverdance around the garden that day, and fair play to Granny Bee, Michael Flatley himself wouldn't lift the legs any higher. Off came Granny's pink bloomers – the fleas had made their way up the legs. We scratched the whole way back to Ballintogher where Granny lined us all up on her back street to disrobe down to our underwear and we had to leave our Sunday best lying there. Before we could enter the house, we were washed down. Out came the DDT to kill the fleas on us and our clothes. It was an awful white powdery stuff with the worst smell. It was banned some years later because it was deemed dangerous to humans and animals.

Our flea fiasco dealt with, Dad got on to the county council to tell them about the flea infestation in the house. When they had dealt with that, sadly, we had to move in. It was horrible. We scrubbed everything from top to bottom. All the floors downstairs were stone and it was my job to scrub those. I was good at that – Granny had taught me well. The stairs were plain old worn wood but in the two bedrooms upstairs, the wooden floors were red rotten. If you went up there, which we rarely did, you had to keep to the walls for fear of falling through. Dad brought home some empty orange crates and built them into the shape of a couch, threw a bedspread over it and there was our sofa. We had a small metal dining table and four chairs, and that was it. The kitchen had a small cooker and a worktop with a sink. There was a little open fire in the living area, which we loved at night. Mum, Dad, Barbara and I didn't need a lot to be happy, just each other's company with stories and jokes. We shared the bedroom downstairs, with Mum and Dad's bed at the end of our bed. It took a few weeks, but we made that house our home.

Where we lived was just two houses down from where a Traveller family lived. The older woman, with her long plaited hair and woollen shawl, would call in to Mum if she'd received a letter in the post and needed it read. I'd sometimes arrive home from school to see the two of them sitting by the fire, chatting and drinking tea. She fascinated me. I'd only ever seen anyone like that in the Western movies I loved, about cowboys and Indians, as we called them then. At night, my sister and I would kneel on two chairs to look out the window, to watch the Traveller family sit around an open fire in the front garden of their house.

Some days Dad would collect Barbara from school. Once, he arrived to find that she'd already left, but no one knew where she'd gone. She was six years old, so there was instant panic. Dad quickly set about looking for her and so did I. We checked back home with Mum and she wasn't there. Now we were all panicking, even going to the gardaí for help. Some hours later, we heard the sounds of a horse's hooves and laughter, and there she was, swinging her little legs off the back of the Traveller family's cart. She'd gone off with them after school for a spin and was full of chat, telling us all about it. We were so relieved to see her that she didn't get told off. One of Barbara's greatest qualities was that she treated people equally. It didn't matter who you were or where you came from, in Barbara's eyes we were all exactly the same. If she liked and befriended you, she'd do anything for you, and always shared what she could with anyone who needed it, even when sometimes she might have needed help herself.

We hadn't been in the house in Ballymote very long, maybe a month, when Mum first started showing signs of sickness. She was now in bed most of the time. She'd have the odd good day when she'd feel up to looking after us and the house. But those days got fewer and fewer. She had headaches, fevers, dizzy spells. The doctor told her to rest in bed and that most likely she was going through 'the change'. She was only thirty-eight, though. She was never sent to hospital or for any tests. She still managed as best she could to hold on to her wicked sense of humour, playing pranks on us when she was well enough. Over the four months we lived in that house, her health deteriorated rapidly. This was especially hard on Barbara because Mum doted on her. I started to become more responsible for Barbara as Mum was no longer able to cook or clean. I'd have to stay back from school or be called home early to look after them both.

Everything as we knew it was changing, and my sister found that hard to process at six years of age. It was coming up to Christmas and my parents and I decided we'd go to Wales, where most of the family had moved when the show stopped touring. We decided we'd leave Ballymote on New Year's Eve.

We went through the motions of Christmas, and Mum and I managed to make it into Ballymote for a little Christmas shopping. As usual, we didn't have a lot of money, but we bought small gifts to exchange on Christmas morning. I will never forget looking into a shop window all lit up with Christmas lights and decorated with tinsel, and Mum noticing me gazing at a tiny little heart on a chain. She asked if I would like to have it for Christmas. I said it was much too expensive, but she caught me by the hand and led me into the shop, where she asked to see the pendant in the window. She held it up against my neck, then handed the shopkeeper some money, saying, 'We'll take this. Merry Christmas!' as she placed it in my hand. I was so happy; if you'd given me the Taylor-Burton diamond, it wouldn't have felt any better. I couldn't help but worry, though, what Mum had done without for me to have it.

We spent Christmas with Granny, as always, and she was sad to learn we would be leaving again. It would be better, however, for Mum and my sister to be back with all the family, much like when we were all together on the show. I would miss some things about Ballymote. I loved Colaiste Muire, where Sister Veronica, although very strict, was really kind to me. I loved the students, the classes and teachers. None of them knew back then what my family and I were going through or about our awful struggles, and how would they?

Christmas was a sad one, as we had packed what little we had to leave the house after only four months and prepare for our journey to Wales. I know that we drove on New Year's Eve in very bad weather to Dún Laoghaire for the sailing to Holyhead. For some reason, which I can't recall, we went on as foot passengers with our luggage, everything we had packed into two tea chests, and the car was left behind. Maybe Dad didn't have enough to pay for the car passage. On the crossing, Mum was still not at all well, but we got through it as best we could. Eventually, we arrived in Holyhead and, with some help, managed to get all our stuff onto the pier. It was very late at night and it was snowing heavily. We didn't have long to wait for Uncle Jack to arrive and we were very happy to see him.

# 7

# WALES

The journey to Wales seemed endless as Uncle Jack drove slowly through the heavy snowfall. We were all squeezed into his car with our earthly belongings in the two tea chests tied to the back. Eventually we arrived at our destination: Caegarw caravan site. As we piled into Aunt May and Uncle Jack's mobile home, I was astonished to see how lovely it was. There was a separate full kitchen, a living room, bathroom and two bedrooms. We were excited to meet our young cousins and sat around chatting, eating and laughing. Uncle Jack and Aunt May were going to put us up until Dad got a job and we could afford a wagon of some kind. The next day, we met up with Dad's sister Liz, her husband, Simon, and more of our younger cousins, who also lived at Caegarw. We were the only Irish family there but there were enough of us to keep each other company – six adults and eleven children. It was a well-maintained site and most people kept pretty gardens and had nice homes.

Caegarw was near a small village called Pyle, about a fifteen-minute walk away. After a few weeks, Dad got a job as a mechanic in a local scrapyard. Barbara and I started school with our cousins, Barbara attending the junior school in St Joseph's, Port Talbot while I went to St Joseph's comprehensive school. Before long, my dad arrived with a caravan for us that he'd picked up at the scrapyard, and I can tell you it needed a lot of doing up and cleaning. It had a very small kitchen, a small living area with a drop-down bed for my sister and me, and a little bedroom for our parents. So here we were, starting all over yet again with not a penny in our pockets. But it had never been any other way. My father wasn't idle one day in his life, yet we always lived from day to day.

Unfortunately, the move did nothing for my mum's health. In fact, she got worse. The headaches were so bad that she'd ask Dad to tie something tight around her head to help with the pain. She wouldn't go to a doctor but someone – I never found out who – recommended a doctor to call out to her. He was a strange sort of man and I disliked him right from the beginning. He gave Mum a bottle of tablets, which I later found out weren't even legal. My mum was not depressed but sick. The tablets were only sedating her, but of course in her pain, she was only too glad to get them. Still, though, no tests or hospitals.

This went on for about a year and it was sheer hell. There were times when Mum would be up and about and able to function. As well as the day jobs, the family formed a band to play in the clubs at night for some extra money: Dad on drums, May on guitar, Jack on accordion and sometimes Liz would join in on accordion also. Both Jack and Liz had great voices and personalities. Four nights a week, I would also be there to sing and do a bit of Irish dancing. I did my homework in the interval.

Although I'd always done well at school, I found it extremely difficult in St Joseph's. Based on my school report, I was placed in the highest-ability class, called '4 North'. That sounded great but the students were only a little over a year away from their exams and I had missed the first two years. What with that and minding my mum and sister, and singing at night, catching up was impossible. Strangely, I never really wanted to sing. I had my heart set on becoming a schoolteacher. Singing was just something I always did and it held no challenge or excitement for me.

There was a terrible stigma attached to living on the caravan site and to being Irish. We were bullied and taunted. We would all wait outside the caravan site for the bus to take us the eight miles to school. We'd stand in the aisle as no one would let us sit down. At school, the taunting was worse. We would be teased with a song from a television advert, 'Irish Bacon, Lean and Tasty'. At morning assembly no one would stand beside us, saying we smelled bad. It was humiliating, but we just took it all. I thought maybe we were not as good as anyone else.

The school lunches are embedded in my memory. As I queued up outside the dining hall staring at it all, I could overhear the other students saying, 'Do we really have to eat this slop again?' and 'It's disgusting.' I'd reply that yes, it was the worst food I'd tasted, but the truth of it was that, other than Granny Bee's cooking, it was the best I'd ever eaten. I loved all the new dishes I'd never heard of before – cottage pie with peas and gravy, Cornish pasty and chips, cheese, egg and tomato pie, casserole. There was also a different dessert every day. I'd only ever had jelly and ice cream on Sundays. For me, it was like Christmas every day. And of course, this was my main meal for the day; there certainly wouldn't be anything like that at home.

My sixteenth birthday was upon me. I had ordered a new coat from a catalogue but when it arrived, it was too long. I pulled my bed down from the wall, spread out the coat neatly and tacked up the hem up. I lifted the coat to try it on only to discover that I'd sewn it to the bedspread. It seemed I'd inherited my father's sewing skills. The day also arrived to sit the exams. I knew it was a waste of time even going in, but I did. I glanced at the questions, signed the blank sheet and sat there learning new songs instead. That was my last day in school.

I went looking for a job immediately. We needed the money and anyway, I wasn't going to give up on my ambition to have a life like everybody else. Nothing at the work recruitment office appealed to me, but I spotted an advert in the local paper for an accountant's clerk at a local office that looked after some quarries. I was interviewed by a lovely woman. She patiently listened to my lengthy explanation in relation to my education and my recent exams. I plucked up the courage to ask if she would consider giving me a written exam in lieu of the exam results from school. She thought for a few minutes, and then said 'Why not?' I believe she was amused at my forwardness, a craft I'd learned on the show and which has always served me well. As best I could, I completed the written and maths questions she'd prepared. As I waited, I wasn't optimistic, as nothing had come that easy in my life. She beckoned me back into the office, and I sat down, shaking like a leaf. With a big smile she said, 'You did good, and I am going to take you on trial, starting on Monday.'

I was in shock. I'd gotten the job I dreamed of, just like that. She went on to tell me that I would start as an accountant's clerk, using ledgers to log the daily, weekly and monthly takings from two of their quarries at a company called Hobbs. I'd have my own desk. It was all wonderful and I couldn't wait to tell my family.

The offices were in an old but characterful house in the countryside, set in wonderful gardens which I loved to look out on every day. I got the minibus to work every day and even had a uniform. I could also continue my work at night with the family band. My weekly pay was £8.50 and I also earned £10 per night for Mum and Dad by singing, but that pay packet from Hobbs every week made me so proud. Arriving at work those first few weeks was thrilling for me. The hours were 9am to 5pm. On the first day, I was surprised to see a woman pushing a trolley through the offices, going from desk to desk. She brought tea and coffee. I thought she was an angel from heaven. She also had my favourite, a Kit-Kat. Not only did I have a job, a desk, a calculator, a uniform and two quarries, but now I'd also be getting coffee and a Kit-Kat twice a day, and all at the age of sixteen. I enjoyed the work so much that quite often I'd take a shorter lunch break to get extra work done, much to the annoyance of some of my co-workers. It wasn't all good, to be honest. Sadly, once some of them found out where I lived, and I was obviously Irish, it made me a target for hurtful remarks and bad jokes. So, instead of making new friends, I spent most of my free time on my own in the beautiful gardens. I deeply appreciated my boss for giving me this chance, and I know she appreciated my dedication.

All the while, my mum was getting worse. She came to the clubs with us for the gigs for the first time in her life, and she, Lizzy and May would have a few drinks. She began to have aggressive outbursts, which was completely unlike her. One night coming back from a club gig, she started fighting with Dad. She made him stop the car, and then put her foot through the radio. She got out and kicked the headlights until she broke the glass. It was horrible. I'd never seen anyone act like that, let alone my mum. Dad was distraught. Our lives became a constant turmoil. As had happened in

Ballymote, I started having to leave work to look after Mum. My boss was a saint: she let me bring my calculator and figures home and then I'd just have to enter them into the ledger the next day.

One particular evening, Mum was in bed with one of Dad's ties wound around her head to help with the pain. She appeared to be speaking backwards and one of her eyes was turned a little. Of course she needed an ambulance, but she was being so difficult that we didn't want to upset her more than she already was. Dad stayed up with her. I went to work the next morning to bring in my figures but not long after I got into work, Dad called me to say Mum was having seizures. She was brought by ambulance to Morriston Hospital near Swansea. Dad collected me from work. It was distressing as this was the first time any of us had had to go to hospital. We were in the waiting room a long time and, though my father was trying to be strong, I could see how nervous and upset he was. Finally, we got to meet her doctor, a Dr Cast. He was so mild-mannered and soft-spoken that we were immediately put at ease. He told us that they had done some X-rays and scans and that my mum had a large clot on the brain that appeared to have been there for some time.

This was what was causing her symptoms – the severe headaches, blurred vision, dizziness, the impact on her speech and then eventually the seizures. Dr Cast said he needed to operate immediately or Mum would die and, even if she survived the surgery, he couldn't guarantee how well she would recover. We were in total shock, but we trusted Dr Cast. We had a couple of minutes to visit with my mother, although she really wasn't aware of us. As I held her hand, I was riddled with guilt. We had hardly ever had a disagreement, but just a few days earlier, we'd had words. She would become very agitated over the slightest thing and, out of nowhere, had asked me to move out. I'd said,

'Mum, I'm only sixteen. I'll leave when I'm eighteen.' I hadn't meant it and, as I held her hand, I prayed that she hadn't meant it either.

I won't even try to explain how we were feeling, between worry and tiredness. Mum's operation went as well as could be hoped for but the clot was very large and had caused some brain damage. It was a few hours before we were brought into a room to see her. It was shocking to see her lying there, tubes everywhere, the left side of her head shaved and stitched in a semicircle. I remember thinking we needed a miracle. We sat quietly beside her and just prayed.

We didn't know it then, but our lives were about to change forever. When Mum woke up, she was a different person. She couldn't speak or walk properly or use one side of her body. As soon as I could, I tried to say how sorry I was that we'd had words, but she didn't understand. I didn't return to my beloved job but instead spent most of the next six months at the hospital with Mum, and would sleep on a bench in the corridor. Dad continued working and visiting afterwards, sometimes bringing Barbara with him to see Mum. Over the next few months, with a lot of hard work from the amazing neurology team at Morriston Hospital, she was again able to walk and talk.

We spent Christmas Day 1970 with Mum in her hospital room. That might sound dreary, but it really wasn't. At this stage, we knew the staff very well so we were among friends. Mum's room was nicely decorated and we had Christmas party hats, a first for us. We were served a lovely full Christmas lunch, better than if we'd been at home. The song playing in the background was John Lennon's 'Happy Xmas (War is Over)' and now whenever I hear that song, it brings me right back to that Christmas Day in Mum's hospital room. Songs do that, don't they? Considering everything, it was a very special and happy Christmas. Mum had pulled through and we were all together. The icing on the cake was the special moment when Santa brought Barbara her Christmas present after lunch.

Shortly afterwards, Mum was transferred to a smaller hospital nearer to us in preparation for returning home. Social services had inspected our home and said it wasn't fit for purpose, so Dad had to come up with the money to get our first mobile home. It was lovely: a bedroom for Mum and Dad, a small kitchen-cum-dining area, a bathroom, and a living room with a sofa bed for my sister and me. Dad and I went to see Mum and brought her clothes for her journey home the next day. She was in great form and chatting about coming home. Very late that night there was a knock on the door. The farmer who owned the site we lived on had taken a call from the hospital: Mum had taken a turn and we were to go straight in.

When we arrived, it was horrendous. Mum was having seizures and wasn't conscious. It seemed impossible that we had been talking with her only a few hours earlier. Dad and I took it in turns to sit with her. We asked that she be transferred back to Dr Cast in Morriston but we were told she wouldn't survive the journey. I became overwhelmed with grief and got up to leave the room but only made it to the doorway. When I woke up, I was lying on a couch; I had fainted. A nurse got me to drink a glass of water and said I'd only been out for a minute. My father was as white as a ghost; I suppose he thought I was gone as well.

After another worrying night spent in a waiting room, we were told that Mum had improved enough to make the journey to Morriston. Our prayers had been answered. There, Dr Cast and his team immediately started scans and tests on Mum and it was quickly discovered that she had meningitis and needed more surgery. Dr Cast said that after the surgery,

Mum had been given tablets to prevent any infection, so he was confused. Instinctively, I picked up her handbag and looked inside. To my horror, I discovered all of the tablets in a box. She'd stopped taking them without telling anyone. Dr Cast was furious: why would she do such a thing? Well, we'll never know the answer to that. After six months of hard work and on the eve of getting her home, this was a cruel blow. I went to visit her after the surgery. My mum was gone forever. The physical person was there in some form, but her mind was somewhere else. She was not aware of where she was or what had happened.

After some time, she eventually came home and our lives became about caring for her – dressing, hygiene, feeding and exercise. Dad and I became full-time careers with absolutely no help from anyone else, physically or financially. As a break for me and for Mum, I would walk with her to Aunt Lizzy's or Aunt May's for a visit, but she couldn't settle anywhere for long.

We managed as best we could. Mum couldn't be left alone at all and the funny and loving mother we'd always known was now always fighting with us, always imagining we were doing stuff behind her back. Dad continued to do the clubs, but I stayed home to mind the family. I was now promoted to chief cook and bottle washer. It never at any stage occurred to us, nor was it suggested to us, that Mum be cared for in a facility. We did the best we could, but sure what did we know about caring for someone so dependent?

Out of the blue, I was asked to join a very popular Welsh group called The Jaguars. It was a chance of a lifetime for us. I reluctantly talked to Dad and we decided it was only fair that I give it a go. From my fixed-rate weekly wages, I'd support the family, and Dad would take care of Mum and Barbara. The band had a residency at The Golden Garter in Wythenshawe,

Manchester, the third-biggest cabaret supper club in the UK, which had opened two years earlier, in 1968.

I moved to Manchester to sing six nights a week with The Jaguars. There were three guys and three girls in the band and we would play on one of the smaller stages on either side of the large main stage in between the main artists, and for dancing at the end of the night. It was a spectacular place, with a lavish gold and crimson carpet and gilding throughout the room. The main stage came out in a semicircle and was dressed in beautiful ruffled curtains that would roll up when the main band played the intro for the star artist. It would be the same star act for the six nights: stars like Cliff Richard, Lulu, Dusty Springfield, Olivia Newton John, Tony Christie, Roy Orbison, Frank Ifield, The Shadows, Tommy Cooper, Val Doonican and Roger Whittaker, to name a few! The room could seat 1,400 people per night and I don't ever remember it not being sold out. You got a choice of full dinner menu, either three or five courses, along with cocktails, champagne or whatever your preference was, served at an exquisitely set table.

The Jaguars would start the night on one of the semicircle stages and an MC would announce us or whatever was happening next from the main stage. After us, Shep's Banjo Boys would entertain on the other stage. I'd only ever seen a place like this in the movies. Next up on the main stage were three women from Australia, who shared a dressing room with us. I was transfixed every night watching them transform themselves into super-models. Hair pinned back, first they did their make-up. It was a work of art. Then out came the wigs, beautiful long hair which they attached like it was their own. To finish, they would step into gorgeous, sexy sequinned outfits. The singer wore a gold sequinned leotard and the two dancers wore short, flowy costumes. I reckoned they were in their late thirties and I remember being impressed that they danced so well, as I thought they were old. I used to sneak out every night to watch them. Their performance was stunning! I learned much about professionalism, make-up and costumes.

I relished working at the Golden Garter and meeting people, including some of the biggest stars of the time. Unfortunately, Dad wasn't managing too well at home. It was all too much for him. I was heartbroken when I had to leave the band and return home to Caegarw to help him.

Another dream shattered, but it was the right thing to do. Dad went back to working in the scrapyard. A year or so went by like that and we struggled along, Barbara going to school, Dad working and me at home. It was very hard to listen to Mum talking and giving out endlessly about things that weren't actually happening, and blaming me or my sister but mostly Dad. I know that she couldn't help it but honestly, it was hell on a daily basis. Eventually, I lost it. I had a total meltdown. I remember crying loudly and trying to pull the sink off the wall in the bathroom out of frustration. Dad brought me next door to Aunt May's to calm down. She put me into bed and went to make me a mug of tea. I was sitting up, rocking to and fro and repeating 'I can't'. I just wanted to be sent away somewhere and be locked up away from all this pain.

Granny Bee came to visit with her son, Seamus, and she blamed me for what had happened to Mum. Someone in the family had told her about the disagreement Mum and I had had just before she was admitted to hospital. Granny Bee pretty much ignored me through the whole visit instead of noticing how much I was struggling. But I had flirted with insanity and decided that it wasn't for me. I got on with the job at hand and I've been able to do that ever since.

When I turned eighteen, I was invited to audition for a position in a group, Steve Hare and the Bunnies (that's not sexist at all, is it?). It was a typical Welsh cabaret show with Steve, the lone male singer, and three girl singers. The manager, Ron Williams, played the Hammond organ and there was also a drummer. I sang a few songs and after the audition Ron offered me a place in the group. Good, steady work and wages. It was then confirmed that I would be replacing Bonnie Tyler as lead female singer. She'd had to quit because of nodules on her vocal cords. After surgery, she'd been left with that deep, husky, raspy voice which made her world famous. I never met her, but I inherited all her costumes. We needed the money, so I took the job. I would stay with Mum and Barbara until Dad came home, then I'd catch a bus for the forty-minute journey to Swansea, where Ron and the rest of the group would pick me up. Ron and his wife Beatrice were the sweetest people and after each show, I would stay over at Ron and Beatie's.

They had a lovely home and made me welcome. I felt like I'd been adopted! Beatie would give me hot cocoa before bed. The bed was pre-heated with an electric blanket, another first for me. Dad would pick me up around 8am every day, while Mum still slept. He'd drop me home and I would take over day duties. That was the routine every night I had a gig, which was four or five nights every week. The Bunnies were popular, and we had a wide variety of music. We'd sing the hits of the day and I would also do the Shirley Bassey hits. There was even some comedy in the show, which always went down well. Our many costume changes were fairly sexy: we'd start off in sparkly shorts and tops, then wear long dresses, then bikinis with fringing and finish the show in (wait for it!) bunny-girl outfits, complete with white fluffy tails.

I spent a very happy year with the Bunnies and would have stayed longer if I could have. We got a residency three nights a week in a big nightclub in Llanelli called The Glen. On one night we sang upstairs in the cabaret room and on the other nights in the large club for dancing. The crowd were mostly regular and local. There was a really nice young guy there most nights who always asked me for a date. I always said no. To be honest, where would I have got the time? Eventually, I agreed and he offered to pick me up outside The Tap pub. I saw him approach and nervously waited for him to stop and get me, but to my surprise he looked at me and drove straight past. This happened three times until I practically had to throw myself in front of his car. When I opened the car door to sit in, he looked confused and said, 'Is that you?' to which I replied, 'Yes! What do you mean?' Then it struck me that he had only ever seen me in sequins, a long blonde wig, false eyelashes, boots and a whole lot of make-up. Here I was with shoulder-length brown hair, wearing a sweater and jeans and very little make-up. No wonder he didn't recognise me. It was a very awkward date and I ended up watching rugby in the pub with his friends. Needless to say, there was no second date.

There was a handsome entertainments manager in The Glen, who was maybe six years older than me. He also asked me out, but I declined. For one thing, I heard he'd separated recently from his wife; besides, I didn't have time to socialise. Ron, our manager, didn't encourage that sort of thing. His name was Peter Phillips. He also wrote a review column for the *New Musical Express*. Well, he was very charming and persistent. One night while I was on my break and sipping a Coke, he came up behind my chair and held a buttered bap on either side of my head. He said if I didn't go on a date with him, he'd put butter through my hair. He had invitations to see

Paul McCartney and Wings in the theatre in Cardiff as he was writing an article on the concert, and on the album *Red Rose Speedway* and the single 'Live and Let Die'. I agreed to one date.

I couldn't wait to see Wings and I bought a lovely yellow two-piece trouser suit for the concert. Peter picked me up in a taxi from my flat in Pyle on 13 May 1973 and off we went. We had great seats, in the middle section of the second row. Surprisingly, it wasn't a very big theatre, but I think Paul McCartney loved the intimacy of performing to a small crowd. I don't think the Beatles had ever sung to an audience without being screamed at. The opening act for Wings was a slim old lady in a ballerina's tutu and, I assume, her elderly husband in a black tail suit, and four poodles doing tricks. It was quite bizarre. I wasn't sure if we were to take it seriously. Paul McCartney came on with Wings: Linda McCartney on keyboards, Henry McCullough on guitar and Denny Laine of the Moody Blues. It was an amazing night and the crowd just went crazy. Peter was lovely and I would see him often at The Glen because we both worked there. I liked him a lot and believe that the feeling was mutual, but before it got too serious, we ended it. It would have been too complicated. As it turned out, Mum's consultant, Dr Cast, told my dad they couldn't do anything more for Mum and he recommended that we bring her back home to Ballintogher.

Mum, Dad and Barbara travelled on ahead to Granny's. I stayed in Wales for a few months to work out my notice with the Bunnies, sell our mobile home and get a smaller caravan to send to Ireland. With a heavy heart, I did all of that and then returned home to Ballintogher to join my family.

A funny and ridiculous story about that journey was that I had promised my sister a Pekingese puppy. I duly bought a beautiful six-week-old tan-coloured puppy, brought him to the vet to be vaccinated and obtain papers for his travels and a little carry basket. At the airport, I discovered I'd left the puppy's paperwork behind. I was wearing a large fake-fur coat, so I just put the puppy down my sweater. The wee fella slept until shortly after take-off, when he gave the odd little bark and started moving. What I must have looked like, with moving breasts, I can't imagine! Barbara couldn't have been happier with her new puppy, whom she called Ching. If I tried that stunt today, I'd be put in jail!

# 8

# THE FAIRWAYS & MIKE KELLY

t's a strange story how I came to join The Fairways showband. Having returned to Ballintogher in Sligo, and aged just nineteen, I decided to retire from show business. I'd already been a performer for the best part of sixteen years and I was tired. I didn't really see a future in it, with having to look after my mum and raise my sister, who was now eleven and attending Ballintogher National School. However, after a few weeks I was completely broke and, for the most part, my family were relying on me financially. Dad had his little garage, but it was only starting up and took a while to bring in revenue of any kind, a few pounds here and there. For as long as I can remember growing up, we struggled financially as a family, at times not even having enough to eat. We always ate well on a Sunday for some reason, but it was downhill the rest of the week.

I placed a small advert in the *Sligo Champion,* looking for musicians to start a small pub band. To my surprise, I got a good number of replies and after meeting with some of them, I decided on three musicians. The first was a guy from America, Gerry Gallagher, on lead guitar. At this time I decided to have a stage name and Gerry encouraged me to choose the name Sandy. So, in 1973, Sandy Duskey became the front-person of a small group called Easy Listening. Playing a variety of popular well-known songs, we became very busy within a short time. I would bring the PA system, such as it was, in the back of the car, a little red and cream Austin my dad had bought for me.

One night we were playing in a local lounge, Coolera House. We went on to a full house to play our first set. When we took a break, Michael, the owner, said that a man called Tom Kelly had rung, explaining that he was the manager of The Fairways showband and that he wanted to hear me sing. He asked Michael to leave the phone off the hook for a while so that he could listen. I thought this was hilarious and promptly forgot about it. After the gig, though, Tom Kelly rang back. He told me that his brother Liam had heard me sing the week before and had suggested that Tom look me up. The Fairways showband were looking for a new girl singer and he asked if I'd audition. I immediately said, 'Thank you, but no.' I was happy in my small group playing locally, making a few bob and still being able to care for my mum and Barbara. A few days went by and Tom rang me again, this time on the public phone at the top of Ballintogher village. It's funny to think of it now but I used that phone box as an office. I'd ring around for bookings, pretending to be Sandy Duskey's manager. On other occasions, like the day Tom called, someone living nearby or passing would hear the phone ringing, answer it and then, if it was for me, they'd come all the way to the bottom of the village to get me. Isn't it a million miles from where we are today with all our technology?

Anyway, Tom tried to convince me to audition with The Fairways, and again I said no. Until he mentioned that there would be £30 expenses for me if I did it, so I agreed. Delighted with myself on the way home to tell Dad, I was thinking I'd do the audition, get my £30 and turn down the job. I was sure I'd get the audition: apart from my show background, I'd gained a wealth of experience in Wales. I asked my best friend, Margaret Craig, to come with me. My father wasn't too excited about it; after all, he'd been through this before, having to mind my mum and Barbara when I'd go out singing at night. I assured him that I had no intention of taking the job and was only going for the £30.

The following week, The Fairways were playing in a hall in Newport, County Mayo and I went to audition that evening before the dance. It was June 1974 and I was twenty years old. Margaret and I headed off in my little Austin and we chatted and laughed the whole way there. When we arrived, the band were just finishing setting up. I was wearing a brown shirt and my best yellow trouser suit (the one I'd worn to go see Paul McCartney's Wings), a long string of yellow beads around my neck and, of course, my platform shoes. I think I even put on false eyelashes. But I was also on another mission. I'd been to see Margo's band the week before in Drumshanbo and the guitar vocalist was really good. His name was Frank McCaffery and I got speaking with him after the dance. A real gentleman, he walked me to my car and I told him about my upcoming audition with The Fairways and he promised to call over to the dance and we could chat some more.

While The Fairways were setting up, the current girl singer came to sit with Margaret and me. It felt really awkward and I was sorry that I was there to audition in front of her.

The Fairways were a pop showband: Gary Street on lead male vocals, Tom Kelly on piano (he was also the manager), Tom's brother Mike Kelly on bass, Hugh McCormack on lead guitar and Johnny Crean on drums, all typical long-haired pop musicians of the time. Because I'd spent several years in South Wales, I wasn't up to speed on the music scene at home and hadn't heard of them, but in fact they were very successful and well known on the showband circuit throughout the country. The audition was great fun, as I knew a lot of the songs from my time in Wales. Tom asked me if I knew the Peters and Lee duet 'Welcome Home'. Thankfully, I'd been singing it already. The harmony line, which I would take, was really distinctive. Gary Street and I sang the duet and it went great. I sang about six songs in all and that was the audition done. I went to sit with Margaret and wait for the band to start. Tom came to sit with us and chatted. He was very soft-spoken and I thought him a very genuine person. He said he thought I had potential and that he would really like me to join The Fairways show-band as front singer with Gary. I told him that I'd have to go home and talk it over with my dad. So Margaret and I waited for half of the dance, I said goodnight to Frank McCaffery, and we headed back to Sligo.

I was torn. The small group I'd started with Gerry Gallagher was together only about three months, and I didn't want to leave it and let the others down. But I chatted it over with my dad. Tom was offering me a weekly wage of £25. We needed the money, so we decided I should give it a try. After a few weeks of rehearsals, I left Easy Listening and joined The Fairways showband, for what was supposed to be a trial period for us all.

I ended up staying in the band until 1983, by which time Gary Street had gone back to the UK and we had become The Duskey Sisters.

During my years with The Fairways, we travelled the length and breadth of Ireland. Back in the 1970s, the roads were so bad, oftentimes we'd leave our homes as early as 11am to drive to a hall or marquee in Cork or Kerry. The six of us travelled together in a Transit van, the equipment and instruments in a compartment in the back and then seats for us. The boys would start by carrying in all the gear. Back then, the equipment was big and heavy and the walk to the stage was rarely easy to undertake. Around two hours later, the equipment was all set up, including some lighting, and we were ready to soundcheck, which regularly turned into a rock jam session.

The Fairways' programme was usually chart pop material and some classic rock. There would almost always be tea and sandwiches supplied for us in the hall before the dance started. At times you consumed the sandwiches at your own peril, for there was no telling how long they'd been sitting there. I have to say, though, we were fed well a lot of the time. Then we'd wait the couple of hours for the hall to open and the people to arrive, around 11pm or sometimes midnight. It was a sight to behold when the enthusiastic crowd would arrive in their droves: lads in their best Sunday suits and Brylcreemed hair, and girls in brightly coloured miniskirts or dresses, high heels and hair back-combed to sit as full and as high as possible. From our vantage point on the stage, we were entertained all night by the dancers. I used to brace myself when I'd call a new set. The girls would all be standing on one side of the hall, the lads on the other. As soon as we struck the first note, there'd be a stampede of guys charging across the floor to grab the hand of the girl they wanted to ask out to dance. There was always a great atmosphere and they'd dance till maybe half past two in the morning. We'd spend at least an hour then sitting on the front of the stage chatting to our fans and signing autographs. The lads in the band packed the gear, and then it was the long trip home. During peak periods of the year, we could work six or seven nights a week. Tom Kelly did most of the driving, as well as playing piano and managing the band. He was an incredibly hard worker, and still is. I'd drive to Ballina, leave my car at Tom's house and travel with the band. I'd get back into my car on our return at all hours and drive home to Ballintogher. I don't know how I did it. I was young, I suppose.

Mike Kelly and I sat in the row of seats behind the driver. We were the same age and became great friends in a very short time. He is a really good bass player and was great at putting together chord charts and arrangements for all the songs we'd need to learn. Mike knew the pressure I was under at home looking after my mother and was very supportive and a good listener on my down days. I don't honestly know if I'd have survived those years without Mike's friendship. He also became my protector. It wasn't easy travelling in all-male company all hours of the day and night. The conversation and jokes could sometimes be over the line but, in fairness, Tom and Mike made sure that I was neither embarrassed nor upset. Believe it or not, life on the show and in the fit-up road-show culture was very sheltered and disciplined. But I was also quiet and an expert at avoiding any kind of potential danger. That instinct had been instilled in me early and has served me well through all my life.

I began to look forward to my chats with Mike on those long journeys. It was sometimes like we were the only ones in the van. I saw him as a great friend and confidant. The band would always stop midway on the longer journeys for a cold drink or snack at some shop and petrol pumps. On one hot day, Mike and I were standing at the back of the van eating ice cream cones. Everything was normal, until out he came with, 'Will you go with me?' Shocked, I replied, 'Go where?' He said, 'Can I take you on a date?' Well, I nearly fainted. I swear to God, I was weak at the knees, and that was the end of my ice cream. I blurted out, 'Oh no, sorry, Mike. We're just great friends and anyway, you know my situation at home, I wouldn't be free to go on a date. As well as that, my father is very strict. And to be totally honest, in our culture we're expected to date within show-people circles and my father would be horrified if number one, I dated a "Josser" (a normal person) and number two, if I was seeing someone in the band. So thank you for asking, but, no.' Well, you'd think I had hit him with a mallet. He just stood there speechless. And right after he had plucked up the courage to ask me, he then had to sit beside me in the van, after being rejected. In my heart, I was very fond of Mike as a real friend, but I didn't think of him as a boyfriend. The next few weeks were very awkward between us. There was no laughing or joking out of Mike and he even stopped going for the tea and sandwiches, which wasn't at all like him.

One evening, after the soundcheck was done, Mike and I sat across from each other in the hall, the dance floor in between us. I tried smiling, but he just looked down at the floor like someone lost. So I thought I'd ask my dad if I could go on one date. Mike couldn't drive, so we decided that he could travel back to Sligo with me one night and could stay in Granny Bee's spare room. I cooked a breakfast fry for Mike, as I knew he liked a fry in the morning. He came over to the caravan and started eating, then said with shock, 'You didn't fry the tomato!' That should have been a clue right there: if something on his plate wasn't to his liking, you'd hear about it. From the get-go, my father wasn't too happy and God help my mother, she didn't understand anything that was happening around her. Oddly enough, Granny Bee liked Mike straight away. We weren't working that night so I asked my dad if we could go to the cinema in Sligo and he said yes. That was our first date and we had a great time. We knew each other well and had lots in common with the band and music, so it really wasn't any effort to get along. We set off to Ballina together the next day to join the band for our next gig. Only this time we weren't friends, but boyfriend and girlfriend.

Tom Kelly and his wife, Patricia, were happy for us, but the rest of the band certainly weren't. You could have cut the atmosphere with a knife in the van. In the beginning, I got on with Gary Street and we co-fronted The Fairways well together. Our duets were great and our voices blended perfectly as we sang the most popular songs of the day. Pretty soon, though, I found Gary very difficult to work with. The audience were convinced we were married because we had so much fun on stage but the truth of it was that we hardly spoke to each other off stage. It must have been hard for him as the lead singer having to share the limelight with me. I'd say he didn't expect me to be so popular.

We went up to Eamonn Andrews' studios in Dublin to record our first single together. We were to do a duet on a song Gary wrote, called 'Coco's Drum', and I was to record a Cliff Richard song, 'Come Back, Billie Jo' for the B-side. It was my first time recording. A few weeks later, Tom told me that Brian Molloy, of the record company Hawk Records, had decided to put my song on the A-side of the single and release it as my debut record. Gary was furious and let us all know how he felt. Not long afterwards, the whole band travelled to Drumshanbo to audition for *The Late Late Show*, which was travelling around the country carrying out auditions. My friend Charlie McGettigan told me years later that he was also at the audition and that Gary and The Fairways nearly blew the roof off the hall with 'House of the Rising Sun'. I also sang a solo. A few weeks later, *The Late Late* rang Tom Kelly to invite me to be a guest on the show, on my own, and shortly after, I made my first of many appearances on *The Late Late Show*, hosted by Gay Byrne. I'd been to RTÉ to sing when I was eleven, but this time I would be singing my first record, 'Come Back, Billie Jo'. I wore a maxi dress with blue feathers around the hem and a neck scarf of the same feathers. Another guest that evening was Yvonne Costello, who was Miss Ireland at the time. We were in the make-up room together and she had her dog with her. He took a shine to my feathers and made off with a mouthful before I could stop him. I had to guard them all night or my dress would have been bald by the time I sang.

It was exciting to be singing live on the biggest television show in Ireland. Gay Byrne was wonderful and a gracious host. The response to the appearance was huge and when I stepped onto the stage the next night to sing 'Come Back, Billie Jo' with The Fairways, I was overwhelmed by the audience's reaction, who were clapping and cheering and singing along. I had the feeling that my career might just be on the move in the right direction. But it would be a long and sometimes difficult journey. Gary was increasingly unhappy with my popularity. The sad thing is, he didn't need to feel that way because he was an amazing talent. He left The Fairways in 1976 and returned to England, where he passed away in 2003.

My relationship with Mike lasted longer than the one date. He was understanding and had a kind nature and I was becoming very close to him. Mike was living in a B&B in Ballina at the time and so I would collect him to meet up with the rest of the band at Tom's house and sometimes he would travel back to Ballintogher with me after the gig and stay with

Granny Bee. She'd have a list of chores for him to do around the house. She liked him because he came from a real and proper family, not like my dad. In fact, Mike and Granny Bee remained good friends right up until she passed away in 2011. Mike would spend most of his visit in Granny's, as my mum was very irritable and unpredictable, making it really difficult to have anyone visit.

When I started working with The Fairways, Dad, Mum, Barbara and I travelled up to Portnoo in Donegal to upgrade our caravan to a mobile home with amenities like the one in Wales. The man who sold the mobile homes was one of the kindest people I'd ever met. The mobile home we liked best was new, had a double bedroom at one end, a beautiful sitting room with coffee table, armchair, sofa bed and a fireplace with an electric fire. The fitted kitchen was next to that, complete with fridge, small dining table and chairs and a gas cooker. Next to the kitchen was a twin bedroom, then a lovely bathroom with shower, sink and toilet. But it was priced at £2,000. We had bought our caravan from the same man the previous year. He said, 'I'll do you a good deal. I'll deliver this mobile home to Ballintogher and collect the caravan. I'll charge you fifteen hundred for this one and, Sandy, you can pay me twenty-five pounds a month until it's paid for.' We were ecstatic. That man knew he'd really not done the best deal for himself, but he could plainly see we were struggling. He was a good man. We rushed home to prepare for the delivery of our wonderful new home. When it arrived, it just about fitted into the garden. A friend of Dad's, Jimmy Mulvaney, helped settle it in with his tractor. Thanks to my job with The Fairways, we now had a beautiful home and Mike could sneak in the kitchen door to sit and chat to me while I cooked. My mother sat blissfully unaware, smoking her cigarettes and watching television.

We were doing really good business with The Fairways and Dad was making some money in his garage. Our lives became a little easier, thankfully. But we cared for Mum on our own: no doctor or nurse called and we had no financial help at all. Eventually, Mum got a cheque for £3 a month disability allowance, but it went straight into her handbag, never to see the light of day. Granny Bee made it clear we weren't to use Mum's money for anything towards our own cost of living. Actually, those cheques remained in Mum's handbag for several years. A social worker called a few times, not to see if Mum needed anything or if we could manage, but to ask if the £3 a month was needed now that I had a record in the charts. I don't want to sound bitter because I'm not that sort of person, but honestly, for those eight years with Mum we had to paddle our own canoe entirely.

The routine working with The Fairways at night and minding Mum and Barbara during the day worked well. I had some of my stage outfits from Wales, including a red hot-pants suit of Bonnie Tyler's that I had acquired from the Bunnies, which I wore with knee-high red platform boots. One night on stage I fell over in the platforms and couldn't get back up. Mike, who continued playing the bass with one hand, leaned over and picked me up. Mostly, I wore a variety of maxi dresses and flared trousers with a backless top in the same colour and silk material. Make-up was great fun too. These were the days when we wore lots of glitter around our eyes and on our hair. Then, to finish off the look, I'd strategically place small coloured stars under my eyes on my cheekbones. All of this glamour had to be achieved in a corner of a dressing room, with a small mirror on my vanity case. The band always dressed trendily and smartly too. We tried a few different male singers after Gary. One, a singer from Dublin called Gary Anthony, stands out in my mind. He was handsome, a good singer and had great stage presence. He did a fantastic job on the Neil Diamond songs. He and I got on well and worked together perfectly. I continued to record for Hawk Records and thankfully had chart success, with enough airplay to enhance my profile and increase our work. Tom Kelly worked very hard behind the scenes on my promotion, getting me airplay, TV and radio slots. Mike and I would spend hours by the record player learning new material and discussing new ideas. Some of the singles The Fairways did included 'Hey Jude', 'Let It Shine', 'Love Me Just A Little Bit' and 'Not With You'. Gary Anthony was very popular with the fans, but unfortunately, he didn't drive and found the commute too hard after about a year, when he left the band to return to the cabaret scene in Dublin. I didn't see him again for years.

My relationship with Mike was going well, and after about four months of being together we got engaged. Mike was a nervous wreck when he asked my father if we could get married. My dad – reluctantly – said yes. I had already met Mike's parents, Rose and Bill, a good few times and thought they were the warmest, nicest people. Rose Kelly was a real character; a retired librarian, she could recite all the great poems with such conviction she'd bang the kitchen table with her fist, all while making dinner. Bill Kelly was a quiet man who sold insurance. Between them, they also ran a little farm. The first time I went up to Cloonrea, near Castlerea, to meet them, I asked Rose if there was anything I could help with. Like a shot, she said, 'Yes, please. I have some sheets and pillowcases in the front room that need ironing.' And that's how I spent the next few hours. There was always a great welcome in their house, and they were very good to my mum whenever I brought her. We all got along just fine.

Mike and I headed off from Sligo to Connolly Station in Dublin on our first train journey together, on a mission to find an engagement ring. We went to Appleby's Jewellers on Grafton Street and I picked a ring that I just loved, a wide gold band with a cluster of diamonds. I'm sure we must have got dinner somewhere modest and as neither of us drank, there was no clubbing but we went to a concert to celebrate, one of the glam rock bands that were big at the time.

It was another several years before we got married. To be totally honest, although I really loved Mike, I wasn't entirely sure I wanted to get married at all. I've always felt a bit weird about it and would have been a lot more comfortable with us living together, but back then it really wasn't the thing to do. Besides, I didn't want to annoy my father. Typical though, some years later, after my mum passed away, Dad went to live with his new partner, Maisie McDaniel.

In 1976, my sister, Barbara, was fifteen years old. She had come to hate school so much that she refused to go and, in her very wilful way, announced that she was going to join The Fairways with me. During her life, I very rarely refused my sister anything, so I agreed to take her on a trial basis, and Tom Kelly gave me the OK. The first gig she came to was in a hall. We all went early, having chosen some songs for her to learn, and we rehearsed. As soon as she started singing, I ran around the hall as quick as I could to close all the windows, in case anyone would hear and think it was me. It was so bad she'd have kept people away from the gig. But she worked hard, looked amazing and, in a short time, she fitted in great. By now, Tom Kelly was managing us full time. A girl from Donegal, Trisha Boyle, joined on piano, so we now had three girls and three guys.

On 20 September 1977, Mike and I got married. We were both twenty-three. By today's standards we were very young, but back then it was the norm. Once the date was decided on, there was very little planning done. Of course, we would be married in St Theresa's Church in Ballintogher, where I had been baptised. Margaret Craig and Barbara would be my bridesmaids, and Tom and Patricia's three-year-old daughter Sylvan would be our flower girl. Mike's brothers, Liam and Tom, were the groomsmen. The Forest Park Hotel in Boyle (which no longer exists) was decided on for the reception. All invitations sent out, it was time for me to buy my wedding dress. The experience was a far cry from *Say Yes to the Dress*. We were on our way to Cork for a gig and we stopped in Limerick for burgers. The band and Barbara went for their snack and I went in to a shop I had spotted that sold wedding dresses. There were two middle-aged ladies who were very nice and helpful, though they did look a little baffled that I'd popped in by myself. I tried on maybe three dresses and settled on a cream-coloured, high-necked smock dress with a short veil and a tiara of pearl-like flowers. It took me all of twenty minutes and cost me £37 for the lot. I still have that dress and veil: it's plain, but cute in a vintage sort of way. I got my outfit parcelled up and returned to the van for the journey on to the gig and that was that!

On the day before our wedding, my family started to arrive from Wales, including Aunt May and Uncle Jack, Uncle Simon and Aunt Liz, Uncle Pat and Aunt Sandra. The reality of what was about to happen started to set in. I'd arranged a church rehearsal that evening and went through all the instructions, even acting them out. Everyone would go to the church, except Mum, who would wait behind until the reception, as she wouldn't be able for the church. Cousin Simon (who would later be part of The Dus-keys) and my sister decorated my car, a blue Ford Granada, for my journey to the church, with Uncle Jack driving and Dad with me in the back.

On the morning of 20 September, I had all my clothes and make-up in the mobile home Mike and I had bought and placed in Hannon's garden, which we had also bought with a view to building a house for us all, especially Mum. There was a flurry of family buzzing around that morning. My first job was to get my mum ready. She had no idea what was going on and was very reluctant to get dressed. We had to compromise and let her wear her tea-cosy hat – hardly mother-of-the-bride style! I went back to our own mobile home to start putting on my make-up on and doing my hair, only to find that Barbara had made off with my make-up bag, to get herself ready. This was a habit she adopted through our whole working lives. Thankfully, Margaret Craig was there to help me. All ready, and with everyone making their way to the church, I went out to look for my father and Jack. My car was parked outside, but there was no sign of Dad or Jack. I looked up the village and there they were, laughing and having a great old time, making their way back down the street from Moran's pub. I beckoned them to hurry, as everyone was waiting in the church. Mother of the divine Jesus, we couldn't find the keys anywhere. Dad and Jack said, 'Hold on there, we'll be back in a minute.' To my horror, back they came, tearing up the road in Dad's car. They pulled up beside me and said, 'Jump in!' But the back of the car was filthy, everything from spanners to engine grease. I said, 'There's no way I'm getting in there in my wedding dress.' Dad said, 'Grand,' and they headed off to the church without me. So much for my rehearsal the evening before!

Just then, Tom Kelly's car came into view. I ran towards him, waving, and thank God he saw me and drove me to the church. When we pulled up at the school, Mrs Dowling-Long was standing at the church gate with all her pupils to wish me well, which was lovely, but there was no sign of my father. I made my way up the steps and sent Tom to find him. He and Jack were sitting in the front pew waiting for me, looking at their watches.

Poor Mike must have wondered if I was coming at all. Finally, Dad arrived out, and the last few words my loving father had for his daughter before he walked her down the aisle were, 'Where the hell were you?'

Thankfully, everything went smoothly after that, with ceremony and pictures done at the church. Sadly, Mum and Dad couldn't join us at the main table for the reception, but Dad did come up to make his speech and I went to sit with them for a while. It was wretched that Mum didn't know where she was and why we were there. But there was no point in upsetting her or myself by trying to explain. We had a lovely day and danced for a couple of hours to a live band. Of course, by the time my family and our band took turns to entertain, there really wasn't that much for the hired musicians to do.

Soon it was time for us to head off. We hadn't planned anything because of Mum. Mike's brother Cathal and his wife, Marian, lived in Swords, County Dublin and had offered to put us up for a few days. I drove us away as a married couple. Because we were tired, we stopped off for the night in Longford. There wasn't much romance; we chatted about the day and, as I drifted off to sleep, I gazed at my wedding band wondering if this ring and what it stood for would make my life any easier.

The next morning, we decided to head for Jury's Hotel in Ballsbridge, Dublin, as we had an extra few bob, and the day after, we went to Cathal and Marian's house and got a Chinese takeaway, which was also a rare treat. Dad phoned that night to say that Mum had refused to eat anything or take her medication since I left. This had never happened before, even when I'd be on the road with the band.

So the next morning we went back home, after a two-day honeymoon with a Chinese takeaway to add to the excitement. We began our married life, but it was very difficult. When we weren't working, Mike would have to sit alone in our mobile home, only coming up to Mum and Dad's at mealtimes. I'd go down and join him when Mum went to bed for the night. For the next two years, the only quality time we spent together was travelling in the van to gigs.

Mike has always been and still is my best friend. We worked together a lot, but as my career took off, I was away from home more and more. He was there for a lot of the high points: meeting and working with Johnny Cash, The Grand Ole Opry, the Eurovision and my TV series. He was my bass player for years, a truly great musician, then moved on to sound engineering for my shows. At one point, he and his brother Tom ran a recording studio, which was built at the side of our house. Daniel O'Donnell recorded his first record there, Margo recorded an album there, Charlie McGettigan and Jargon too, and a host of other artists. Sometimes Mike would be a stay-at-home dad to our two children, Willie, who was born in September 1979, and Barbara, who was born in September 1981. (Sadly, Mum didn't live to see either of them, as she passed away five months before Willie was born.) For a period of my career, Mike took on the management role and booked my shows and tours.

We had met at twenty and given the challenges we had with my mum, a daughter with special needs, working all the hours that God sent and travelling all over, our marriage was very strained for quite some time. I say honestly, Mike was a lovely, quiet man to live with and a great father to our two children. He was happy to let me pursue my career, in the hope that it would enhance all our lives. Over our married years, when at home, I focused much of my attention on the children, especially our daughter. Mike knew that I wasn't happy, but he was, even though things weren't ideal.

When the kids were in their early twenties, I decided that I wanted a separation. It was very difficult to tell Mike and even harder to tell Willie. We didn't tell Barbara, as she wouldn't have understood. Although Mike knew our marriage hadn't been right for a long time, he was devastated and it took a while for him to come to terms with the fact that I was leaving. Willie, too, was very hurt – no child wants to see their parents separate and it affects them for life. I continued to be in the family home when Barbara was there and for all family celebrations, always at Christmas too. We've never missed a Christmas together as a family. Once Mike accepted that this was how it was going to be, we got along really well.

We went together to Sligo courthouse to have the divorce granted and sat together chatting as we waited for our case to be called. Afterwards, we went to a nearby pub where I had a glass of wine, Mike a cup of tea. It was sad, but it was done with respect from both sides.

We still work together from time to time. We have even been on a couple of holidays. If I need someone to drive me to a gig, Mike is always happy to bring me. We're still great friends and confidants, after half a century.

Mike battled cancer in 2022 and thankfully has made a great recovery. That diagnosis made me think about the amazing history we created together. At my age, I won't have the time or the want to build all that again. That said, we both agreed we'd not get married again, at least not to each other.

# 9

# SOMETHING'S LOST, BUT SOMETHING'S GAINED

In January 1979, Mike and I had some wonderful news: we were expecting our first child. We were over the moon. At this same time, Mum was in the Richmond in Dublin with a second brain haemorrhage and Dad was with her. A few weeks earlier, when Mum was in Sligo General Hospital, a woman invited me to join her Padre Pio prayer group for healing the sick. She took Mum's name and address and I forgot about it until a week later, when a letter arrived in the post with a Padre Pio prayer card and a little relic, a piece of Padro Pio's robe.

I brought it with me and travelled in the ambulance with Mum to Dublin, who was having continuous, violent seizures. When we arrived, while the staff brought Mum to her bed, I don't know why but I walked up and down the long, busy corridor, asking people where the monastery with the Franciscan Capuchin monks was, but no one knew. In the distance, coming towards me was a monk in Capuchin robes. He looked to be in a hurry, but I begged him to visit my mother. His answer stunned me, and I could see he was shocked, too. He explained that a family had requested that a monk from the monastery bring over one of Padre Pio's bloodstained gloves, which he famously wore because of his stigmata, to bless a sick relative in the hospital. The monk had been to every single ward but no such person was in the Richmond Hospital with the name he had been given.

What were the chances? I took him to Mum's bed, where she was still convulsing and non-responsive. Pulling the curtains around, he invited me to join him in prayer for my mum. I felt a calm descend, knowing that we would not be on this journey alone. When he finished praying, he said, 'I have to tell you this may not mean that your mother will live but it does mean she will go peacefully, should that time come.' I have carried those prayer cards with me ever since; everywhere I go, they sit on the locker beside my bed.

In 1979, we renamed Sandy Duskey and The Fairways as The Duskey Sisters, and brought in a third female vocalist to the band. Now we could cover a huge range of chart material and various other styles of music while also introducing some good dance routines.

The Duskey Sisters were booked to go to England for a short tour in early 1979, but I was suffering from severe morning sickness and could hardly get out of bed, never mind travel. The band left and there I was on my own. Granny Bee was really not impressed that I had brought this on myself when I should have been minding my mother. She was still trying to forgive me for wearing a halter-neck dress on *The Late Late Show* and for the photograph that appeared in the *Sunday World* of me wearing Bonnie Tyler's red hot-pants suit. The *Sunday World* sold out in Gilmartin's shop in Ballintogher within minutes. Granny Bee decided that I had disgraced the family and now that I'd gone and gotten myself pregnant, she wasn't going to be spoiling me. I stayed in bed for almost a week. I was three months pregnant and rapidly losing weight.

Anyone who's been through this will understand what I mean. I just lay there in the dark for what seemed like an eternity, praying to get some relief from the sickness. There was no phone or any form of communication, so I had very little idea of what was going on with the band in England or Mum in Dublin and, to be honest, I was too sick to care. Late one night, I thought I heard the van pull up. The door opened and Mike appeared with a large white teddy bear. 'I'm home!' he said, not realising just how sick I had been. I told him in no uncertain terms where to go and where to put his teddy bear. He didn't reappear until the next day when I'd calmed down. Barbara sat with me that night but, at the age of seventeen, she had little understanding. I appreciated having her there, all the same.

The next day, everyone realised just how bad I actually was. I was completely dehydrated and I noticed I was losing a little blood. Mike brought me to Mrs Willis, our very good neighbour, and she was more than happy to help. I rang a GP and explained my symptoms. He told me I had miscarried the baby and that I needed to go straight into hospital for a DNC. I didn't know what that was, but soon discovered that when you have a miscarriage, they bring you to the theatre to clean your womb, under a general anaesthetic.

I was admitted to a private room and some tests were carried out. Mike left to let me rest. Just before I was brought to theatre for the DNC, my doctor decided to run a few more tests. After about half an hour, he came back to where I was waiting in a side room and said, 'You're still carrying your baby.' I couldn't believe it. I was so happy, so relieved! I went back to my room, propped myself up on two pillows and waited for Mike to return. He was probably dreading seeing me as I should have been in the depths of grief. Instead, what greeted him was me smiling like the Queen of Sheba. I told him that we still had our baby and he was over the moon with joy. However, I had to stay in hospital for four weeks on a drip and bed rest because I was so dehydrated and there was still the risk of losing my baby. And so The Duskey Sisters had to continue without me.

In fairness, they did a good job in my absence, but had to accept a lesser fee as I was not there. As soon as I was strong enough and released from the hospital, I went straight back out on the road with the band. Thanks to my doctor, I was able to manage my sickness and get back to work. We were very busy, thankfully, but we still made time to visit Mum in Dublin as much as possible. Dad, of course, stayed by her side the whole time.

In April that year, the surgeon in the Richmond sent my mum back to Sligo General and from there she was sent to St John's Nursing Home. Granny Bee was furious when she heard and said, 'You've sent your mother to the workhouse,' because, in her day, that's what St John's was. Mum was now completely bedridden and her mind was in another world altogether. It was heartbreaking but at least she was at peace, as all the aggression was gone. She had the best of care at St John's. Sister Nathy was the nun in charge of Mum's ward, an absolute saint and very kind to everyone, as were all the staff.

We visited Mum every single day. The first day I saw her, she was wearing a floral nightdress, her hair neatly styled, and her nails painted with a pale pink nail varnish. I'd never seen her wearing nail polish before. She was smiling and looking up at the ceilings with her arms slightly stretched out. She appeared to be trying to catch something that only she could see. I longed to tell her that she was going to be a grandmother, but there wasn't any chance she would understand, so I didn't. When it was time for me to leave, she asked, 'Where are you going?' When I told her I was going to a gig, she replied, 'Get me my shoes, I'll come with you.' I left her that day with the heaviest of hearts, knowing she was nearing the end of her journey. The doctors had told us that Mum would maybe have a year left.

Mike and I had planned to build a house in our field, Hannon's garden, for the whole family, with special facilities for looking after Mum. This latest news changed everything, though. Mike and I decided to buy a house immediately and take Mum home. We looked at three houses in total. My favourite was one beside Lough Gill, but Mike would not agree because it was £2,000 more than the one we ended up buying. We decided on a three-bedroom house in Carrowgobbadagh, with beautiful views for Mum to see from her bed. In a short time we realised that we could not have asked for better neighbours, John and Marie Mulligan. They are among my closest friends; our children grew up together and have remained lifelong friends.

During the process of buying the house, we were taking turns sitting by my mother's bedside. By now she was completely unresponsive. Still, we had to leave and play our gigs. One day in May, when I was four months pregnant, we were to play in Banna Beach in Kerry. I had a bad feeling and did not want to leave. Eventually, I was persuaded to go, so we went, did our gig and went to bed at the hotel. Tom Kelly was with us. Early the next morning, there was a loud knock on Tom's door. I woke Mike and said, 'Mum's dead.' I just knew before I was even told. Mike fetched Barbara and

I broke the news to her. We cried and all we could think of was getting back to see her as quickly as possible. Everyone sat in silence around the hotel breakfast table before heading off on the longest journey. Anyone who's experienced a journey that is leading to heartbreak will know how it feels.

At St John's, the pain was etched on my father's face as he hugged Barbara and me, tears streaming down his cheeks. Mum was only forty-seven years old, but she looked much younger than that, at peace at last and her suffering over. But we were broken. I was also very angry. I should have been there when she took her last breath, but no, yet again the show had to go on. How many more times would I hear that?

A few days after Mum's funeral, Dad, Mike, Barbara and I were sitting around the table in our mobile home, talking about how changed our lives would be now that Mum was gone. It's a peculiar feeling when your whole existence revolves around one person and daily routines are planned to suit their needs. We all felt the same: on the one hand, there was the awful sense of loss, but on the other, there was this overwhelming sense of freedom. That might sound cruel, but that's how it was. We could now do anything we wanted, or go anywhere we pleased. This wonderful sense of freedom lasted for about a week, when the awful pain of grief really took hold and we realised Mum was gone forever.

Our new house in Carrowgobbadagh lay empty for a month after Mum's funeral. None of us had the heart to even see it. Healthwise, I was feeling a lot better and was able to continue working. But now that our baby was due in just four months, we had to begin the task of moving into our house. This was a huge deal for my dad, Barbara and me, as it was the first time we'd had a home without wheels on it. It took some time to learn how to utilise all that space but we all settled in very well, with help from our neighbours.

It must have been strange for them to have musicians move in next door.

I worked up until ten days before my baby was born. The last show I played was the open-air stage at the Rose of Tralee festival. Just before we went on stage, my sister said, 'Thank God it's your last night, you look like an egg with legs!' and she was right. Our baby was due on our second wedding anniversary and of course we hoped the baby would arrive on time. But the day came and went. After a meal to celebrate our anniversary, we turned in for the night, but as soon as I got into the bed, I felt my waters break. It was ten past midnight. Mike couldn't drive at the time, so I got him to wake my father to bring me to the hospital. I grabbed a towel and went to stand on it in the kitchen. Then, very casually, Dad walked in, glanced at me leaking all over the towel and said, 'Are you sure you're in labour? This is not how it happened with your mother.' He proceeded to fill the kettle to make himself a cup of tea. There was no sign of Mike. I found him in the sitting room, dusting the ornaments with a cloth. I was the only half-sane person in the house! I ordered them to grab my case, get the car and bring me to the hospital.

I was shown into the labour ward by two nurses and that's where I remained in absolute agony until eight o'clock the next morning when Dr Donovan arrived. By that time, I was delirious with the pain and Dr Donovan decided to sedate me for the delivery. I was delighted because at that point, death had felt like the better option. When I woke up, I met my son. At visiting time, Dad and Mike came in and were thrilled to see him. Thank God, William was a healthy baby. A week later, we brought him home to meet the rest of the family and even Granny Bee was smitten. My sister had an immediate bond with her nephew. It was an amazing thing to have happiness like this in our lives – the first time in a long time. Bringing Willie home gave us a new and bright chapter to look forward to.

The next few weeks in our house consisted of prams, cots, nappies, bottles and everything to do with having a newborn in a home. When I went back to work, Dad offered to mind Willie, which in hindsight might not have been the brightest of ideas. The first night we got home from a gig, we found my dad asleep on the couch beside Willie in his cot, and lined up in front of the fire were the baby's bottles, nappies and saucepans. He had decided to set up a full nursery in the comfort of the living room, to save having to move in and out of the kitchen, and was using the saucepans to heat the bottles on the open fire. Another night when I came home, I lifted Willie from his cot, only to hear a crackling sound coming from him. Under his babygrow, he was wrapped in newspaper. Even stranger, the child smelled of whiskey. I asked my dad what was going on, he happily replied, 'Well, the child is very chesty and I didn't have any brown paper, so I popped him into the *Sligo Champion* and gave him a spoon of whiskey to help him sleep. That's the way your mother used to do it.' I said to Mike, 'This might be a good time to hire a babysitter.' Which is exactly what we did.

During Willie's early years growing up, he was surrounded by music as we did all our rehearsals in our home. He even came with us to some shows. Like any child, he absorbed everything going on around him. When we'd bring him to gigs, he'd set up camp behind the drummer; as soon as he could walk, he'd head off down to the tearoom for sandwiches with the lads. During the gigs, though, it was getting hard to keep him out of the band. When the guitar player stepped forward to take a solo, Willie would immediately jump into his spot to play his plastic toy guitar, much to the amusement of the audience.

In 1981, there was great excitement for us when The Duskey Sisters were asked to record a demo for the National Song Contest. This was the first time we were invited to enter the contest. Our song was called 'Where Does That Love Come From', a fairly typical Eurovision Song Contest entry. We were delighted to get the news that we were picked to take part in the Irish National Song Contest, presented by Mike Murphy. Costumes organised, dance routines rehearsed, we arrived at the RTÉ television studios to perform the song live with the RTÉ National Concert Orchestra. We had a fantastic time and did really well, coming third. Shortly after the contest, I found out I was expecting my second child.

# 10

# MY DAUGHTER BARBARA – SOMETIMES MIRACLES HIDE

T hankfully, this time I was not nearly as sick as during my first pregnancy. So, with a healthy diet and a freezer full of ice lollies, I was able to continue with the band. I engaged Dr Donovan as my gynaecologist as he had taken such great care of me with my first baby. I had great trust in him, and that's important. It was less than a week to my due date and, at my appointment with Dr Donovan, the last thing he said to me was to stay close to home until the baby was born. Of course, his advice fell on deaf ears. The Duskeys were singing in the Castlebar Song Contest and I had already made up my mind to go. I wasn't going to miss that.

At every chance, my sister changed the style or colour of her hair, so on the day of the contest, I brought her to a hairdresser in Sligo for a change of colour. She wanted a silvery blonde. Unfortunately, after two hours, her hair was a slate grey. She was horrified and rushed out of the salon, with me after her. In my haste, I tripped and fell on one of the steps. Barbara helped me up and it appeared that the only harm done was to my sister's hair. I managed to talk her round and we headed off to Castlebar.

The place was packed but Mike and I were lucky enough to get seats in the front row. The contest was fantastic and our band did us proud. I was having a great night, even though The Duskeys didn't win. During the show, I got the odd twinge of back pain. It was quick and sharp but I didn't worry. If the worst came to the worst, Castlebar General Hospital was right beside me. I said nothing and we made the journey back home. Through the night the pain came and went, but still I didn't panic.

The next day, I took a warm bath and noticed I was bleeding. I rang Dr Donovan and he told me to come straight into the hospital to the maternity ward. I'd been such an idiot! Why hadn't I gone straight in after leaving Castlebar? When I arrived on the labour ward, Dr Donovan was standing there in white wellies and the nurses were all in plastic aprons. That didn't look good. Dr Donovan glared at me and said he had read in the paper that I'd been in Castlebar. I'm not going to go into the detail about the horror of the next few hours, but let's just say the wellies were a good choice.

My family were all waiting in a side room, including my dad. The doctor told them that the fall had caused internal bleeding. I had lost a lot of blood and it would be touch and go for me and my baby. Because of Dr Donovan's expertise and quick action, my baby and I were okay and our beautiful little girl was born on 29 September 1981. We called her Barbara Rose May, after my mum, Mike's mum and Aunt May.

She was the cutest little baby and William, who was just two years old when he first met his sister, was thrilled. We had no inkling of all the struggles in life that Barbara would have and how having Barbara in our lives would make us a totally different family.

We were very excited to bring our little daughter home, but fairly soon, excitement turned to concern. My baby was blinking a lot and blowing little bubbles with her mouth. I thought she was having little seizures – this looked similar to the seizures my mother had had after her surgery. Of course, I brought her straight to the emergency department in Sligo General. They didn't find anything wrong with my baby, so we were sent home. This routine continued for a number of weeks and we had a path worn to the hospital. To me, she seemed to be getting worse. Very late one night, she turned blue and became limp. Only Uncle Jack and I were at home. Jack carried Barbara wrapped up in a blanket as I drove to the hospital. He kept telling me not to worry, but as he cradled the baby, tears rolled down his face.

At the hospital, I pleaded with them to do some sort of scan on her head. I had this instinctive gut-wrenching feeling that there was something wrong with her brain. They didn't have a scanner at the time, so they did an X-ray. It showed up a shadow covering a third of the brain. We had to travel to Crumlin Children's Hospital immediately. I went with Barbara in the ambulance. In the hospital, she had a little cubicle to herself, so it was easy for me to stay with her all the time. Mike visited when he could, but he continued working with the band through this period, so he wasn't always with us. Willie remained at home with the nanny, Olivia. I documented the seizures every day and I still have the charts. Anytime I come across them, I'm astonished at how much my little baby went through.

Barbara spent most of her time in hospital over the next few years. There was very little help outside the hospital, so we had to learn as we went along. We'd already been on a similar journey with Mum, but we still didn't have a diagnosis for Barbara, so we were clinging to hope for a good outcome. I tried to show as little emotion as possible to the doctors as I'd learned that the stronger you come across, the more information you'll get. I did my crying behind closed doors, and there was a lot of that.

There was heavy snow in Dublin that year and transport in Dublin was limited, so I spent a lot of time just staying with Barbara. Mike was between visiting his father, Bill, who was gravely ill in hospital, visiting Barbara and working in the band. This one night, we were called into the office. Barbara had been to the Richmond Hospital (where my mother had been) for a brain scan. The doctor told us that our daughter had a cyst on her brain, which was filling with fluid and growing in size, and so it was putting pressure on the rest of the brain and causing more damage. The longer this went on, the more damage the pressure would probably cause. I've often wondered that if the cyst had been found sooner, how likely would it be that Barbara would be leading a different life right now. What if they had been able to do a CT scan in Sligo when I had first become concerned? What if she had been referred to the Richmond sooner for the scan? If this had happened in more recent times, I'd have had a scan whilst pregnant. Maybe they could have helped her. What if? What if? What if? I have a lot of these perpetually troubling questions in my life, but they don't change anything.

Here we were in the Richmond Hospital, Mike and I, walking up that same corridor we'd been with Mum, but now with our baby daughter.

Sad as it was, I knew that she would have the best chance here because the hospital had some of the best neurosurgical teams in the world and I trusted them. The surgeon told us that they would operate to try and remove the cyst, but if they couldn't, he would put in a permanent shunt to drain it.

On a very cold January day, at four months old, Barbara had her first surgery. I can't remember how long the surgery was, but it seemed like forever to us. They couldn't remove the cyst due to its location on the brain so, unfortunately, they had to put in the shunt. It was as it was and what could anyone do to change it? Thankfully, she came through the surgery well enough. I knew the journey that lay ahead from what had happened with Mum, with the shunt and seizures and the sorts of things that could go wrong and the changes that would have to be made as she grew, but we still had a lot of questions for the doctors. Barbara's diagnosis wasn't really straightforward. Having asked all questions on our carefully written list, we were told that it wasn't possible to say at that stage if she would be able to walk or talk, nor could they tell as she grew. We would have to wait and watch. I found myself comparing her to other children the same age to monitor her development.

During this period, I made the decision to leave The Duskeys. It wasn't an easy decision, but I had to be with Barbara. Then Tom Kelly got a call from RTÉ to say that we had been picked again to enter the National Song Contest, with the song 'Here Today, Gone Tomorrow'. A record label, run by Shay Hennessy, also became interested. So Tom, Shay and the band all rallied around to persuade me to do the song contest so they would at least have the three girls. We also invited our cousin Simon to join us. I agreed to just the song contest. To be honest, I was sure we wouldn't win.

Between the times I spent with Barbara at the hospital, we put together our dance routine and rehearsed for hours back at home in my house in Sligo. Willie was only two and a half years old at the time, but the poor child had watched the routine so many times up and down the sitting room that, all of a sudden, he hopped off his seat, grabbed a hairbrush and worked his way into our line-up to do the routine with us. It was hilarious! He knew every move from watching us.

The night of the contest was very exciting, with people voting all over the country. We were so sure we wouldn't win that Tom Kelly had booked us a dance in the National Ballroom in Dublin that same night, shortly after the contest. All the songs and performers were great and the atmosphere was fantastic. Then, as the votes started to come in, we saw that we were doing well. With a sudden burst of excitement, we thought, 'Hold on a second, we're actually in with a chance of winning this.' Mike Murphy was a terrific presenter, keeping everyone, both in the studio and at home, on a high. It was like an All-Ireland football final. We couldn't believe what we were seeing as we crept up to the top of the leader board. The final jury sent up their vote and it was over: we were the 1982 winners of the National Song Contest and on our way to Eurovision in Harrogate!

Everyone was congratulating us, Tom and Shay were over the moon, as were Sally and Dick Keating, the song's writers. We were elated. We did a quick interview with Mike Murphy as we were called back on stage and presented with flowers and then we sang the song again. What a high! With the contest over, all the contestants were invited to a celebration party in the RTÉ canteen. It was only then that we remembered we had a gig. We couldn't go to our own party. Instead, we were whisked off to the National Ballroom, still in costume, where our band was waiting on stage for us to arrive. The place was packed and we slowly made our way through the crowd to the stage. People were cheering and clapping, and there was a fantastic atmosphere. Now for the next dilemma: the band hadn't learned the song, as we hadn't expected we'd win. So we just launched into it, unaccompanied. There was so much excitement it didn't matter. We had one of the best gigs ever that night.

The next few weeks were hectic. Barbara was still in hospital, so I had to juggle my visits to her with meetings, interviews and recordings. We began working with a choreographer and a stylist for our Eurovision outfits. We were flown to every airport in Ireland for press receptions, all while still doing our gigs. It looked like I was going to have to rejoin the band for a while. We spent several nights in a recording studio with Shay Hennessy, making an album, and took it in turns to sleep on the studio floor. Shortly before the Eurovision, our friends in Ballintogher in Sligo had a big bonfire for us and brought us through the village on the back of a trailer pulled by a tractor – that was a fun night. We had several fittings for our costumes, but we much preferred what we'd worn in the National Song Contest. We had put a lot of thought into those outfits: silver sequinned catsuits, with white shimmery tops and silver headbands for the girls; and Simon (who went by the stage name of Danny) wore a silver sequinned waistcoat to match. But we didn't really have a choice, because the RTÉ Eurovision team picked the designer and costumes. You might remember the green satin jumpsuits with sequins and green satin high heels for the girls, while Danny wore a yellow two-piece suit. They didn't seem glamorous enough, but it was too late to replace them, so we just got on with it.

It was time for us to record the promo video. Remembering that Sheeba the year before had had a really cool video, wearing fur coats and being driven in a limousine, we couldn't wait to see what RTÉ had planned for us. We were picked up in a minibus and brought to Dublin Zoo very early in the morning, before it opened. On arrival, we were met by a make-up artist and stylist, Evelyn Lunny. This is when we discovered that we'd be wearing overalls and wellies. We weren't going to be wearing high fashion or driven around in a limousine. We were going to be feeding the animals. We were each given a bucket of fish to feed the seals, brushes to clean out the elephant enclosure and we had to be filmed in front of a chimp that kept pooping in his hand and throwing it at us. But it turned out to be a fun day all the same.

It really wasn't sitting easy with me to be going off to the Eurovision in the UK while Barbara was still recovering. Just a few days before we were due to leave, the doctors said she needed more surgery, that there was a problem with the shunt, but it wasn't anything to worry about. I felt like the worst mother in the world as I prepared to go into the Eurovision, but it would have been letting too many people down to back out. As was part of the Eurovision tradition, we appeared on *The Late Late Show* prior to leaving. Our last gig was in the Baymount in Strandhill, a home send-off for us. And what a night it was, absolutely packed with all our friends, family and fans, who had come out to wish us well.

Initially, it was a little disappointing not to be flying off to an exotic location, but in reality, we were delighted to be going anywhere. In all, between family and RTÉ staff, there were at least twenty of us travelling. The staff at Dublin Airport couldn't have been nicer. The airport put on a reception in a private room for the press to take pictures and chat, and then we were on our way. Harrogate was lovely and, as you can imagine, there was some buzz as all of the participating countries arrived. We shared our hotel with the

Swedish contestants and entourage. The whole place was a hive of activity with the press, artists, fans and musicians – it was really something to see.

The contest was held in the Harrogate International Centre, its first major event, as it had only recently been opened. It could seat 2,000. We were brought over to see it with Ian McGarry and Tom McGrath, head of light entertainment in RTÉ. Tom was a legend who spearheaded many of RTÉ's top shows, including *The Late Late Show* and the National Song Contest, so it was great for us to have an opportunity to work with him. After all, he had picked 'All Kinds of Everything' as an entry and Dana to sing it. He was a no-nonsense kind of person and took his work seriously. The Harrogate Centre was stunning, with fabulous staging and lighting, a full orchestra – we could hardly wait to get going!

In the few days before the competition, our team kept us busy with rehearsals, photo opportunities and meeting the press. We loved every minute of it. In the midst of the usual questions – what did we think our chances were, did we like Harrogate, etc. – out of the blue, a reporter asked me how my daughter was doing and if her illness would affect my performance. I was shocked. I somehow kept my composure and answered that my daughter was doing well and that I would be singing for her on the night. The news spread like wildfire through the press so, of course, that line of questioning continued.

Our host city had many trips and parties for us and we availed of it all. One of the nicest evenings we spent was at Castle Howard, the ancestral home of the Howard family for over 300 years. We had seen it on the TV series *Brideshead Revisited* the year before. Quite a spectacle was arranged for us: the grounds were full of people in period costume – jesters, peasants, musicians, dancers – and huge bonfires. At dusk, we were given a tour of the castle, room by room, with actors in magnificent costumes. To finish the night, there was a banquet and drinks. That night stayed with me for a very long time.

At our first rehearsal, Noel Keelaghan joined the orchestra as our conductor. Things went great, except that when we did our first side step of the dance moves, four of us went across the stage but only three came back. I had misjudged the stage and fallen off, which was hilarious. At the end of rehearsals, everyone in our team was happy and so were we. There was a bit of buzz about us now, which was exciting. The night before the actual contest, they did a full mock contest with a live audience, to make sure all would go smoothly for the live show. It was really fun because that night on the scoreboard, we all got top scores. Then it was early to bed after checking in on Barbara back in the Richmond.

The next day, I was called to an early morning meeting with the RTÉ team, who told me that they now agreed with us about our costumes. They would not have us wear the crossover flowy tops, but would have the beautiful hand-sewn sequin motifs taken off the tops and sewn on to the jumpsuits instead. The wardrobe department pulled out all the stops and got our costumes sorted on time.

There were eighteen countries participating and we were number seventeen in the running order. We felt happy with our performance and felt we had done our best. With the songs over, we sat with the other contestants to watch the votes come in. First vote and Ireland received one point. As we were on camera for the world to see, we couldn't show our dismay. To make things worse, we were sitting right in front of Nicole from Germany. All we could hear for the entire night was, 'Germany, ten points!', 'Germany, twelve points!' and so of course the cameras were focused on our area.

In the end, we came eleventh, which was not at all bad, especially by today's standards. We'd had a ball. Early the next morning, we travelled back to Dublin. We had an abundance of flowers and decided to bring them all to the Richmond Hospital for Barbara. Every single person on that flight carried a bouquet of flowers on their knee. Unlike our departure from Dublin Airport, there was no reception or welcoming party. We thought it was funny at the time.

Mike and I went straight to the hospital to see Barbara. Already, the Eurovision was far from our minds and we were firmly back to reality. She'd had her surgery and we were told she was doing really well. She was in her cubicle and it would break your heart to have seen this beautiful little baby, so small and helpless, with an incision running all the way down one side of her head and stitched back up. No one wants that for their child. I felt physical pain just looking at her. I wept and felt incredibly guilty for not having been there with her. She has had many surgeries since then and I have not missed one. I shouldn't have missed this one, but I couldn't change it, so I focused on Barbara's recovery. Mike and I sat with her all night.

Another month or so went by with us juggling gigs and hospital visits, until Barbara came home. For the most part, Barbara was a very quiet baby, unlike her brother, Willie. When she was at home, she really was very easy to look after. However, with a baby with special needs, you're more alert and always worry more. As time moved on, there were more visits to the doctor and stays in the hospital when the shunt gave problems. Thankfully, we were to learn that Barbara could walk and talk and play. She spent a lot of time with the other children in Carrowgobbadagh. They treated her as they did each other and she'd go off playing with them every day. John and Marie Mulligan next door had five children; Sean was and still is Willie's

Sharing a moment with Big Tom during the photo shoot for our duet, 'If I Needed You', in 1983.

*Below left*: With my Gold Star Award in 1985 (picture by Jim Eccles, *Sligo Champion*). *Below right*: The cover for my 1984 single, 'Baby Don't Go'.

*Left*: With my trophy for winning the International Award at Fan Fair in Nashville in 1985.

*Below left:* The first time I sang on The Grand Ole Opry, Nashville, in 1989.

*Below right:* With Shay Hennessy and the gold record for 'Crazy' in 1989.

The night in 1989 when I met Johnny Cash for the first time and sang on stage with him, after he called me at the radio station and invited me to Omagh.

Backstage at The Point Depot in 1989: (l–r) my sister Barbara, Jessi Colter, Waylon Jennings and me.

At a memorable party at Johnny Cash and June Carter's home in June 1989.
(L–r): Barbara, June Carter and me.


*Below left:* The Grand Ole Opry tickets I didn't use in 1989 because Johnny and
June invited us to a party at their house in Nashville. That was the night Johnny
asked me to record 'Woodcarver' with him.
*Below right*: With Johnny Cash at his house that same night in 1989.

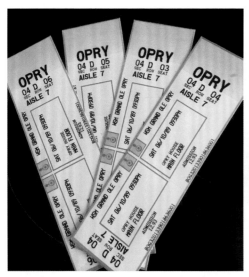

### JOHNNY CASH

Hi, Sandy,

Thanks for the C.D., cassette, poster and soap. Smells good.

I love our record, and I'm looking forward to hearing the whole album.

I'm doing great. I hope you and your family are fine.

Looking forward to seeing you in March. Hope we can do something together. (Musically, that is.)

Have a happy Holiday.

Much Love
John

12/8/89

*Above:* With Johnny Cash at his house party in 1989. (L–r): My son Willie, me, Johnny Cash and my sister Barbara.

*Left:* One of many personal letters from Johnny Cash to me, which are among my most treasured possessions.

*Above*: Recording 'Woodcarver' with Johnny Cash at Bradley's Barn in 1990.

*Left:* The original lyric sheet we used in studio for the 'Woodcarver' duet recording.

# JOHNNY CASH

Hendersonville
Tn.
Nov. 16 1990

Dear Jandy,

As promised, here is something I made you. I dont know what to call it, except to say that it is based on the design of a Sioux Indian "Spirit Mantle."

The four silver conchos represent the four winds. They are Navajo. The eagles are for high achievement, or good luck. The Indian and buffalo buttons are made from nickels. The large circle is Zuni Indian, and a symbol of the sun, for life. Blue is for spirituality and red is for passion. For life, music, love, work, people, etc.

I miss you.

The time with you was really nice.

Have a nice christmas.

With much Love

John

The letter of explanation from Johnny Cash regarding the spirit mantle he made for me.

*Above:* Rehearsing with Harold Bradley in Bradley's Barn studios in 1990.

*Left:* With Harold (left) and his brother, legendary producer Owen Bradley (right), at Bradley's Barn in 1990.

best friend, and Martina has always been Barbara's best friend. They'd be over and back between the houses, a tradition that carries on to this day, even at Christmas.

Barbara attended St Joseph's school for special needs children in Sligo. It is a fantastic school with amazing staff and, although she didn't interact much in class, she took everything in. At eighteen, she started attending the Sligo Family Resource Centre in Ballytivnan and loved it there. The amazing staff were just wonderful in how they cared for Barbara. She came touring with me on the road a lot of the time, to England, Scotland, Wales and all over Ireland. She even came to Nashville a few times and once she came with me to the Patsy Cline weekend in Winchester, Virginia to present the fan club with $5,000 she had raised herself in a raffle. Barbara knows so many people all over and they adore her.

Now, those who have met her know that her language can be very col-ourful and she has no problem telling anybody where to go if they get on the wrong side of her. She came with us on one of our tours in Scotland, and Angus, the Duke of Hamilton and Keeper of the Keys of Edinburgh Castle for Queen Elizabeth II, was at our show. He was a personal friend of George Hamilton IV and a fan, and so he and his wife Kay came back-stage to say hello. I had already met them a few times, but it was Barbara's first time. Herself and the duke got on great, so much so that he invited Barbara to a lunch in her honour at his home, Lennoxlove Castle, the next day. I immediately said, 'Thank you, but we couldn't possibly intrude.' He was having none of it, however, and insisted that George IV, Barbara and I come for lunch.

George IV drove us out to the castle. It was really impressive. It was the duke's childhood home and he had shown George and me around before.

He had war memorabilia and artefacts that had belonged to Mary, Queen of Scots, in particular a beautiful ring with a large oval stone. I've always regretted not asking the duke if I could try it on! Barbara was highly entertained by all this as we made our way to a smaller dining room where a table was set for us. The duke had invited a friend and his wife to join us, so there were seven of us sitting down. The gentlemen were wearing shirts and cravats and were speaking with very aristocratic English accents. The duke had the cook make pizza in Barbara's honour and, as we sat there chatting, Barbara kept saying, 'Mum, no one is talking to me,' so I said, 'Don't worry. It'll be your turn to talk soon.' To entertain Barbara, the duke started telling some jokes and I thought to myself, 'Please no, don't let Barbara tell a joke.'

The day so far had gone off without a hitch and the next thing I hear Barbara pipe up, saying she had a joke. I thought George would choke on his pizza. She asked, 'Why did the chicken cross the road?' There were a few guesses, until the duke asked Barbara to tell them why the chicken crossed the road, to which she replied, 'I don't know.' And we all burst out laughing. I felt sweet relief and then, as I thanked God, she said, 'If ye think that one was good, wait till you hear the fucking next one.' Thank goodness, they all just laughed, and the duke then rescued us from the situation by saying, 'We also sometimes use the f-word, especially when we are out hunting.' It was so funny.

When Barbara was first diagnosed, I was completely broken. We didn't know what her life would be. We just had to wait it out as she grew and developed. I'm grateful for the fact that she does have some quality to her everyday life. We are a lot luckier than some and I remind myself of that constantly, but I'd be telling you a lie if I said it hasn't been challenging.

Like any mother, I would have loved for Barbara to have more in her life. I wish she'd been able to join her childhood friends on their teenage nights out, on their journeys through education, careers, boyfriends, getting married, having children, earning their own money, learning to drive and have a car. The simple things. For her to have the independence to make choices like everyone else. I hate it when parents get frustrated with their children for things like staying out too late without saying where they were or what they were doing. I've always known where Barbara is. I've watched her standing at the window looking at her peers going out, and looking sad. I was always in tears for her. Our neighbours, the Mulligans, said recently that they and their children were lucky to have lived beside Barbara and many say the same about having Barbara as a friend: she enhances their lives. I also think she has enriched my life, and although there has been hardship, there is nothing I would change.

When Barbara was eighteen years old, we slowly introduced her into respite care, starting one night a month. That first day she went from St Joseph's school, I was parked out of sight and followed behind to watch her. It was one of the hardest things I've ever done. I was sick in the pit of my stomach and crying as she went into the respite house. I knew she didn't have a full understanding of what was happening, so all I could do was go home and sob. We had come to this huge decision because I had spent several weeks in hospital with dangerously high blood pressure, after falling ill at a show one night. I wasn't allowed out of bed and all that time made me think of what would happen to Barbara if I had a heart attack or a stroke. I had sheltered her but she needed to find some kind of independence.

It was Valentine's Day and Mike and I were going out for a meal for the first time without Barbara. By 6pm, I couldn't take any more worrying, so I got into the car and drove off to collect her and bring her to the restaurant, so she joined us for the Valentine's meal as she always did. Eventually, I tried again and pretty soon, Barbara and I were just about coping with the separation. Over the next few years, the respite stays increased over time and Barbara moved to a different respite house. During that period, there were problems with her behaviour in care. Her outbursts at home could also be disruptive, but in her defence, we had never gotten any help with managing it. We hadn't a clue. Bringing up any child can be difficult, but bringing up a child with special needs is a whole different thing and there is no handbook.

Barbara is a very intelligent and caring person, but she must find it frustrating not to be like everyone else. She knows that she is different. Her frustration sometimes comes out in anger and she cannot help that. At least now there is much more awareness for people with special needs and life is easier for them and their families in many respects. However, there is still a long road to go. So many families out there need more help and support, but because these people don't have a voice, they go unheard. Barbara and those like her never ask for much, and I will never understand why their families have to fight for their rights.

We have been blessed that Barbara has had a lovely respite home to go to when needed. She has her friends there and she loves them deeply. The staff are loving and kind, and are a second family to her. It still hurts to watch her walk up to the door, sometimes turning back to tell me to f– off. But that's just Barbara, always saying what she thinks!

As a family, we are all incredibly proud of Barbara's personal achievements in winning medals in the Special Olympics, for bowling and swimming, and at national level too. Over the years, many in my audiences have caught a glimpse of Barbara's medals when she is present, as she never leaves the house without them.

We are a far better family for having Barbara in our lives. Whether it's the excitement of planning her next big birthday bash or Santa's annual visit on Christmas Day, our house has always had a different set of priorities than most. In the world of show business, where sometimes life can be glamorised, Barbara has always kept us with our feet firmly on the ground.

Sometimes miracles hide.

# 11

# GONE COUNTRY

After the Eurovision, The Duskeys were extremely busy, playing many festivals and venues around the country. On one afternoon in July 1983, we were all in the van on our way to Cork city for a gig. Not far outside Sligo, on a treacherous, narrow stretch of road heading towards Tubbercurry, our driver went to overtake an articulated lorry carrying huge steel girders, on its way to Knock Airport, which was being built at the time. As we were overtaking, our van's bonnet somehow unlatched and flew up over the windscreen, completely blocking our driver's view. The van veered in front of the lorry and both we and the lorry went across the ditch, down into a field, with both vehicles landing on their sides. It all happened in an instant. We were in shock, but instinctively we knew we needed to get out of the van quickly. Being on its side, its doors were of little use, but the windscreen had fallen out of the front, so we climbed out that way, except my sister, Barbara, who had to be helped out. As we lay on the grass in the field, it was plain to see that Barbara was in a lot of pain. Local people came and helped us and finally some ambulances arrived to take the most badly injured to Sligo General Hospital. Most of us walked away from the accident with few or no injuries. I had whiplash, but Barbara had been in the front passenger seat and had taken most of the impact. She had very serious spinal cord injuries and had to stay in hospital for six months in a body cast. I was the only singer in the band who could get back to work relatively quickly but, in reality, the writing was on the wall for The Duskeys at this point. It was clear that it was coming to an end.

Even before the accident, I had decided to pursue a career in country music. A lot of my friends thought I was mad at the time. We were doing good-enough business with The Duskeys, but my heart was leaning more and more towards country music. Even in The Duskey Sisters, I would sing songs from Crystal Gayle, Linda Ronstadt and Emmylou Harris. Tom Kelly was still my manager, but I knew that for a career in country music, I would need a manager in that genre and Tom was very much an expert in pop music at that time.

Big Tom was a huge star at the time and I met with his manager, Kevin McCooey, thinking I might as well shoot for the top. Mike and I met Kevin and his wife, Marian, and it didn't take Kevin long to decide to put together a band for me and launch me as a country artist. I was thrilled, but it was with a heavy heart that I had to tell Tom Kelly I was changing management. Tom had always been good to me and a great friend; after all, we were family and had worked together for nine years. The gentleman that Tom is, he took the news very well. I finished up my dates for him and, in 1983, began working on a whole new programme.

It wasn't long before I was playing my first gigs as a country artist. I would travel up to Oram Hall in Castleblayney – Big Tom country! – to rehearse with my new band: Martin Cleary on guitar and pedal steel, Ginger Morgan (of The Mainliners) on bass, Mike Kelly on keyboards. This was the first time I'd fronted my own band, which was really exciting. I made a decision to drop the name Duskey, as it would have kept that pop connection. Instead, I went with Sandy Kelly. My father was not at all impressed that I'd dropped Duskey, but he got over it in time.

Big Tom was an incredible person. He was kind, mild mannered and extremely funny. He agreed to record a couple of duets with me, and Kevin picked out two songs: 'If I Needed You', a Townes Van Zandt song, and for the B-side, a song called 'Fools'. This would be my first release as a country artist. Rehearsals in full swing, I took a little time out to go to Tom's recording studio in Castleblayney to record the duets with him. John Ryan produced the songs and, with the music all recorded, it was time for Tom and me to record our vocals. I was nervous, of course, but Tom was so laid-back, it didn't take long for me to relax. Just Kevin, Tom, John, Mike Kelly and I remained in the studio to work. It was quite dark in the singing booth. Tom had his headphones on and was sitting on a high stool. I stood facing him with my headphones on. John started the track and we sang. I could hardly believe how well our voices matched. Tom looked happy and Kevin McCooey was grinning like a Cheshire cat in the control room, so I knew it was working. Then, in the middle of a line, a mouse ran across my foot and I nearly blew the ears off Big Tom with an unmerciful scream. The poor man nearly fell off his stool. I apologised and said, 'I just got an awful fright.' Tom said, 'Hold on there, I'll sort that out.' Back in he comes with a bottle of Harvey's Bristol Cream. 'Take a mouthful of that and you'll be grand.' I did as advised and since then, I've had a great liking for that sherry. It reminded me of all the wakes I went to as a child with Granny Bee!

About a week later, Tom and I got photos taken for the cover of the single. Kevin did a great job launching my new band. I had new photographs, new outfits, PA system, lights and a van. He also pointed out to me that, for the photos, I shouldn't sit too close to Tom because some of his female fans wouldn't like it. I thought he was joking but quickly realised he was quite serious. Tom had a huge and very loyal fan base, but a small number of them were very protective and didn't much like the idea of him sharing the stage with a female.

'If I Needed You' was released in 1983 and went to No 1 in the country charts. This was a great boost to my profile and promoters were more inclined to give me a chance and book me for live shows on the country circuit. For the most part, Kevin guided me on what to sing. It was a totally different programme than I'd been used to, mainly country classics, songs by Dolly Parton, Tammy Wynette and Patsy Cline. It took a while for me to settle into the music and feel as comfortable as I'd wanted, but Ginger Morgan and Martin Cleary were a great help. Although not really into country music, some of my loyal fans stuck with me on my difficult journey.

The country music audiences were also totally different. In some cases, I don't think they knew what to make of me. For a start, I was very animated on stage, as I had always been. But back then in country music, artists didn't move around that much on stage. I remember Paschal Mooney coming up to the stage one night and calling me over, telling me as nicely as he could that he'd never seen a country artist lifting their knees that high and that possibly I needed to slow up a bit and concentrate on the singing. I took his advice as best I could. Paschal was a huge support to me and I visited him in Drumshanbo and spent several hours going through songs that would be suitable for my programme and to record. Paschal also had a wonderful show on RTÉ Radio 1 called *Keep it Country* and he would select a number of bands and artists to appear. Thankfully, I was one of those picked. It was my first time as a country music artist to meet other musicians. I wondered what they made of me. I'm pretty sure a couple of them weren't that impressed with my take on country music.

The band and myself were working hard trying to make inroads into the scene, and thanks to Big Tom and Kevin, it got easier. After the duet with Tom, I brought out a single, a song called 'Reasons'. It did really well and got a great amount of airplay. People even began asking for the song at my gigs. Coming across a song that people love so much is amazing. To hear it requested on the radio, have people to ask you to sing it at shows and hear them sing along with you is honestly a great feeling. We recorded some more singles – 'On My Mind', 'Dancing Your Memory Away', 'You're Making Me Believe in Love Again' – all recorded at Windmill Lane and produced by John Ryan.

Kevin decided it was time for me to bring out my first solo album, *Paradise Tonight*. We recorded some more songs at Aigle Studios in Dublin and used a very popular, more contemporary producer, Nicky Ryan. He had a lovely studio on the top floor of his gorgeous Victorian house and he also hired a huge mobile studio, Eerie Mobile Music. It was huge fun recording those songs. Nicky Ryan was different in his approach to producing and not at all afraid to be creative and different. Every morning when I'd arrive to work on the songs, I'd enter the house through the kitchen, where Nicky's wife, Roma, would be there with the children, and a lovely smell of home cooking and spices.

There was also a really lovely but quiet young woman sitting on the large window ledge, with legs outstretched and reading a book. I'd always say hello and she'd answer in a soft voice with a Donegal accent. Each day that passed, we chatted a little more. She told me her name was Enya and that she was living there for the moment, writing songs and recording with Nicky. She seemed to be very much part of the family and I really liked her. There was something very different about her presence, very calming and peaceful, as was the whole place really. When I went in to record the vocals on 'I Will Always Love You', all the lights in the studio were off and the place had beautifully lit candles everywhere. It was a bit different from recording in Big Tom's studio with a mouse running across my foot and me drinking sherry. One evening after I'd finished recording, Nicky said, 'I want to let you hear what Enya and I have been working on.' We sat in the studio and he played music that I'd never heard the likes of before, Enya's hauntingly beautiful voice, which had been multi-tracked and accompanied by layered keyboards. Of course, her music became hugely successful, that same music I'd heard at the studio, which made Enya the best-selling Irish solo artist in history and the second overall behind U2.

I was now signed to CBS Records and my album *Paradise Tonight* was a huge radio success. The DJs and presenters loved some of the singles, especially 'Baby Don't Go'. Unfortunately, the sales didn't equal the airplay. The album was mainly crossover country and I don't think the Irish country music fans were ready for that. Looking at it now, the large picture on the vinyl cover of me in a minidress, up to my knees in the sea at Portmarnock, holding my shoes over one shoulder, it was more Shania Twain in the mid-1990s than an Irish country singer in the mid-1980s. But it was what I wanted to do and what I believed in. In that respect, I've always taken the road less travelled, right or wrong. There was a chain of shops in the UK that sold stylish and contemporary clothes but with a Native American flavour: mock suede minidresses, leather belts, accessories and even boots. I loved the look and thought it suited the music. Besides, no one else was wearing the same style.

My sister, Barbara, was married to David Duffy, of Tom Duffy's Circus, at the time. I thought it would make a really cool picture for my next album if I was walking with a young lion. They had a young but large lion cub called Socrates, and David arranged for me to visit Socrates a couple of times, to let him get used to me. He was beautiful and he loved my sister, so that gave me confidence. The day of the photo shoot arrived. Tom, David and Barbara gathered round as Mike took a few pictures to give us a sense of how it might look on an album cover. Out comes the lion cub on a long chain lead, but the second that lead was handed to me, I was terrified. I'd forgotten to factor in playfulness. Socrates made a run at me and grabbed me around the legs with his two huge front paws, knocking me to the ground. Still terrified and holding the lead, I looked up at him staring down at me while he licked my face. It was the most frightening experience of my life. Thankfully, David rescued me. The photos Mike took were hilarious, me with a lion on the end of a lead, staying as far away from him as I could. Standing in the sea on the first album and trying to get away from a lion on the second, maybe not a great look. It seems my little scheming ideas from childhood were still part of my DNA.

In 1985, I was invited to represent Ireland at the European Country Gold Star Awards. Ireland had a good reputation in the competition, as Susan McCann had won in 1982 and Philomena Begley in 1983. Paschal

Mooney was on the judges' panel. Of course, he couldn't vote for the Irish contestant but he was invaluable with his advice and support. As we headed off to Belgium – Kevin and Marian McCooey, Paschal and myself – Paschal advised me, as gently as he could, not to get my hopes up, even though Ireland had won it twice in recent years. I was happy just to be getting a free trip to Belgium. I'd come up with the idea of putting together press packs, much as we'd done for Eurovision with The Duskeys. I got bios printed up, an 8 x 10" PR photograph, and also included the vinyl of the *Paradise Tonight* album, all neatly presented in a nice folder.

As soon as we arrived at the hotel, although it was evening, Kevin and I were taken to the amusement park where the contest would be held in a couple of days' time. Apparently, we were the last contestants to arrive. To my horror, they wanted to film me on a roller-coaster ride, with a camera-man beside me. Under no circumstances was I going to get into that seat. It was beginning to get dark and the producer begged me to do it. I agreed to go if Kevin sat beside me. In we got and the cameraman hunched down in the seat in front of us to film my fun journey. That's not how it worked out, though. They got a promo film of me looking scared out of my mind and, as we came back down, I screamed the f-word at the top of my voice. In the end, they settled for filming me on a small slide. Happy days!

The next morning, we made our way over to where the contest would take place. It was a glorious day and the performances would be on an open-air stage. I could see the judges' seats and tables set out, so before they arrived, I placed one of my press packs on each table. Rehearsals went really well. I sang 'I Will Always Love You' and wore fitted white jeans with a white, fringed Western shirt and white cowgirl boots. The standard of the other artists was really good, so I resigned myself to the fact that I might not win. The previous year's winner had got a car, though, and I was a little envious of that.

We were all rarin' to go the next day as we journeyed again to the park for the competition. There was a great buzz around the place. When it was my turn to sing, I got up and gave it my best. I wasn't at all nervous, just enjoying being there. At the end we were all brought up on stage to await the voting results. They called out third place, second place, then … 'First place, Ireland'. I'd won the Gold Star Award! Paschal was delighted, Kevin and Marian were hugging and jumping up and down. Then Kevin ran up on the stage, lifted me up and swung me around. I was presented with the Gold Star and flowers, and once again sang my song. It was a pretty big deal back then and it was shown on television in all the participating countries. Susan McCann was the first winner for Ireland and Louise Morrissey won the Gold Star the last year it was held.

Unfortunately, there was no car prize that year, but I was far too happy to mind. Back at my hotel, though, in my excitement, I plonked the Gold Star on a glass table beside my bed and shattered the table. I'd underestimated the weight of the trophy. Winning this award and RTÉ's broadcasting of the whole contest really helped me become more accepted by the country music fans at home. A promoter from Norway was at the contest and booked me and the band for a three-week tour in Norway later that year. Everything was moving in the right direction and we were ready.

Being ambitious, I decided in 1986 to submit material to be considered for a festival I'd heard about, Fan Fair in Nashville. I knew only the bare minimum: that some of the top Irish country music artists had performed there and that it was a very prestigious event, with most of the big country stars in America performing over that week. I represented myself, using a different name, as I'd done some years previously in the phone box in Ballintogher. This time I used my daughter's name, Barbara Kelly, to act as PR agent for Sandy Kelly. I sat at my kitchen table and wrote a letter to the Country Music Association (CMA) telling them that 'Sandy Kelly, a new country music artist here in Ireland, would like to be considered for the International Show at Fan Fair 1986.' I included a bio and press kit with the album *Paradise Tonight*, just as I'd done for the Gold Star Awards. I headed to the post office and, for the first time in my life, I posted a package to Nashville.

One of the things that excites me most about this business is that you never know what's going to come up from one day to the next. Many weeks passed and I was getting on with gigs and family life in Sligo. Then a letter arrived from Nashville. I was nearly afraid to open it, filled with anxiety and excitement at the same time. It could be bad news, or was there any chance at all that it would be good news? The contents of this letter could change my life, one way or another. Little did I know then just how much. Carefully opening the envelope to avoid damaging the big CMA logo on the corner, I read: 'We the selection board at the CMA are delighted to invite Sandy Kelly to represent Ireland on our International Show at Fan Fair this June 1986.' I must have read it ten times before I actually believed it. I called Mike to show him the letter and the two of us were dancing around the kitchen. I rang Kevin and he was over the moon as well.

Finally, having calmed ourselves down, I sat down to try and figure out what it would involve. We didn't have the internet back then, so I rang my good friend Paschal Mooney. I knew that he'd advise me well about my trip to Nashville. He told me that it was indeed a great honour to be invited to perform at Fan Fair by the CMA and that I should start my preparations immediately. I really don't know how I'd have managed without him. Listening to him speak about Nashville, I could hardly contain my excitement. I would be singing in a huge open-air stadium to thousands of country music fans and backed by some of Nashville's most famous musicians. At last, I'd be able to visit the 'Home of Country Music'.

But my excitement soon came crashing back down to earth. Within days, the CMA phoned to say that an objection had been lodged by another artist from Ireland, who said I shouldn't qualify because I was a pop singer and not a country artist. The judging panel would review my application and would let me know in a few days. Can you imagine how disappointed and hurt I was? Yes, I'd had a career in pop music, but I had been doing country music for almost three years now. I wasn't the only artist to change genre; to name just two, Kenny Rodgers and George Hamilton IV both had careers in pop music before they moved into country. I made all of the phone calls that I needed to and explained my position honestly. And then I waited for the phone call from Nashville. I could barely think of anything else. But finally, the call came. The panel had considered all the facts and listened again to my album, and they considered me as country as any other artist on the show and were reconfirming my invitation. A few years later when I started working with the bandleader in Nashville, Harold Bradley, he told me all about the objection and what had transpired.

Once again, thank God, I was going to Nashville!

I called Paschal to revisit what exactly I needed to do in preparation. Happily, he and Sheila Mooney were going there at the same time, so we'd travel together. The CMA paid for Mike and me to fly to Nashville and also for all transport on arrival, plus seven nights' accommodation at the Park Suites Hotel.

Performing with my sister Barbara (right) in Lebanon for the Irish peacekeeping forces in 1990.

With my band and Irish peacekeeping forces in Lebanon in 1990. (L–r) Sergeant Dick McCarty, Barbara, Eugene McMullan, me, Mike Kelly, Company Quartermaster Sergeant Richie Barry, Gerry Mooney and Mick McCarney.

One of the highlights for me on my RTÉ show, *Sandy*, was recording in Markree Castle in Sligo in 1990 with the Carter Cash family. (L–r): John Carter Cash, June Carter, me, Helen Carter and Anita Carter.

Singing with Johnny Cash in Markree Castle for my TV series.

*Left:* Johnny Cash and June Carter kindly posed for a photo with my daughter and me during a break in recording at Markree Castle.

*Below:* On stage in Belfast's Ulster Hall in 1991. (L–r): Me, June Carter, Johnny Cash, Helen Carter and Anita Carter.

*Left:* A 1992 promotional photo with Tommy Cash for Cash Country Theater in Branson, USA.

*Below:* With my children Barbara and Willie on a trip home from Branson for Willie's confirmation in 1992.

*Above:* Performing with the legendary Willie Nelson at the Rocky Gap Festival, Virginia, USA, in 1991; *below:* A view of the huge crowd at the same festival. I'm on stage with The Jordanaires.

From the set of my TV series, *Sandy.* *(All photographs © RTÉ)*

(L–r) Gloria, me, Louise Morrissey and Philomena Begley.

(L–r) Me, Emmylou Harris, Paddy Moloney and Dolores Keane.

With Charley Pride.

*Top:* On set with the dancers.

*Middle (l–r):* With Ralph McTell and Joe Dolan.

*Bottom:* With Ronnie Drew.

Recording 'Crazy' with Willie Nelson at Bradley's Barn in 1994.

*Bottom left:* (l–r) Willie Nelson, Charlie Dick (Patsy Cline's widower), me and
Harold Bradley in 1994.
*Bottom right:* My sister Barbara with her hero Willie Nelson outside Bradley's
Barn in 1994.

At Dublin Airport, when we checked in, because of Paschal's profile we all got upgraded to first class! We got champagne, goodie bags and even a pair of green socks for the journey to add to our comfort. It was like the honeymoon Mike and I had never had. Paschal and Sheila were perfect company and we would stay with them the first few nights at a friend's house, producer Tom Pick and his wife, Sally, before checking in to our official hotel.

Nashville was gobsmacking: country music blaring out all over the arrivals hall, people walking around in cowboy hats, jeans and boots, just like something out of a Western movie. There were pictures everywhere of every country music star you could think of: Patsy Cline, Johnny Cash, Dolly Parton, Willie Nelson, Waylon Jennings and more. Tom and Sally Pick couldn't have been nicer and made us very welcome in their home just outside Nashville. We'd barely dropped our cases when Tom brought us all down to Music Row, to see the shops, publishing companies, record companies, bars and museums. The place was a hive of activity. It felt like a dream: it was everything I'd hoped it would be and more! There was the Country Music Hall of Fame, which houses all the original documents, photos, costumes and instruments of the most famous artists in the history of country music, and here was I standing with only a pane of glass between me and Patsy Cline's Western fringed stage costumes, boots and jewellery. What I wouldn't have given to try on one of those outfits!

After a few days of sightseeing and music city tours, it was time for Mike and me to move to the Park Suites Hotel with all the other artists from Europe. The hotel has tropical gardens and fountains inside. Our suite was huge, with a living and kitchen area. There were I don't even know how many channels on the television, and this at a time when we had only three channels at home. We loved the country music channel there and watching videos of all the different artists. The telephone was great fun too: when you'd get back to your room, if the little red light on the phone was flashing, it meant you had a message, or maybe a few. Over the next couple of years, those little red lights went from hardly flashing at all to flashing a lot as I began to make friends in the Nashville community. On this particular trip, the messages were mostly from the CMA with details regarding rehearsals and the show. It was June, so it was really hot and it was also my first encounter with air-conditioning. The temperature was far too hot outside, but too cold inside. When we'd be in a restaurant, I'd have to keep popping out to get warm.

Finally, all the artists were grouped together to meet at the hotel and then we were brought to the rehearsal rooms. We met the musicians: Harold Bradley, the bandleader; Charlie McCoy on harmonica; Pig Robins on piano; and, would you believe, The Jordanaires were on backing vocals! This male vocal quartet had recorded with Elvis and Patsy Cline and with all the big record labels. We had two songs each. Mine were Dolly Parton's 'I Will Always Love You' and Bill Monroe's 'Blue Moon of Kentucky'. Harold Bradley impressed me a lot. A very soft-spoken and gentle-mannered man, but you knew instantly that he didn't suffer fools and expected one hundred per cent from anyone he worked with. I later found out that Harold, his brother Owen Bradley, and Chet Atkins were the founders of what's called 'The Nashville Sound'. Known as 'The A-Team', they were the studio band that played on all the major hit records at the time, with Elvis, Roy Orbison, Brenda Lee, Patsy Cline – everyone, really. Harold told me a story about when they were recording with Elvis down in RCA Studios in Nashville. Some Elvis fans got information that he was in town and hundreds of women gathered outside the studio, screaming for him like a mob. When Harold peeped out, there was a load of girls jumping up and down on his brand-new Cadillac. He nearly had a heart attack! Security had to be called to calm them down. We were definitely in the company of music royalty at Fan Fair '86.

Thankfully, I didn't know any of this at the time or it might have been too daunting to sing a Patsy Cline song, knowing I was being backed by the musicians who had played on the original record. Blissfully unaware, I sang my heart out and enjoyed every moment. Singing for the first time with these musicians gave me a better understanding of what people meant by 'The Nashville Sound': it was totally unique.

After rehearsals, Mike and I headed out to the Fan Fair arena to see what it was all about, and we were in for a real treat! At the Nashville Fairgrounds there were two huge dual stages, set right in front of a stretch of the NASCAR racetrack, with meet-and-greet huts surrounding the track. It was all on a massive scale. Up to 50,000 fans would meet and hear their favourite country stars. A lot of things have changed in country music since then and not all, in my opinion, for the better; today, you have to pre-book and pay extra to meet your favourite singer. Stars used to be willing and happy to meet people and sign autographs. It was a big part of the experience for the fans and, after all, country music is 'music of the people'. Mike and I had a fantastic day walking around listening to music, looking through all the stalls with clothes, boots, albums and, of course, eating fried chicken.

The next morning, we got ready for the show. We were to arrive at the park early, before it opened, to soundcheck and run through the songs. My outfit was the one I'd worn for the Gold Star Awards – white Western shirt, white fitted jeans and cowboy boots. It had been a lucky outfit for me before! Country music was blaring from the speakers on the main stage and, as I made my way up to the gigantic stage, a mixture of fear and exhilaration hit me. I'd played some pretty big festivals before, but nothing on this scale. Backstage there was an open area with tables and chairs to relax and socialise. It was another beautiful day. I was shown to my cabin dressing room and began my usual pre-show rituals, laying out a hand towel to place my make-up on, hair products, relics of my favourite saints and pictures of my children. I hung up my costume and placed my boots out before going back outside to wait my turn to soundcheck and rehearse. There was someone there to look after us at all times, which, I must admit, made me feel a little important. What it must be like to be Tammy Wynette!

When my turn came, I climbed the steps to the stage. My God, it was so big, it was quite the walk to my microphone in the middle. I must have looked tiny. Shoulders back, deep breath and off I went. I turned to the band and said 'hi' and they greeted me with their Southern charm. Looking out over the seating area was overwhelming: rows and rows of seats to accommodate thousands of people. Anyway, I snapped out of my trance and went over to speak with Harold Bradley about my performance. I suggested that I sing 'Blue Moon Of Kentucky' first and then 'I Will Always Love You'. Harold said, 'Sandy, you will kill them with the last song.' I wasn't sure what he meant by that, but I hoped it was good. I rehearsed my two songs and the sound of everything was so big and full, I thought that if they had the windows open at home in Sligo, they'd surely hear me.

The host of the show that year was Charley Pride. It was such an honour to meet him. He was nice and extremely funny, and immediately put us all at ease. The fans began filing in and, before long, the seats were steadily filling up. A sea of people, certainly an awful lot more than I'd ever performed to before. I got suited up, make-up on, curlers out and ready to go. The band started the concert with a medley of classic country songs, each taking a solo, including The Jordanaires singing a fantastic version of 'An American Trilogy' in their amazing close-knit harmony style; it would have brought a tear to a stone. I was placed near the end of the programme and as I stood on the side of the stage, I could hardly wait for Charley Pride to call my name.

When it finally came, out I went in my all-white Western outfit, not looking much like the elf from the show now, I thought. The welcome shown to me from the American audience was huge and I was filled with pride to be representing my country and determined to do my very best. My first song went really well and then I spoke to the audience a little, knowing that they liked the Irish. I'd have loved to sing more songs, but anyway, I started into 'I Will Always Love You'. I introduced the song by telling them that I had won the European Gold Star Award singing it.

Every magical moment singing with that band was musical heaven. I finished the song to loud cheers and applause. I couldn't believe my eyes when every single person rose to their feet and gave me a standing ovation! I burst into tears as I stood there watching and, as I turned to leave the stage, I saw that the band were also standing and applauding. Charley Pride then planted a kiss on my cheek to add to my out-of-body experience. At this rate, I wouldn't need a plane at all to fly home; I was as high as a kite.

I went to thank the band, making special time to speak to Harold Bradley, although I still had no idea of his history and success in music. I said my goodbyes, feeling happy at the success of the day, but sad that most likely I'd never meet these people again. At the meet-and-greet booth, a long line of fans waited to meet us. We were all there for several hours (but I do talk a lot!). All in all, it was one of the best days in my life.

I'd been keeping a close eye on what I was spending, as we didn't have a lot of money, but before we left Nashville, I really wanted to make one last visit to a Western store I liked, The Alamo. I'd spotted a leather fringed jacket and a shirt. The jacket was $250 and the shirt $60, which, in 1986, was a hell of a lot of money to me, but I bought both. One thing that was a bit strange about the shop was that they asked for my name and postal address to keep me updated about new styles. I gave them the information and went on my way. I was very sad to leave Nashville, in tears as the plane took off, thinking I'd never be back. But at least I was bringing home some new and precious memories.

Back in Sligo, it was just wonderful to see Willie and Barbara and their delight at the gifts we'd brought them. A few weeks later, I started getting letters from The Alamo that were nothing at all to do with Western wear, but weird religious stuff, very anti-Catholic and saying some terrible things about any type of society outside his cult, The Alamo Christian Foundation. I was confused and shocked. I discovered that this supposed designer to the stars, Tony Alamo, was in fact a cult leader. He was later sentenced to 175 years in prison for his many crimes, the worst being sexually assaulting many young girls whom he considered his wives. He died in prison aged 82 in 2017.

Everything was back to normal at home but I kept thinking, what if I wrote a letter to Harold Bradley? Would it even reach him and, if so, would I hear back from him? I decided to just go for it. I wrote to thank him for his help and kindness on our visit to Nashville, that it had been a dream come true for me, and just how much it meant to me to have had the chance to work with them all. Then I asked if he might be at all interested in producing an album for me in the future. I had no idea how life-changing that question would be. I wasn't even sure how I would finance such a project, but I'd worry about that later if it worked out. I've never allowed myself to worry about anything that hasn't happened yet.

After a few weeks, a letter arrived from Harold Bradley. You can imagine my excitement as I opened it. The best news! Harold would be delighted to produce my next album. Now all I had to do was find some way to finance it and travel back to Nashville. Neither would be easy. My previous and first album, *Paradise Tonight*, was out on CBS Ireland and they were still releasing singles from it. I was now into my third year of being managed by Kevin McCooey. I knew he had a lot of confidence in my career moving forward and he did a great job at managing me in Ireland and the UK. But now that I'd got a taste of what was happening in Nashville, my ambitions were aiming higher and further afield. My mum, Babs, was born in America and I'd always harboured a desire to live there for a while. My career in country music was about to take on a whole new chapter and lead me on a roller coaster of a journey!

# 12

# THE POWER OF A PRAYER

They say dreams can't really come true, but I now know for sure that, if you work hard enough and dream big enough, they do. I've always been a dreamer – I get that from my dad.

It was 1989. I had been working on my career in country music since 1983, with some success, but not yet everything that I'd hoped for. I had one of the best country bands in Ireland and we were as busy as most other bands with work. We had just come off a fantastic support tour with Waylon Jennings and Jessi Colter. I had released my second country album and was back working with Shay Hennessy. Shay insisted that I record four Patsy Cline tracks, 'Faded Love', 'Sweet Dreams', 'I Fall To Pieces' and 'Crazy'. We released 'Crazy' as a single and I was due to drive around the radio stations to promote it.

In the meantime, I'd been invited to open a fair day at Cloonamahon in County Sligo, a former monastery, but now a facility for people with special needs. Afterwards, I took a walk around the gardens and grounds with the priest, and I wish I could remember his name. He had such a positive effect on me that day. He was chatting about religion and I said, 'Father, I have to be honest with you, I'm not the world's best practising Catholic.' He stopped, looked at me and said, 'Neither am I.' Then we both laughed. He handed me what looked like a piece of jewellery, circular and gold in colour. He said, 'Here is a very special relic. It's of Gerard Majella.' (Whom I'd never heard of.) I later found out he'd been born in 1726 in Italy and died aged only 29 years. I looked at the relic, with decoration all around, glass covering the relic and below that a mother-of-pearl sequin, which I thought was funny. I said to the priest, 'Are you sure this isn't Elvis?' He went on to tell me that it was a fragment of bone, which I wasn't too excited to be carrying around in my handbag at the time. As I walked away, he said, 'Sandy, there is a prayer meeting here tomorrow night with a very special lady who has spiritual powers.' I replied, 'Thank you, but I don't think so, Father.' I returned home, just a few miles away, and began to think about my life.

It had been a difficult few years trying to get my country music career off the ground, not easy keeping up with bills and the continuous worry over my daughter, Barbara, her ongoing health issues and her future. I kept thinking of the conversation with the priest. Later on, I said to Mike, 'You know what? I'm going to go to that prayer meeting and ask for prayers for Barbara.' So the next night Mike and I headed off to the prayer meeting. I wasn't really expecting much and, truth be told, I felt a little uncomfortable. I'd always prayed, but in a much more personal way. Anyway, we arrived into the small church and sat down, but I felt so uneasy, as though everyone was looking at me. The room was full. A woman came in and went up on the altar and started talking and praying. Then she invited people to come up to ask for special prayers. There was a steady line of people and a couple of times the person asking for the prayer would faint and there were four men to catch them. I remember thinking how embarrassing it was for them. Then the priest quietly asked me if I'd like to put forward my request, so I summoned the courage to go and ask for prayers for my daughter. Up I went, still feeling very uncomfortable and as if all eyes were on me. But I'd just say what I had to say and leave, and at least I'd have done what I'd come for.

I approached the woman, who looked very pleasant, and quietly said that I would like to pray for my daughter, Barbara, that she would be okay and have a good life. The woman started to pray over me, then very quickly touched my forehead. Well, as soon as she did that, back I went! I'm not sure what happened, it was like slow motion falling back. I'm not sure if I blacked out or fainted. I can't even explain the feeling – somewhere between drunk and floating – but when I opened my eyes there were four men kneeling, two on either side of me. I could see them hazily and hear the woman praying over me, but I couldn't move. When I came back to myself, all I wanted to do was leave as quickly as possible. I was mortified.

When I was able to think and move again, I said to Mike, 'I have to go, I have to go.' We left as quietly as we could. On the way home, I felt really weird, still kind of in a trance and floaty. I tried to explain it to Mike but it was impossible. After all, I wasn't that kind of person. I've always been open to prayer and have always prayed, but in my own way and in my own personal space. Honestly, I felt that I had experienced something that night, but I was already writing it off as my imagination.

It was an early start the next morning. Checking I had enough copies of my new single 'Crazy' and of course bios and pictures, in case a fan might be lurking somewhere waiting for an autograph, I headed off towards Cavan. Looking every inch the country star in my Levi's and Western jacket, I'd finished off the outfit with a pair of steel-tipped cowgirl boots that Harold Bradley had bought for me in Nashville. Off I went in my Toyota Carina to knock on the doors of every pirate radio station I could find to ask them to play 'Crazy'. I have to admit that although Shay Hennessy, my record boss and friend, practically had to drag me to the studio to record it, I was very proud of it. Frank McNamara had produced it, with the cream of the Irish Concert Orchestra weaving their magical sounds as I sang.

I had been to several stations and this was the last one on my list. The DJ kindly asked me to do an interview before he played the track. As I gathered my bits and pieces to leave, in the distance a phone rang. The DJ answered it. He came back in and said, 'Sandy, there's an American guy on the phone for you.' I said, 'What? Are you sure?' I took the phone and cautiously said, 'Hello.' A deep American voice replied, 'Hi, is this Sandy Kelly? I'm Johnny Cash.' To which I said, 'No, it's Dolly Parton. Pull the other one!' This smart buck taking the mick wasn't going to catch me out! Again, the voice said, 'Really, I'm Johnny Cash.' 'Yeah' says I, 'Who are you trying to kid?' Again, the reply, 'I really am Johnny Cash.'

I could feel the ground going from under me. 'Are you really Johnny Cash?' 'Hon, I've been trying to tell you that!' Jesus, Mary and Joseph, I was talking to Johnny Cash, on the phone, from a pirate radio station somewhere in Cavan! The blood drained from the DJ's face when he heard me say, 'Sorry, Mr Cash, I thought it was someone messing.' 'June and I were travelling in the car, we heard your song and interview, and liked it very much. So we'd love for you to come see us tonight at our concert in Omagh.' Trying desperately to catch my breath to answer, 'Thank you, Mr Cash. Of course, I'll be there.' I'd figure out how I'd do all that later. At this point I could only get out the words 'yes', 'no' and 'thank you' out of my mouth. I was in shock and the DJ hadn't moved or uttered a word since he'd realised he had also just been talking to Johnny Cash.

Well, I was all over the place leaving the radio station, a million things going through my head like a hurricane. I sat in the car for a few minutes to pull myself together and make a plan. Time was of the essence, every decision vital. First, I had to find a phone box, call Mike and repeat everything that had just happened to convince myself it wasn't a dream. I asked him to go to my wardrobe and take out the new black leather skirt suit I'd bought for my first big support tour, with Waylon Jennings and Jessi Colter. If there'd been mobile phones then, I'd have rung half the country to tell them I was going to meet Johnny Cash and June Carter. In my head, I practised what I'd say to Johnny when I met him, something interesting, intelligent. What the hell would I say? 'Nice to meet you, I love your music.' No. 'Thank you for inviting me, I'm looking forward to the concert.' No. 'I never dreamt I'd ever meet you.' No. '"Walk The Line" is one of my favourites.' Oh God, no! It was all terrible. I didn't want to be too cheeky, but I wanted to sound confident. To hell with it, I'd have to wing it. Sure I might not even see him at all, I thought. One thing was for sure, though, I needed to get a photograph because I'd never see him again and who'd believe any of it if I didn't have a photograph?

I met Mike at a pub near the venue. I changed in the ladies' and put on some make-up, and then made my way to the stage door. I said nervously to one of the security guards, 'I'm Sandy Kelly and Johnny Cash invited me to be here tonight.' To my astonishment, he said, 'Yes, Mr Cash is expecting you.' Well, did I ever think I'd hear that sentence coming out of anyone's mouth! I was brought backstage and could hear the buzz of the fans front of house, finding their seats to await the arrival of their hero, and here was I, waiting outside his dressing room to meet him. 'Thirty minutes to curtain up!' All of a sudden I was calm and automatically switched to professional mode, although my body was still flooded with every emotion I possessed. For the moment, though, I was still in control. Just then, I spotted a well-known photographer. I grabbed him and said, 'You see that door? Johnny Cash will walk out any minute. I'll line myself up beside him and, as quick as you can, take a picture of the two of us. I'll never get this chance again.' 'Okay', he says. Big camera, lens and all strategically positioned on his chest, finger on the button ready for action. The dressing-room door opens, all eyes focus in that direction and I'm facing the door. A warrior-like figure emerges, at least ten feet tall (to me), piercing eyes, black hair, long black coat and black leather knee-high boots. All brought together by a wide belt with a large Native American style silver buckle. As I was scrambling to get my mouth in gear, he held out his hand to grasp mine and said, 'You must be Sandy Kelly. Waylon told me all about you.' 'Thank you so much for inviting me Mr Cash.' I turned to get lined up for the photo, but Mother of the Divine Jesus, the photographer was stretched out on the floor, the camera still positioned on his chest. He'd fainted at the sight of his idol. The last I saw of him, the security guards were carrying him, camera and all, out the exit door and laying him across the bonnet of a car. But what the hell would I do now to get my picture?

Johnny said to his manager, Lou Robin, 'Round up the band, bring them to my dressing room.' As he escorted me through the door, thankfully, I was able to keep my composure, though I felt quite lightheaded and my heart felt like it was going to jump out of my chest. I managed anyway to put one foot in front of the other and get through the door to the dressing room, followed closely by Johnny Cash. Saints preserve us, if any of my family or friends could see me now, I thought. Pretty soon, the band arrived in with sheets of paper in hand. I was thinking maybe I shouldn't really be here while they're practising, so I said, 'Maybe I'd better go out and get my seat while I still can.' Johnny let out a big belly laugh and said, 'Sandy, you won't be needing a seat. You'll be on stage singing with me.'

For once in my life, I was speechless, glued to the floor. He said, 'Come on back in here and let me hear your four best Patsy Cline songs with the guys here.' (This was lucky, as I knew only four Patsy Cline songs at this stage!) I thought to myself, 'Pull yourself together, pull yourself together' and I did. The showman's daughter in me kicked in and I was ready. The guys in the band were lovely and Johnny was so gracious and kind. I knew that within minutes he'd be stepping onto the stage to the roar of his fans. Quickly I said, '"Crazy", "I Fall To Pieces", "Faded Love" and "Sweet Dreams".' There were no problems at all as I sang quickly through them with the band. These Nashville musicians would have been playing these songs all their musical lives.

Within minutes, I saw June Carter and her sisters Anita and Helen coming towards us. I'd only ever seen them on an album cover or on television. Such beautiful Hollywood-like women, all dressed in long flowing dresses, Anita's floral and chic, Helen's more formal and classic. June was an absolute picture in her long silk and satin dress. Every inch the star! It was plain to see why Johnny loved her so much, and her smile beamed with beauty and warmth. At the side of stage, they stopped to greet me. June said, 'You must be Sandy. John and I love your version of "Crazy". So nice to meet you.' There was no showbiz-superstar nonsense with any of them, just a warm, wholesome welcome.

Almost eight o'clock, everyone standing by, it's show time. A few announcements, 'Ladies and gentlemen, please take your seats, this evening's performance will begin shortly.' Feeling a mixture of great happiness and fear, I stood at the side of stage to watch the concert and wait to be introduced. I had no idea when. Johnny delivered hit after hit: 'Folsom Prison Blues', 'Cry, Cry, Cry', 'Ring of Fire', 'Get Rhythm', 'I Still Miss Someone', 'A Boy Named Sue'. It was sheer magic to see how, in a very strong and charismatic but still humble way, he held the audience in the palm of his hand and they were having the night of their lives. June and her sisters took to the stage to a wonderful welcome and performed a set of beautiful Carter Family songs. Music that as children they had toured all over America with. Mother Maybelle and A.P. Carter had cemented their place in history as the first vocal group to become major stars, recording their debut album in 1927. Here I was seeing Mother Maybelle's daughters. I was in the company of country music royalty. Honestly, it was like a dream, but if it was, I didn't want to wake up.

June, Anita and Helen were amazing, and then it was my turn. I blessed myself, said a quick prayer to any saint I could think of, also asking Patsy Cline for her help as I had once before, just before I recorded my vocal on 'Crazy'. I could hear Johnny telling the story of how they had heard me that day on the radio. Then, 'Please welcome to the stage Sandy Kelly!' People cheering and clapping, you'd think it was an All-Ireland final. I suppose I was one of their own and they were proud. I could feel their support and so I was going to give my set all that I could. I loved every moment of it, Johnny and June standing watching – such an honour for me.

I stood side of stage after my set to watch the rest of the concert. The Johnny Cash show certainly gave 100 per cent. Johnny and June singing 'Jackson' brought the house down. June could be very funny on stage and the audience loved it. She stood with me when she finished. I knew that she'd been one of Patsy Cline's closest friends and so I asked her about Patsy. She told me how close they had been and how heartbroken she was when Patsy died. She also said that Patsy had once said to her that she believed she'd die young.

I plucked up the courage to ask June how tonight had come about and what had prompted them to invite me to meet them. I told her what a shock it had been to get the phone call from Johnny and the invitation to come meet them. June answered, 'Sandy, when John and I heard you sing Patsy's "Crazy" and heard you speak, we both felt an immediate spiritual connection and that we'd like to meet you.' She said they had done shows all over the world, but this was the first time Johnny had picked out someone to meet with them and sing on the show that same night. It was unusual. That night was the last show of their tour, and the audience didn't want them to leave the stage. Anita, Helen and June invited me back to their dressing room before they left and shared some wonderful stories about their friendship with Patsy.

There was a flurry of activity outside the dressing rooms with the crew packing up and loading the truck, musicians gathering up their personal belongings and costumes being packed away on the bus for the journey back to Dublin and then the return flight to Nashville. I began saying my goodbyes to June, Anita, Helen and then the band. I made my way to Johnny's room, where he and his manager were. Although we'd only just met, I already felt a connection. I was emotional but kept it together as I thanked him and June for asking me to join them on stage and for their kindness. Johnny asked if I had any plans to visit Nashville any time soon. As luck would have it – and luck was on my side once more – I was able to answer yes. The CMA had invited me to perform at Fan Fair again, the very next month, June 1989. To my surprise and delight, Johnny said, 'Well, when you get to Nashville, June and I want you to come out to our home in Hendersonville and visit with us.' Writing down his private number on a piece of paper, he said, 'We will look forward to seeing you again soon.'

Well, now the tears ran down my face and I could no longer keep my composure. Only when I saw them get on the coach and wave did the reality of the last eight hours hit me, and also the relevance of what had happened the night before at the prayer meeting in Cloonamahon. I am convinced that praying that night changed everything for me.

# 13

# 'WOODCARVER'

**B**ack in Sligo, after the incredible experience of meeting Johnny and June, my preparations got under way for travelling to Nashville for my second appearance at Fan Fair. I talked to my manager, Kieran Cavanagh, and Shay Hennessy, to keep them in the loop. Live gigs were going well and we were doing a residency two nights a week in Bad Bob's in Dublin, all on the heels of the success of my current record, 'Crazy'. It was going to be a much different trip to Nashville this time around. I'd be meeting with Johnny and June again and reconnecting with dear friends, whereas on the first trip in 1986 I hadn't known anyone. It would be super special. On this trip we had a little more money, so my son, Willie, and my sister, Barbara, would travel with Mike and me. Willie, nine at this point, loved the large airplane and the long flight with TV screens and hot food: a hotel with wings.

Willie's eyes nearly popped out of his head as we walked through Nashville Airport. A representative of the CMA collected us and, once we were out on the highway, Willie was mesmerised by all the big cars and huge trucks. We were booked into the Embassy Suites. In the week that we'd be there, I had only one day off. But it was fun for everyone hanging out at the stadium where Fan Fair was being held: music everywhere day and night, stalls selling just about everything to do with country music and, of course, all kinds of food. Mike, Barbara and Willie had a ball.

Believe it or not, hadn't I stupidly lost the piece of paper Johnny had given me with their private number! When I went to the CMA office to check in, at the end of our meeting, I quite innocently asked, 'Oh, by the way, would you happen to have Johnny Cash's phone number? He gave it to me about a month ago in Ireland and said that I was to call him when I got to Nashville and come out to the house to visit himself and June.' The woman looked at me for a moment. 'You're serious, aren't you?' she said, then burst out laughing. 'Have you any idea how many folk come in here looking for Johnny Cash's number?' I said, 'Honestly, he really did want to see me.' But I wasn't getting anywhere, so I just left it and focused on the show. I thought it was probably too good to be true anyway. Nothing against Johnny Cash, but people do say things that sometimes don't materialise.

On the morning of our big show, we all made our way to the stadium. I'd already met up with Harold, the band and The Jordanaires. By this time we'd all been recording together and so I felt a lot more comfortable and less intimidated. Harold had taken me under his wing and mentored me. He'd even taken us all out to dinner. So that morning, making my way to the stage, it was a whole different ball game. Willie and Barbara were backstage, it was a lovely sunny day and music was blaring out of the speakers all over the stadium. One by one, the artists soundchecked and we got ready. Kathy Mattea was there, with whom I'd done a show back home, alongside The Bellamy Brothers. She remembered me and so we got along really well. The audience, thousands of them, piled in. The show was fantastic and, just like last time, I went to the signing booth to meet fans afterwards. It was so much fun, I was there for several hours.

Later, I told Harold about losing Johnny Cash's number and the whole story. He said, 'Look Sandy, I know what you're saying is true, but trying to reach out to Johnny Cash would be almost impossible.' I knew it too. We made our way back to our hotel and, as the following night would be our last before returning home, with what little money we had left, I decided to treat us all to a visit to the Grand Ole Opry. I'd never been and we were all excited to finally see a show at the 'Mother Church of Country Music'. We went downtown to buy our tickets that evening.

The next morning, the phone rang in our hotel room. It was the woman from the CMA, Pam. She said, 'Sandy, you're not going to believe who's looking for you – Johnny Cash just rang here to see if we knew where you were. He and June are having a party and they want you to go out to the house.' I told her that we were leaving to go back to Ireland in the morning. Pam said, 'That's fine, the party is today and I told them I would drive you and your family out to Hendersonville. It's all arranged!' So Pam had some-how gotten herself invited by driving us out there. I got off the phone and Barbara said, 'Did I just hear you say that we're all going to Johnny Cash's house?' I said, 'Yep. You'd better get the curlers in.'

We had a quick breakfast and started to get ready to visit the Cash family home. How would you even get your head around that?

Pam arrived to pick us up and we made the trip out to Hendersonville. Pam knew where the house was. Hendersonville, outside Nashville, is a lovely area. As we arrived at the large, gated home, the beauty of it took my breath away. It was the home of everyone's dreams. There was a man guiding us towards the parking area, which was already full of cars. I think we must have been the last to arrive. There was a fine walk up to the house, a tennis court next to the house and on it a magnificent marquee. June was standing there, greeting everyone. She had beautifully coloured Hawaiian flower garlands, leis, on her arms and placed one over each of our heads. It was a lovely way to be greeted.

I could hear lots of chatter and I remember wondering if they'd even remember who we were. I just stood for a moment to take it all in. There was a sea of beautifully decorated tables, all done in an elegant country style. There were a lot of people and as I glanced around the room, I recognised many faces from the album covers in my living room. I saw Dottie West first, star of the Grand Old Opry. I could hear Johnny Cash singing; he was on a little stage, black shirt and trousers and, of course, the Hawaiian lei. Just him playing his guitar and singing for their guests. We were seated at our table and told to help ourselves to food from the magnificent array of dishes, all cooked from Mother Maybelle's own recipes. For those of you who don't know, Mother Maybelle, June's mum, was legendary in the world of country music as a member of the Carter Family band. This was a party June had put together to honour her mum and to launch her cookbook.

We sat and listened to Johnny and then a succession of other well-known singers took to the stage to sing for us. Then I heard Johnny say, 'We were over in Ireland recently and June and I met this little girl called Sandy Kelly and we invited her here to sing with us. We just loved her voice and

I'd love for you all to hear her.' Christ, I nearly fell off the chair. As usual, I pulled myself together and, to the sound of applause from people I admire so much, I made my way to the stage. Johnny reached out his hand to help me up. There was a guy playing acoustic guitar, I sang a few songs and, to the amusement of everyone, I told the story of how I'd met John and June. They loved my Irish accent. I looked down at our table where Mike, Barbara and Willie were beaming. Once I got over my shock and fear, I really enjoyed it. It's not often that you sing with Johnny Cash at his house, with June Carter, Roseanne Cash and Rodney Crowell, to name a few, sitting at the front table watching you.

When I sat back down, Johnny's manager, Lou Robin, came over and whispered to me that Johnny wanted us to stay on after the party and visit with him and June over at the house. I hesitated for a moment, because we had those tickets for our first and maybe last visit to the Opry, for the 9.30pm show. But what was there to think twice about really? If Johnny Cash invites you and your family to stay on and have coffee with him, well, that's what you do. I was a bit frustrated that I'd spent the money – which was a whole lot of money to us then – but with such a special invitation being extended, I quickly got over it.

With the party over, people started leaving. John and June stood at the door, thanking everyone as they left and gifting them a Mother Maybelle cookbook, personally signed by June. They were the perfect hosts. When everyone was gone, we walked over to the house with Johnny. It's very hard to fully describe how beautiful the house was, a mansion really. Sitting on the edge of Old Hickory Lake, built with dark wood, complemented by stone walkways and buildings, it stood very tall, maybe three floors in parts, and it spread down along the lakeshore. There was a stone walkway leading down to a seating area and a boat dock on the shore. I know that Johnny enjoyed fishing, so he must have loved living here. There was also a swimming pool.

In the kitchen by the fire, there was a big rocking chair and Johnny sat in that. June made coffee and we sat down and had a long chat about Ireland and Sligo. Johnny was interesting to talk to and, in turn, was interested in finding out about people. We all felt a little intimidated sitting there in the Cash family kitchen, casually chatting. June invited us to walk around the rest of their home ourselves and have a look. Off we went, room to room, each decorated to perfection with stunning drapes made in all kinds of rich fabrics, and crystal chandeliers. We made our way down a spiralling wooden staircase into the most fabulous dining room I've ever seen. There must have been at least twenty chairs around the long wooden table, which was laid for a lavish dinner. June's tableware all looked antique. All the rooms that faced out onto the lake had huge floor-to-ceiling windows.

We didn't want to overstay our welcome, but before we could leave, Johnny said, 'Sandy, I have a song that I want to record with you.' I said, 'Can you please say that again!?' He laughed and said, 'I have a song that I've been meaning to record with Emmylou Harris, but I think it would really suit your voice.' Handing me a cassette tape with the word 'Wood-carver' written on it, he said, 'Take it and listen to it and if you like it, come back and we'll record it together.' Speechless again! We hugged and I told him how much this meant to me and said, 'I don't care what the song is like. I'd be thrilled to record "Three Blind Mice" with you.' He and June both laughed at that. So we parted by saying, 'See you again soon.' The whole day had been fantastic – what an experience and what great memories! Back in the car, we were all full of chat, even Pam from the CMA was super happy. She could hardly believe what she just witnessed.

Back at our hotel, I was able to listen to the song. I don't have words to explain how I felt, but I imagine it was like winning a gold medal at the Olympics. I was so emotional, yet so unbelievably happy. Sitting with the small tape recorder that Harold Bradley gave me, I could have cried as I listened:

Woodcarver, carve me the house of my dreams,

Carve me a valley, make me a stream,

That runs through the mountains and under the trees,

Woodcarver do this for me ...

The song was perfect. I understood why Johnny thought it would work. Johnny was the woodcarver and I was the girl asking him to carve her dreams. It was incredibly beautiful. I rang Kieran, my manager, and Shay at the record company, and I rang my dad, as he was a huge Johnny Cash fan. He was so proud. I didn't sleep a wink that night!

Before I left Nashville Airport, I called my record producer, Harold, to tell him that Johnny had found me and to share the great news with him. He was thrilled for me and said that opportunities like this were extremely rare and that Johnny must have really liked my voice. When I got back home, I got straight into working with my band again. It was fantastic to get home to Barbara too. We had a nanny who lived with us, Olivia Canning from Ballinamore. Olivia was a fan of mine and when we advertised for a nanny, she applied. We knew her well and liked her, and we trusted her with the children.

We were doing well and attracting good crowds at home, but I had to keep the news about Johnny to myself until the recording was done. That

August, I headed back to Nashville to record. Johnny had asked if I had a preference for a producer and a studio and, of course, I said, 'Harold Bradley and Bradley's Barn'. He was very happy with that choice. This time, Kieran, Shay and the television producer Ian McGarry would come along to start filming a documentary for RTÉ called *The Showman's Daughter*, which would include footage of the recording of 'Woodcarver'. As you can imagine, we were all in great form and really looking forward to the sessions. Harold had been in touch with Johnny about the key and arrangement for the song. Arriving in Nashville, I immediately got back into learning the song. I knew it already but wanted to be very comfortable recording it. Well, as comfortable as you can be with Johnny Cash standing beside you!

Next morning, Harold collected me from the hotel early, so that we'd be ready to start long before Johnny got there. When we got to the studio, the fear and nerves started. This was only the third time we'd met; I didn't really know him well. While Harold got the studio ready with the sound engineer, his nephew Bobby Bradley, I laid out my make-up in the ladies'. This studio was also used for filming; Jessica Lange had recorded there for the 1985 Patsy Cline biopic *Sweet Dreams*. I was outside having a coffee when an open-top jeep approached, the dust off the road flying up behind it. It pulled up outside the studio and out hopped Johnny Cash. He was by himself, in his trademark black trousers and a dark green denim jacket with badges sewn all over it. I was beyond excited. Inside in the studio, he sat down to chat with everyone in the control room about the recording while he ate a large tub of yoghurt.

Harold had recorded the backing track the day before. The musicians had worked all day on it. Usually when I record, I come in every day with the musicians and sing guide vocals for the songs. That might take a week and then I'd come in on my own to do the final vocals. This would help me get to know the songs and be really comfortable singing them. This time would be different, but I wasn't complaining.

Harold and Bobby played the track for us to listen to, plus a track for *Ring of Fire*, which they had also recorded the previous day. Both sounded fantastic. But I was so petrified, I excused myself and legged it back to the ladies', nervously touching up my make-up and hair. After a while, Harold knocked on the door and said, 'Sandy, are you going to stay in there all day or are you going to come cut a record with Johnny Cash?' I pulled myself together and when I stepped out, there was Johnny sitting on a large leather sofa. He said, 'I promise I won't bite.' And we all laughed.

We sang 'Woodcarver' a couple of times to the track and it sounded great. Johnny felt a little tired, so Harold suggested that he rest for a while before we started recording. The big recording room was decorated like a very lavish sitting room. The lights were dimmed and Johnny lay on the leather sofa. We left him to rest for a few hours and he seemed much more himself afterwards.

It was time to record. Johnny was really easy to work with and in no way demanding. He loved the track and, from the first time we sang together, it all worked perfectly. Our voices blended well and so the story in the song felt natural and sincere. Unlike how it appeared in the video, Johnny and I actually stood opposite each other while we recorded. I won't even try to explain what it's like standing in front of a studio mic, wearing headphones and looking across straight into Johnny Cash's eyes. But I was not going to let him down. I sang my very best and we laughed a lot in between. Johnny was happy and I was relieved to have not disappointed him.

Johnny was very creative and, about the third time we sang it, he went straight into talking the last verse. I don't have to tell you how powerful his voice was. When he spoke, the ground moved. He looked straight at me and said:

Well I can carve you your house, I can carve you your man,
But I can give you much more with these woodcarvin' hands …

Even today, I can conjure up exactly how I felt. Everyone there knew it was a special recording. When we listened to it in the control room, we could sense that we'd created something beautiful.

After eating, it was time for some of the local Nashville press and TV shows to come to interview us. Shay, Kieran and Ian McGarry were also there with a film crew to capture inserts for the documentary and to make a video for 'Woodcarver'. It was work, but fun. I was so busy that I didn't have time to take in all that happened that day. It was only when I was lying in my bed that night, exhausted, that I had time to reflect. I honestly couldn't believe the kindness that was in Johnny Cash. I was getting to know him and learn about the icon so many people adored and still do. On the day we recorded 'Woodcarver', I brought him a bronze figurine of an Irish warrior, because I saw Johnny Cash as a warrior. He gave me an original copy of his first album on Sun Records and signed it.

The next day, Johnny, June and the band left to do some shows and so once again we said our goodbyes, at the studio. But this time I knew for sure we'd be meeting again.

# 14

# MY JOURNEY WITH
# JOHNNY & JUNE

The rest of my Nashville visit was full on, recording shots for *The Show-man's Daughter* documentary. I enjoyed it all, and got to spend time with new friends, especially Harold. It was early 1989 and we had approached RTÉ with the idea of a one-hour TV series of music and chat, which I would host. This idea was approved and the wheels were in motion, so when I got back to Ireland from Nashville, it was straight into the preparation for *Sandy*, my TV series, and the release plan for 'Woodcarver'. There was a very heavy schedule coming up and I just couldn't wait.

'Woodcarver' was released shortly after and, needless to say, having a single coming out with Johnny Cash had a significant impact. The song was a huge success. By this time, my upcoming TV series was also announced, along with a new album. I was flying high. Johnny was coming to the UK and Ireland to play some dates and he invited me to be a guest on the shows, which was fantastic. I got to travel with them on the coach and got to know all the family better. I don't ever remember them being in bad humour – they were always joking around. Johnny and June had a fantastic sense of humour. Their son, John Carter Cash, was also on the tour. On the first night of the UK tour, just before I was due to go on, Johnny appeared out of his dressing room and went over to tell the MC exactly what to say when he announced me on. It was the nicest and most thoughtful thing! I've done a lot of shows with a lot of big names and Johnny is the only one who took a personal interest like that or who had me travel with them. My spot went down great and then the Johnny Cash Show started. He would invite me back out to sing 'Crazy' and then 'Woodcarver' and, to finish, I would join Johnny, June, Anita, Helen and John Carter for a gospel medley at the end of the show. Then it would be onto the bus for the journey back to our hotel.

The coach was no ordinary one, but very lavish, with a kitchen in the back. Johnny would wander down from time to time, open the little fridge and make himself a huge sandwich. The family all loved food and they were all great cooks, including Johnny. On tour, they brought their own chef, who would have the use of the kitchen in each hotel we would stay in. It wasn't pretentious; they just couldn't afford to be sick and miss shows. On the coach, June would sometimes entertain us all with her comedy. As well as being an established singer and musician, she was well known as a comedian, having appeared as such on all the major networks in America. She did a little of it on the show in the UK and always had a new joke for us after the show each night. She would stand in the aisle of the coach and tell the joke with all the animation that was needed. She was a great actress.

Johnny loved to sew as a hobby. He kept his needles and thread in a vintage tin box and he sewed old badges and buttons he'd collected onto his jackets and hats. On stage, he wore a stunning spirit mantle he'd made from suede, leather and pieces of silver. It was blue, red and white. I said to him cheekily one night after the show, 'Will you make me one of those?' and he said, 'I will.' A few months after that tour, a box arrived in the post. There was a handwritten letter, neatly folded, sitting on top of a spirit mantle that he had made for me. The spirit mantle was on a white satin cushion. It took my breath away. I was shocked that he'd remembered and that he'd actually taken the time to make it for me. I couldn't have ever gotten a more beautiful gift. In his letter, he explained the meaning of the spirit mantle and what it would mean to me personally.

On a later tour, I was waiting at the side of the stage with Johnny's sister Reba, who took charge of all of Johnny's personal affairs. I really liked her and she was very good to me. When Johnny introduced me, I came walking towards him, proudly wearing my spirit mantle, as he was wearing his. I thought it would be nice. When he saw me and as I got closer, I could see by his expression he hadn't expected me to wear the spirit mantle. I don't think that anyone else knew he'd made it for me and I instantly realised it was meant as a personal gift. That was the last night I wore it.

The last show of this particular tour was in the National Concert Hall in Dublin. It was nearly Halloween and it was arranged for Johnny, June, John Carter, Helen, Anita and the band to film a guest appearance for my upcoming series *Sandy* in RTÉ. After the concert, I suggested to Lou Robin that, as they had a few days off to film, it might be nice if they travelled to Sligo and stayed at Markree Castle to film there instead of doing it in studio. He immediately said, 'No, that's too far and Johnny won't want to do that.' Now, I know I shouldn't have, but I mentioned it to Johnny. He said, 'How far is Sligo?' I told him it was three hours from Dublin. Without discussing it with anyone, he said, 'Okay, let's go to Sligo!' Lou and some of the others weren't too happy, but when Johnny made a decision, very few went against it. Kieran Cavanagh organised everything with Markree and RTÉ, and Ian McGarry made the arrangements for the film crew.

On the day they arrived, Mike and I drove in front of the coach on the winding road leading to Markree. When the castle came into sight, standing majestically in a light mist, I couldn't have been prouder and couldn't wait for them to see inside. There's a great arch (where the horse-drawn carriages would stop), massive wooden double doors and a long, wide stairway to the reception area, where there's a huge open fireplace. Mike and I left them to settle in. The owners, Charles and Mary Cooper, made them welcome and gave them a bit of history about the castle. I returned to start filming in the early afternoon. We sang on the grand stairs in the reception hall, while June watched from the comfort of an armchair by the huge open fire. It wasn't easy to make the song romantic with her there, but Johnny performed as normal, so I followed suit. And I came out on the right side of June.

When we took a break, John and June met with my dad, who was delighted to meet and chat with his idol, and they also met my daughter, Barbara. They knew all about her, and Johnny really connected with her. He got a kick out of how straight-talking and honest she was. She was eight years old and as cute as a button. The castle was closed while we were filming and, at one point, Johnny was behind the bar in the Long Room, pulling a pint of Guinness for himself. Barbara was on a high stool, swinging her legs and chatting away. Johnny's Guinness poured, just as he's about to savour that unmistakable taste, Barbara says, 'Hey! Where the fuck is my drink?' Well, I was mortified. Johnny nearly choked on his first sip as he roared with laughter and poured a Coke for Barbara.

Next, we filmed Johnny sitting in front of the fireplace, telling the story of 'Forty Shades of Green', and then he sang it, playing acoustic guitar. It was very emotional. Then June, Anita, Helen and John Carter all played together in front of the fireplace. The Cash Carter family were the ultimate professionals, always delivering great performances with ease, never making demands or causing any hassle.

Ian, Shay and Kieran were delighted with what we had filmed that day. I headed off with Ian to do some more filming at home with my family. Then later, Mike and I joined everyone back at Markree for dinner. Over dinner, there was a surprise. Johnny presented me with a beautiful silver and turquoise ring belonging to June, and June gave one of Johnny's bolo ties to Mike. We all had an early night; it had been a long day. The next day was Halloween and the Cash family were busy planning a private party in the castle. Unfortunately, I had to return to Dublin to do a gig in Bad Bob's.

Over the years I've kept a connection with Markree. My sister, Barbara, had her wedding reception there. I'd always had a lovely friendship with Charles and Mary Cooper and when the Corscadden family took over the castle in 2017, that connection has continued. I've sung there at many events and filmed for various channels, had umpteen photo shoots for magazines. There is a room named the Johnny Cash Suite and Johnny and June's signatures are proudly displayed in a glass cabinet for visitors to see.

In March 1991, I toured again with the Johnny Cash Show. One night, I was on stage with June and her sisters, kind of like an honorary Carter, and spotted Johnny at the side of the stage, which was odd because he would normally be back in his dressing room. He wound up a toy mouse and let it off across the stage towards us. June, Helen and Anita just glanced at it and kept singing, obviously used to his little tricks.

The last date on the tour was at Wembley Arena, at the Silk Cut Country Music Festival, but it was a separate date from the rest of the tour and I hadn't been booked for it. When I explained to Johnny, he insisted I stay on the coach with them. And so I went to Wembley for the first time. We arrived at the huge backstage entrance. Everyone backstage was just awestruck. Mervyn Conn, the festival promoter, came over and Johnny said, 'By the way, we have Sandy Kelly on the show tonight.' Mervyn shook my hand to welcome me. I guess when Johnny says you're on the show, you're on the show. That night in Wembley was one of the personal highlights of my career. I sang 'Crazy', then Johnny and I sang 'Woodcarver'. The crowd erupted into huge applause. As I made my way off the stage, I heard the intro of 'Woodcarver' being played again, and Johnny saying, 'Welcome back Sandy Kelly!' Lou Robin later said it was hilarious to see me running across the stage to join Johnny to do the duet for a second time.

After the show, Lou Robin knocked on my door and handed me an envelope, saying, 'This is from Johnny.' In it was £1,000. He knew that I was bringing my children on a short break and he wanted me to have this for them. On another occasion, when I was working with him in Branson, he did the same thing when I was making a quick visit home to Ireland for Willie's confirmation. His kindness had no bounds.

I was singing at River Fest in Nashville around 1991. Afterwards, a woman called May Axton asked to meet me, and invited Harold Bradley and me to her home for lunch the next day. Harold told me that May

Axton was a pretty big deal around Nashville and had a long history in the music industry. She had introduced the nineteen-year-old Elvis to Colonel Tom Parker, and co-wrote 'Heartbreak Hotel' for Elvis. Her home was a huge southern mansion, like something out of *Gone With the Wind*. I thought to myself, 'This is going to be some lunch.' May greeted us at the door with two little poodles, one pink and one blue. The dining room contained a long banquet table with three place settings at one end. We sat and chatted, but as time went on, I noticed there was no smell of cooking, and I was starving. The next thing, the doorbell rang and out May went to open it. She came back in with a couple of delivery pizzas. It was so funny: there we were in this huge mansion with the long dining table, eating pizza.

We visited her office the next day. I was excited to see it as she'd looked after so many of the big country artists. May told me that an artist, Steven Saylor, was working on a painting called *The Celebrity Train*, which would be auctioned for the Carson City Rotary Foundation to raise funds. May asked me if I'd pose for Steven and, of course, I said yes. When Steven arrived, he asked me to sing while I posed, so I sang 'Katie', which I had recorded a few days before.

A year later, while I was in Branson, Steven called to see me, bringing twenty-two of the first prints from the original painting. I sat and signed each one, which were going to the twenty-two artists in the painting. About a year after that again, my own personal, very large and beautifully framed print arrived at my home in Carrowgobbadagh, signed by each of the other celebrities in the painting, including Waylon Jennings, Roy Acuff, Eddy Arnold, Glen Campbell, Kenny Rodgers, Randy Travis, Lorrie Morgan, Juice Newton and Crystal Gayle. I'm glad to say that I still have the painting in safe keeping.

Later in 1991, on my next visit to Nashville, I was invited to sing at the Fidof celebrations. This festival invited eighteen artists or bands from all over Europe to perform in the open air to thousands of people. There was a judging panel and I came in second place, winning a few thousand dollars. During that visit, the artists were all invited to a concert. Roy Clark did the first half, then Waylon Jennings and Johnny Cash did the second half. A few nights before this concert, Waylon and Johnny had done a press conference at the Opryland Hotel. The room was crowded, and I was standing at the very back. But after the press call, Waylon spotted me, grabbed me by the hand and dragged me through the crowd to where Johnny was, saying 'Look who I found!' I swear to God, Waylon was so excited you'd think he'd found the queen of England. Waylon brought me to a little reception in another room and insisted on explaining all the different delicacies and showing me how he made his favourite sandwich. Right up there with Johnny Cash, Waylon Jennings was one of the nicest people I have toured with. I could never explain how down to earth and kind he was.

On the night of the concert, during the interval, after Roy Clark had done his spot, one of Johnny's personal assistants, Hugh Waddell, tapped me on the shoulder and said that John and Waylon wanted me to come backstage. They were sitting at a table, with Jessi Colter sitting nearby. They said they'd like me to join them on stage for a song and suggested 'Good-Hearted Woman', which, thank God, I knew.

The second half started and Waylon went on first. Johnny led me up to the side of the stage to listen. It was just a dream standing there, watching him perform. I can't remember the song, but suddenly Johnny took my hand and said, 'Let's dance!' There I was, slow-dancing with Johnny Cash and listening to Waylon Jennings. Then Johnny went on. Together, they were just unreal, making music and having fun. I was called on for the encore. Could life be any better? It might sound to you that this was all normal for me or that I took it all in my stride. I can assure you that was not the case at all. I savoured every second spent in the company of these unique and talented people.

Also in 1991, I recorded 'Crazy' with Willie Nelson, which was an incredible experience for me. When he'd heard about my success with 'Crazy', he agreed straight away to do the duet. I could hardly believe the good fortune this song was bringing to me: first Johnny Cash, and now Willie Nelson. Willie Nelson had always been my sister's favourite male country singer. When I told her that I was going back to Nashville to record with him, she almost fainted and then begged me to bring her with me, which I did.

On the morning of the recording, I was nervous, naturally, as I'd never met him before. Barbara was busying herself, getting ready. The more time we had, the bigger her hair got. A call came through to say Willie, who'd just got back from a Highwaymen tour, was going to swing by the hotel and pick us up in his tour bus. When I looked at Barbara, she was as white as a ghost. She said she couldn't travel on the bus as she'd probably faint when she saw him. 'Christ', I said, 'Well, I have to go!'

Harold arranged for Barbara to travel separately. I was waiting outside the hotel, when the huge coach pulled up, painted on the outside with portraits of The Highwaymen – Willie Nelson, Johnny Cash, Waylon Jennings and Kris Kristofferson. I couldn't see in, but I stood there, trying to look as cool as possible. The coach door opened and there he was, Willie Nelson, holding a mug of coffee and looking exactly how I imagined. He said, 'Hey Sandy, nice to meet you!' He couldn't have been any more normal. There was a personal assistant guy with him, who looked like a Willie Nelson clone.

As we made our way to the studio, the people in the cars driving by were desperately trying to get a look in but, as I said, you couldn't see into the bus. We listened to the songs we were to record as we drove along.

We arrived at Bradley's Barn studios, which had become a second home to me by this stage. As the coach made its way up the narrow dirt road to the studio, I could see Barbara bent over in a tight skirt, looking into the wing mirror of a car and backcombing her hair. Willie looked out and said, 'Good Lord!' I made no comment, as Willie and I headed for the door of the studio, while Barbara just looked after us. I came back out to get her, and said, 'Barbara, come meet Willie.' She was so star-struck, I practically had to lead her by the hand. Once inside, I said, 'Willie, I'd like to introduce you to my sister, Barbara.' Well, as quick as lighting, she shook hands with the lookalike assistant, who was standing beside Willie. We all started laughing as Willie said, 'Hi, I'm Willie,' taking her hand and shaking it. It was both hilarious and embarrassing.

I feel incredibly lucky to have recorded 'Crazy' again, this time with the person who wrote it, and most of the musicians who originally played on it, Owen Bradley, who originally produced it for Patsy, and Harold, his brother, who was my producer at the time. Charlie, Patsy's husband, came in to hear it and joke around with us. It was a fantastic day, as laid-back as you'd expect from Willie Nelson. We stood around the piano, Owen playing 'Crazy' while Willie and I sang. His style of singing is unique, always coming in after the beat. I had to stop myself from starting the words for him. If memory serves me, when we did the actual recording, singing to each other, he was still holding a mug of coffee.

Willie really seemed to be enjoying the recording, and Harold even gifted him one of his guitars. He was having so much fun that, by the time he was done, we'd recorded four songs: 'Crazy', 'Every Time You Need a Friend', 'Against the Wind' and one other, which is still a secret because it is yet to be released.

In 1993, Harold invited me back to Bradley's Barn to record a duets album and, once again, Shay Hennessy was involved. The name of the album was *Kelly's Heroes*. We spent the whole week recording with a variety of duet partners. Every single person sang their heart out on the songs, and it's something I'll always treasure. We already had the Johnny Cash and Willie Nelson songs recorded, of course, and some of the others I recorded were, 'The World's Greatest Song' with Glen Campbell, a song written by my dear friend Andy Landis; 'I Love You Only' with Gary Morris; 'Jambalaya' with Jett Williams; 'Whisper Your Name' with Randy VanWarmer; 'The Way Old Friends Do' with George Hamilton IV; 'When the Leaves Turn Brown' with Hal Ketchum; 'Half a Mind' with George Hamilton V; and 'Old Flames' with Tommy Cash, with the legendary Chet Atkins playing guitar on a couple of tracks. Most special of all was recording 'Walking After Midnight' with Patsy Cline: we had got Patsy's original recording tapes from Charlie Dick (Patsy's widower) and, with a bit of technical wizardry, I got to duet with her.

I let Johnny know that I was in town. He invited me to join him and his sister Reba at the Opryland Hotel for an awards ceremony and said he'd pick me up at my hotel. The pick-up point was indoors at the back of the hotel, a seated glassed-in area where people waited for taxis. On the stroke of six o'clock, a stunning metallic-blue Rolls-Royce pulled up. Everyone waiting there rushed to the window to look. I waded through the crowd to the car, feeling like Cinderella as Johnny stepped out to take my hand and help me into the car.

Johnny said that Roy Rogers was to get a special award at the ceremony. Now there's a name I couldn't believe I was chatting about – Roy Rogers, a cinema legend and every child's hero! It was another unforgettable night and I met a lot of really lovely people, including Randy Travis.

When it was time to leave, I was told to keep close and walk fast as we made our way through the lobby of the hotel back to the car, which was outside with its engine running. The walk was cordoned off with ropes, with hundreds of fans lined up, taking photos and calling out. Being on the celebrity side of the rope distracted me for a moment and I fell behind. When I got to the large door, all I could see was the Rolls pulling off and fans running after it. Now what would I do? The next thing, the Rolls is flying it back, brakes screeching. Johnny flings the door open and shouts, 'Get in, quick!' It felt like we'd just robbed a bank! At my hotel, Johnny walked me through the lobby and all the way to my room. Dressed all in black, of course, knee-high boots and a long black cape lined in blue satin, there was no mistaking who he was. When I opened my bedroom door, he peeked in to see the pile of clothes thrown on my bed, and said, 'I see you keep a tidy room.' I was mortified and said, 'I couldn't decide what to wear.' He hugged me, kissed me on the cheek and took off down the hall like some sort of a god.

Every time I was in his company, he surprised me. I still don't understand why Johnny enjoyed spending time with me. I think maybe he appreciated my honesty and good humour. I remember doing a show with him in the Slieve Russell in Cavan, which had just opened. Johnny and I were presented with a gold disc for 'Woodcarver'. Johnny was sitting alone in the artists' backstage waiting area, waiting to go on. I sat with him and he said the strangest thing to me: 'Sandy, will you be my friend?' It was spoken with sadness. I replied, 'Honestly, it's very difficult to be your friend because you're surrounded by so many people. It's sometimes impossible to get to the real you.' He just smiled and made no reply.

Although he was loved and adored by so many people, there was a loneliness about him. I will forever remember the many stories he told me. He spoke about his eldest brother, Jack, who'd been tragically killed aged fifteen. This had a profound and lifelong effect on Johnny. Once I asked him how he got the dimple-like mark near his chin, and he said he'd got shot. When he saw my reaction, he burst out laughing. He was just winding me up.

Johnny played what I believe was his last ever show in Ireland at the Olympia in Dublin on 8 February 1993. I was in my kitchen in Carrowgobbadagh, peeling vegetables for a stew, when the phone rang in the hall. It was Reba. She said Johnny wanted to know why I wasn't there. I explained that I wasn't booked for the show, but she said, 'Johnny wants you to get here to sing on tonight's show, so you better get here!' Mike left me to the train and I arrived at the Olympia about two hours before show time. I could hear Johnny talking so I followed the sound of his voice until I found him and then threw my arms around him because I was so happy to see him. He asked what I was going to sing, so I said 'I can't sing tonight. I don't have anything to wear.' Then Reba said, 'Sandy, when Johnny Cash asks you to sing, you don't worry about what you wear.' So it was decided. That night, Kris Kristofferson opened the concert, then Johnny and June and the band started. I fell into the routine as before with the Carter family.

I was sitting on a high stool, watching from the wings, when suddenly the backstage door opened and in walked Bono and the rest of U2. I was completely star-struck. I've always loved Bono and the band. Then somebody's hands came over my eyes and a voice whispered into my ear. It was

Bono, and suddenly I'm reduced to a fourteen-year-old schoolgirl, unable to speak or think straight. Meanwhile, June was on stage with Johnny doing a comedy routine, lifting up her skirt to dance. She had black tights on with a large pattern down the leg. Bono asked me if was it tights or a tattoo. I laughed at that, and then he said, 'I just love Johnny Cash.' To which I replied, 'He loves you too!' Johnny called U2 on stage, led by Bono, who knelt down in front of Johnny and kissed his feet in a declaration of admiration. I suppose I can always say I followed U2 on stage.

On 12 September 2003, I had just finished working on a cruise. My sister, Barbara, met me at Dublin Airport, which was very unusual. She said, 'I've had a call from Tommy Cash and he wants you to call him. Johnny's not well.' I'd had a few calls like that from Tommy over the years, as Johnny's health hadn't been good for a while. I rang Tommy and knew from his voice that it was bad. He gave me the dreaded news: 'Johnny is gone. He passed away earlier today. We didn't want to tell you as you were making your journey home.' It was like being hit by a bolt of lightning. I was devastated. I told Tommy that I wanted to come to Nashville to be there. He said, 'Sandy, we would dearly love to have you here for the celebration of Johnny's life and his funeral.' We were both in floods of tears as we hung up.

I travelled to Nashville straight away and cried all the way there. George Hamilton IV picked me up at Nashville Airport and brought me to my hotel. He understood my sorrow. The service was held on 15 September at noon. I arrived early. It was a private service and there was a lot of security outside. In the church were two big screens, one on either side of the altar, showing home videos of John, June and the family. It was heartbreaking to watch, especially because June had passed away just four months earlier, on 15 May 2003. Lou Robin made his way across the altar, making sure all the wreaths were positioned correctly. He cut a sad figure. After managing Johnny for more than thirty years, Lou was looking after him for the last time. He was surprised to see me but gave me the biggest hug. He was devastated.

I returned to my seat as mourners started to arrive. Some I knew and some I just knew to see. Kris Kristofferson paid tribute to Johnny and Emmylou Harris was one of the guest singers in a beautiful celebration of Johnny's life. Then, one by one, we filed past the casket to pay our respects and say our last goodbye.

At the Memory Gardens in Hendersonville, a piper walked ahead of the casket to the grave. Prayers were said and then we all sang 'Will the Circle Be Unbroken' as the casket was lowered. Something changed in me that day. How could it be that he was gone? Someone so much larger than life, so kind, talented, loved, adored by millions? It made me realise that we should all live our best lives, because it doesn't matter what you have or who you are, we'll end up just the same. I paid my respects to Johnny's family and left to make the sad journey home.

I will carry my love for Johnny and June in my heart for as long as I live. I have visited their grave in the years since, and also the graves of Anita, Helen and, more recently, Harold Bradley. I was truly blessed to have known them and I miss their friendship every single day.

# 15

# *SANDY* – THE TV SERIES

B y 1989, my career had really taken off. As a direct result of Shay Hennessy insisting that I record the Patsy Cline songs and with the help of my manager Kieran Cavanagh and my own many years of experience, opportunities started to present themselves. My recording of 'Crazy' gave me my first gold record, it introduced me to Johnny Cash and June Carter, and it introduced me to the music of Patsy Cline, which I've presented on many stages over the years. 'Crazy' was the reason I met and recorded with Willie Nelson and it was the reason RTÉ offered me my own prime-time TV show, allowing me to reach into the homes of hundreds of thousands of Irish viewers every Sunday night!

Kieran, Shay and I had quite a few meetings to brainstorm and put a concept together for a TV series. Then we brought in producer Ian McGarry. We had first met in 1982 when The Duskeys won the National Song Contest, which Ian directed and produced and, with others from RTÉ, he had travelled with us to Eurovision. So we knew we could work well together. Ian, Shay and Kieran took our ideas to the head of RTÉ light entertainment, David Blake-Knox, whom I'd not yet met.

I got a call from Kieran to say that everything was looking good, but that before David made a final decision on it, he wanted to meet me. We met for lunch and got along really well. At the end of lunch, David shook my hand and said, 'Congratulations. You have your own prime-time RTÉ series.' I was absolutely thrilled. That's the wonderful thing about what we do: if you are persistent, work hard and make personal sacrifices, you have a shot at achieving your dreams.

So 'Crazy' became the biggest-selling Irish record in 1989, 'Woodcarver' with Johnny Cash was released in 1990 and got me my second gold record, and now also in 1990, I began working on my own television series. I was also putting a musical together on the life and music of Patsy Cline. RTÉ afforded me all of the best people, musicians and facilities that they had. This would be a top-class show with music and chat. It was back-breaking work, a huge undertaking from everyone involved – and there were a lot of people involved. So many, in fact, that I didn't even meet some of them. There were set designers, carpenters, electricians, painters, costume designers, wardrobe department, stylist hairdressers, make-up artists, lighting designers, lighting department, camera operators, still photographers, sound engineers and technicians, researchers, a full team of people in the production office, a floor manager, a full team of people in the director's box, a 26-piece studio band, including backing vocalists, the entire RTÉ

Concert Orchestra with Gareth Hudson, six dancers and a choreographer, scriptwriter, links writer, and on and on! The publicist and I had a personal assistant, Janet Gallagher, who was just fantastic in every way.

Immediately, there was an endless list of meetings with people representing all aspects of the show. There was musical content to be chosen and gone through with the musical director, Frank McNamara, and medleys to be chosen for the orchestra, conducted by Gareth Hudson. Brendan Balfe of RTÉ Radio wrote links for me. I was blessed to be in the company of such talented and professional people. To get a series like this to where it needed to be, everyone had to be on top of their game, and that they were. Harold Bradley had taught me a lot about discipline. I'd learned what you needed to bring, like being on time, courteous to those you work with and getting the best from your support team.

There were a lot of people helping me put this show together, but I was the one presenting it and, if it wasn't good or popular with the viewers, that was on me. I didn't think about that, though. I knew the team were the best and trusted them to do their part. I focused on mine and, like a beautiful jigsaw, it all came together. Every episode would have an opening number with the dancers, I'd have quite a few solo songs, plus duets and interviews with Irish and visiting guest artists. The music was really right across the board. Some people in the industry at the time said I should keep to one genre of music, but I've never done that. Growing up on my grandfather's show, you learned to be versatile and to be an entertainer, so that's what I was doing.

The orchestra segments were recorded behind closed doors, while the duets, guests and interviews were in front of a live audience in the studio, with the exception of Johnny Cash and June Carter and their family, which was recorded in Markree Castle in Sligo. Joe Dolan wanted his appearance to be with the orchestra and so too did Daniel O'Donnell. That all worked out great because it was different and it was lovely to record some duets with the orchestra. After rehearsals with the studio band, we would record four shows in front of a live audience every week. On the weekend, I would record four separate medleys with the orchestra, each to be inserted into a show.

We decided early on to include a Patsy Cline song and a piece of her story in every show. I went to Nashville where we recorded all the music for Patsy's songs, with Harold producing and with all but one of Patsy's original session musicians and, of course, the fantastic Jordanaires. The tracks were sent to RTÉ and were used for my show. There was a completely different set designed for this, with a more Western feel. The vocals for the thirteen Patsy songs and intros were all filmed with a live audience in RTÉ in one day. They flew The Jordanaires in from Nashville to be part of the Patsy segments, with my own band in the background, including my sister, Barbara. I sang live and so did The Jordanaires. Their harmonies were incredible, as you'll already know from Elvis and Patsy Cline records. All recorded, these would then be inserted into the respective shows. There was a hell of a lot of work and money involved in getting the programme made to a very high standard.

Another day each week had to be set out for dance routines. This I found the hardest because there was so little time and so much to learn and remember. But Stephanie, the dance choreographer, was brilliant, as were the dancers, and we had a lot of fun. After the daytime rehearsals were done, I'd go straight to my hotel room with four show scripts for that week and I'd sit up late into the night learning song lyrics, links and questions for interviews.

There would also be a full day's rehearsal for each show. Early starts and long days. On show days, I'd be picked up from my hotel around 7.30am and it would be straight to wardrobe, hair and make-up to get that all sorted for my pre-records. Then into studio with my script for the day, which back then resembled the Bible. These days, you'd have an autocue on the cameras, but back when I was presenting, that wasn't available. I had to memorise all my links and, with a music show, unlike other programmes, I couldn't use cue cards, so it all had to be in my head.

Although the shows took every ounce of everything I had in me, I'm still very proud of them. Thankfully, the viewership was huge, even reaching number two in the viewership polls, only behind *The Late Late Show*. Sunday evenings on RTÉ were *Glenroe*, followed by the *Nine O'Clock News* and the *Sandy* show.

Before we'd start recording, I'd come in and meet the audience and sing one or two songs. Things would sometimes go wrong during takes, which was always a great laugh and the audience enjoyed that. I remember The Dubliners were all ready to go and I was standing beside them to do the introduction. I had the whole lot delivered perfectly until I got to, 'Please give a big welcome to …' and I went completely blank. I couldn't remember who I was standing beside. Ronnie Drew just glared at me with those huge electric-blue eyes, and then the whole place erupted in laughter. I wish RTÉ had put all the outtakes together in one extra show – it would have made a hilarious programme.

The budget for the series was very high and so we were able to have amazing guests. I had the opportunity to sing with some of the world's finest stars, which included many of my own favourites. My first time to meet George Hamilton IV and his son, George Hamilton V, was on *Sandy*.

We had mutual friends in Nashville and I discovered that George IV had worked a lot with Patsy Cline and had some great stories.

● Demis Roussos was another guest. Now there was a singer! Born in Egypt but living in Greece, he had long black hair, a black beard and wore a kaftan. He looked every inch the star. His voice was stunningly beautiful and very unique. You might remember two of his hits, 'Forever and Ever' and 'Goodbye My Love, Goodbye'. My duet with him was 'Sometimes When We Touch'. With Leo Sayer, such an electric personality, I sang 'When I Need Love'; with Roly Daniels, the duet was 'Like Strangers' and with Daniel O'Donnell, 'I Want to Dance With You'. One of my favourites was a duet with Rebecca Storm, 'I Know Him So Well', and, of course, 'Woodcarver' with Johnny Cash. I loved duetting with Tony Christie, Red Hurley, Big Tom, Alvin Stardust, Foster and Allen, Ralph McTell and Ronnie Drew. Another highlight was singing 'Sonny's Dream' with Emmylou Harris, and singing with Dolores Keane, and Paddy Moloney. The list goes on: Charley Pride, Shakin' Stevens, Helen Shapiro, Smokie, The Drifters, The Ink Spots, Brendan Bowyer, Joe Dolan, Jim McCann, Philomena Begley, Johnny Logan, Linda Martin, Tony Kenny, Danny La Rue, Randy VanWarmer, Louise Morrissey and Gloria.

We covered the songs of Doris Day, Neil Sedaka, Burt Bacharach, The Beatles, Elvis, Glen Campbell and some contemporary stuff of the time, including U2 and James Taylor. It was so much easier to learn them because I really wanted to sing them, and to sing them with the RTÉ Concert Orchestra, no less. I would sometimes say to Gareth Hudson, the conductor, that the music sounded so beautiful without me, it seemed a shame to sing over it. There is something magical about an orchestra when they start playing; it just lifts your spirits and lights up the whole room.

We included one love song in the show each week, with the orchestra, which we recorded in Windmill Lane studios, if I remember correctly: Foreigner's 'I Want to Know What Love Is', Elton John's 'Candle in the Wind', Juice Newton's 'Angel of the Morning', Olivia Newton John's 'I Honestly Love You', Bryan Adams' 'Everything I Do', and that's just a few.

The dance routine that stands out in my mind is the opening to the show when we did Dolly Parton's '9 to 5', which began with the six female dancers all sitting at typewriters in black office suits. Another time we did a fantastic up-tempo gospel routine with all twelve of the dancers. One of my favourites was a full segment from *Calamity Jane*.

A second *Sandy* series was offered to me later in 1992. This time I knew exactly what to do and everything felt a lot more comfortable after the experience of recording the first series. After the disappointment and problems in Branson (more about that in the next chapter), it was great to have something to focus on straight away. Kieran, Shay and I were working together again, just as before. We went with exactly the same format, the thinking being 'if it's not broke, don't fix it', though instead of celebrating Patsy Cline's life and music, we did Hank Williams'. The whole team and musicians on the series were the same as before, except for the musical director, Andy O'Callaghan having taken over from Frank McNamara.

We always did an Irish showband segment, which was hugely popular with the viewers at home. It allowed them to hear and see once more the artists and musicians who had entertained them the length and breadth of Ireland for years. There was something for everyone on that show. Hundreds and hundreds of fan letters arrived for me every week. Some of them I never saw; my personal assistant, Janet Gallagher, vetted them and took out the weird or offensive ones. There were viewers who had an opinion on everything, including my clothes. Some male viewers wrote suggesting I wear skirts a little shorter and admiring my black tights. Some women wrote to say that they loved a suit or dress I'd worn, telling me about a special occasion they had coming up and how they'd love to have that particular outfit. I always answered to tell them the truth: I didn't own any of the costumes. RTÉ had either bought them or had them designed and made specially for me. I answered hundreds of letters every week. I ordered up little notecards with my name on the front and sat down on a Monday night, my only night at home, and hand-wrote a note to the people I felt I really needed to respond to. Occasionally, the odd person would turn up at my house in Sligo, but not in their thousands, looking for cups of tea, like Daniel's fans.

I've kept a small box of unanswered letters all these years, and only found them during the pandemic. I read through them, feeling bad that I'd never got around to answering them. Remember, I'd received these letters in 1992 and this was now thirty years on. One in particular drew my attention. It was from a Michael Hackett and referred to my grandfather's show. This was most likely why I'd kept it. It was a wonderfully warm letter that described Michael's visit to Dusky Dan's Roadshow. There was a landline phone number at the top, so I'm thinking, if this gentleman can remember being at my grandfather's show and sent me this letter thirty years ago, he has to be a good age or maybe not even be here any more. To hell with it! I picked up the phone and dialled the number, feeling quite nervous. A man answered the phone and I introduced myself and said, 'I'm looking to speak to Mike Hackett, please.' He immediately answered, 'Well, it took you long enough to call me.' The two of us started laughing and we have since stayed in touch.

When I finished each recording, I would go out to the RTÉ reception area ahead of the audience and thank each of them as they left. Then I'd swing by the green room to thank the artists and chat for a moment before a car brought me back to my hotel to read my next script. I wish I could be as disciplined now as I was back then, but I was a lot younger, with an abundance of energy and ambition.

A sadness came over me just after the last show was recorded. Most of the people involved in that show, and indeed the whole series, were gathered in the green room. I'd thanked the audience as they left but before I joined everyone in the green room, I decided to revisit the set on my own. It's always a strange feeling when, as an artist, you sit alone on a theatre stage, in a recording room or, in this case, a television studio, after you've performed or recorded and everyone else is gone.

My show was in the same studio *The Late Late Show* was recorded in, which was presented by Gay Byrne at that time. When we finished on a Thursday night, the studio would be transformed into *The Late Late* studio, and then on a Monday transformed back to a *Sandy* set. In one way, I felt a huge sense of relief that we'd finished another series and that it had been a good one, even better than the first. There was no reason to think that RTÉ wouldn't offer me another series. Though in my heart I knew that nothing had really changed for me: I was financially struggling and physically drained, and could see myself being forced into having to consider other offers outside Ireland.

# 16

# BRANSON – CASH COUNTRY

I had never heard of Branson, Missouri. Taking the very big decision to go there in 1992 and work for ten months wasn't easy for me, but at the time I felt I really didn't have a choice. I had just finished a show in Cork when I got a call from a manager in New York, Jerry Purcell. Let me tell you a bit about him and how we met before I tell you about Branson.

While recording at Bradley's Barn in Nashville in 1991 with producer Harold Bradley, an elderly gentleman called Eddy would drop by the studio every night for a chat and to listen to me put down my vocals. He had some great stories about his own tours and some of the stars he knew and worked with. It transpired that this charming, unassuming visitor was Eddy Arnold, the biggest-selling artist next to Frank Sinatra! Here was the artist who had recorded 'Make The World Go Away' and 'Cattle Call'. It's said he was country music's biggest-selling artist before Garth Brooks came along. We became really good friends. Sadly, this kind and sweet man passed away in 2008.

One night as he was leaving the studio, he sang to me on the front porch, making me feel like I was in a Western movie with John Wayne! Jerry Purcell was Eddy Arnold's manager and Eddy had given him one of my albums. I was unaware of this until my manager in Ireland, Kieran Cavanagh, got a phone call from Jerry in New York to say that he'd like to fly over to Dublin to attend a recording of a couple of my TV shows with a view to bringing me to work in America. This was all happening very quickly and, before I had time to think, Jerry was in Dublin. He duly came out to RTÉ and was very impressed with the set, the band and the guests.

On meeting Mr Purcell for the first time, my gut feeling about him wasn't good. He looked and talked like something out of *The Godfather*. He put himself across as being very complimentary, kind and caring, but my instincts were picking up something totally different. The day after the show, he and Kieran met to chat and then Jerry asked to speak with me alone, which struck me as strange. He told me about all the successful stars he'd worked with over his many years in the business, people like Perry Como, Maya Angelou, Makem & Clancy, Jay Leno, Doris Day and, of course, Eddie Arnold. Jerry had found the song 'I Honestly Love You' for Olivia Newton John. The list went on and on. I was able to confirm all this by talking to Eddy Arnold and Harold Bradley. It was all true and pretty impressive.

He went on to list all the things he could do for my career in America. Then, producing a management contract, he asked me to sign it there and then. I had immediate flashbacks to all the conversations I'd had with my granddad, Dusky Dan, about show business and being careful of who you associated with. With my instincts twanging, there was absolutely no way I was going to sign the contract. I explained that I was already under contract to Kieran Cavanagh and that I was completely booked up at home and in the UK, as well as recording my TV shows and recording in Nashville. So Jerry Purcell left empty-handed.

Undeterred, a few months later Jerry called Kieran to offer me the opportunity to open for Willie Nelson at the Rocky Gap festival in Maryland, USA, in front of 25,000 fans, a festival which Jerry himself had a major part in organising. All expenses paid, he flew me and my band from Ireland, and he brought in The Jordanaires and Harold Bradley from Nashville. It was an amazing experience for me and the band. To my total surprise, when I began to sing 'Crazy', the crowd began cheering and clapping, which I thought was in response to me. But then I heard Willie Nelson's voice joining me on the song. I turned around and there he was, walking towards me with a microphone and singing with me. I was both shocked and delighted; it was the first time I had ever sung with Willie live. It was like something out of a movie! After the concert, Willie invited me onto his tour bus for a coffee and a chat, just like we'd done at Bradley's Barn before. But it was becoming clearer and clearer that Jerry was trying to persuade me to come and work in the States, and the way he was going about it didn't sit well with Kieran.

Although I was really committed to my work at home and to my family, it wasn't all roses in the garden with my career at home at the time. I remember saying to Mike, 'I don't think I can afford to be this famous.' In spite of hit records with 'Crazy', then 'Woodcarver' with Johnny Cash, a top-rating RTÉ television series and working shows, I was struggling to keep up with family bills and my manager's commissions. Everything I did seemed to be costing me a lot of money. I financed my own tours and advertising. When we brought The Jordanaires and Harold Bradley over to join me and my band for an Irish concert tour, even though it looked to have gone well, I ended up losing money. I was working my ass off but sinking financially.

I had just finished a show in Cork when I received a phone call to my hotel room from Jerry Purcell. It was 6 January 1992, Oíche Nollaig na mBan, Women's Little Christmas. We'd had a wonderful night, as we always did in Cork, but everything that was going on weighed heavily on me. I don't know how Jerry tracked me down. He said the phone call had to be in the strictest of confidence and to not even tell Kieran Cavanagh or it would jeopardise the whole thing. He went on to say that he had been contacted by Lou Robin, Johnny Cash's manager, whom I'd met several times. Lou said that Johnny wanted me to come to Branson, Missouri, to be in their new show at Cash Country Theater, but that no one was to know anything about it yet. Feeling as low as I did that night, this was both exciting and terrifying. At that time, I was one of the best-known entertainers in Ireland, yet I was struggling to survive. Such a decision to have to make. The situation at home was putting a strain on my relationship with my manager, Kieran, and now Jerry was telling me that I'd have to decide within forty-eight hours and move to Branson by the end of January. I would have to let my band go, which included my husband and my sister, and turn down my next RTÉ series and cancel all my work for the next year. In return, I was offered a ten-month contract by the theatre in Branson with a great guaranteed fee, plus all travel and expenses and a two-bedroom condominium at a golf resort. I would initially have to leave my family behind, but they could join me once I'd settled in. I said I would have to talk to my family and think about it. The last thing Jerry said was to remember not to discuss this with anyone, especially the Cash family or Lou Robin, because Kieran Cavanagh toured Johnny Cash in Ireland and the UK and Lou Robin didn't want to have any bad feeling. Why I bought into that I'll never understand. Ringing Lou Robin should have been the first thing I did. But I didn't and how I lived to regret that decision.

Mike, my sister and I had a long discussion about it and finally, with a lot of uneasiness, it was decided that really I didn't have a choice but to go and pursue a career in America, as well as at home. To put it simply, I needed the money. This should have been a really happy and exciting time – anyone would jump at the chance to perform with Johnny Cash and June Carter – but I was weighed down with so many problems. To top it all, my dad was waiting to be called in for heart bypass surgery.

I met with Kieran Cavanagh in his office in Dublin. Our professional relationship had become strained as I was finding it difficult to keep up with the commission fees. I told him about Jerry Purcell's phone call and the offer of a ten-month contract at Cash Country Theater. I felt that, if I was upfront about it with him, he would understand that I had to go. We had, at one point, been very good friends. Understandably, he was not happy at all. Jerry Purcell ought to have called Kieran about this and included him, but he hadn't. I promised Kieran that, if all worked out for me in Branson, I would pay him commission and that for any work I did in Ireland and the UK, I would work only with him. He and Jerry Purcell were not on talking terms at this point. The atmosphere between Kieran and me was not that good when I left, although I genuinely believed that everything would turn out okay in time.

When I returned to Sligo, I started preparing to leave for Branson. Every-one was upset but understood. I met with my good friend and owner of

Crashed Records, Shay Hennessy, to tell him about my plans. He was sorry to see me go, but he understood. Then it was time to sit down with my band and tell them. It came as a shock because it was all happening so fast. My sister, Barbara, who was also part of the band, would keep them on and launch a solo career, although that wouldn't be easy either. My last show before leaving was very emotional. There was a fantastic crowd of people who'd come to wish me well, including Shay, but sadly not Kieran. My RTÉ series was running at the time and attracting big viewership numbers, but I had to tell RTÉ that I couldn't do the next series because I'd be in Branson.

Jerry told me that Lou Robin and Johnny Cash wanted to work through him because there were so many other singers over there who would feel they should have been asked and, foolishly, I believed him. A management contract arrived by courier with instructions to sign and return it as soon as possible in order for him to get my US work visa. I wasn't very happy with some of the clauses. For instance, he wanted to sign me up for all territories, even the universe! It's not as though I'd be touring Mars. I brought the contract to my solicitor in Sligo, but in hindsight I should have gone to a music lawyer who was a specialist in management contracts and US law. In fairness, my solicitor did the best he could. We included an addendum to say that the contract excluded Ireland and England, Scotland and Wales, as I had promised Kieran. So, with this clause included, I signed the contract and sent it back.

In a few short weeks, it was time to leave. One of my closest friends, Geraldine Brown, came with me for the first month to keep me company. She had been a great friend over the years and we had travelled together quite a lot. Geraldine is kind and great company and someone I could trust. Mike, Willie and my daughter, Barbara, came to Shannon to see us off. It was difficult and heartbreaking saying goodbye. Willie, then aged twelve, understood what was happening, but Barbara, who was ten, really didn't and so it was very difficult for her. I consoled myself with the hope that our lives would get better.

We landed in New York's JFK Airport, where Jerry Purcell met us with his secretary and some paperwork I needed on arrival. Jerry had planned to travel from New York to Branson with us but couldn't at the last minute. Continuing our journey, we were met in St Louis Airport by a guy who worked at Cash Country Theater, to take us on the two-hour drive to Branson. Well, I was about to discover exactly what Branson was all about. He said, in a great American accent, 'Welcome to Branson, ladies. This is Highway 76 where you'll be working, Sandy.' It looked like a smaller version of Las Vegas, without the gambling. Theatre after theatre, each one bigger than the last. Huge lit-up signs on them all, with names like Andy Williams, Loretta Lynn, The Osmonds, Willie Nelson, Merle Haggard, Mel Tillis and more. Anyone who was anyone in music had a theatre there. It was magical and exciting, and Geraldine and I looked at each other with disbelief. Then our driver said, 'Here it is: Cash Country, where you'll be performing!' Although still under construction, it looked iconic. We didn't stop, as it was evening and we were quite tired.

Our next stop was where I would be living for the next ten months. We pulled up at big security gates on the edge of town, where we were met by a security guard. Over the gates was the name Point Royale Golf Resort. This was a first for me, a golf resort, the last place I'd expect to be. It was fabulous: the houses were all different styles, very quaint, with small but beautiful gardens. Then there were condominiums, all nestled together near the clubhouse. This is where I would be living, in my own condo. I'd never even heard that word before. I was so excited to see inside and it didn't disappoint:

a stunning open-plan kitchen, dining and living-room area, which opened onto a gorgeous wooden deck overlooking the river and trees. On a coffee table in the living room was an arrangement of twenty-four red roses, which read – 'Sandy, welcome to Branson and Cash Country' – and signed 'The Cash Family'. 'Wow,' I thought. There was also a small laundry area, two bedrooms and bathrooms. The master bedroom had a large glass sliding door out onto the deck. It was like something in a magazine. I was thrilled with it, as was Geraldine. I was already imagining Mike and the kids moving over once the theatre opened and I was settled in. There was a phone, of course, and I didn't waste any time in ringing home to let Mike, Willie and Barbara know that we had arrived safely and that it was a really beautiful place.

A lovely gentleman from Cash Country welcomed us and showed us around Point Royale. There was an elaborate clubhouse with a restaurant and an outdoor pool, but, it being February, and colder than I'd ever experienced, they were closed. Our guide told us that a lot of musicians were living here, including Merle Haggard's band and Willie Nelson's, hence all the security, I suppose.

We headed back down to Highway 76, where all the shows were, to meet the producers of the show, plus Tommy Cash, Johnny's youngest sibling, whom I knew least of all the Cash family. We met for dinner – Geraldine and I were absolutely starving. I was quite nervous to meet everyone, but realising that I was in the company of some of the most respected and influential people in the business, I kept my composure. Over dinner we chatted about various things, the music industry in Ireland, etc., before getting down to chatting about Branson and Cash Country and my role in the whole project. It seemed that, although the population of Branson wasn't that large, thousands of fans flocked there every week to attend the shows and see their favourite stars. The first theatre opened in 1934 and since then the town had just grown and grown. It was reassuring how nice everyone was and how genuinely they welcomed me.

I was thankful to have Geraldine with me. The Cash and Carter families hadn't moved there yet and I didn't know anyone. The next day, we were collected and brought to an office at Johnny's new theatre. The building was enormous, much larger than most of the other theatres and very impressive, just what I'd expect for Johnny and June. Although the building was secure, with the foyer and some front rooms completed, except for decoration, the main auditorium was still very much under construction; they were still pouring the concrete for the floors. The stage was absolutely huge and almost regal in appearance. I was thinking the audience would hardly see me up there. At the front of the theatre, in the palatial foyer, was a large, ornate water fountain, surrounded by horses carved in stone or marble.

We finished our tour of the theatre in one of the front upper rooms to have our formal meeting. This was also where we would rehearse for the next six weeks. Tommy Cash was there, of course, and a bass player called Jimmy Tittle, who was married to Katie Cash, Johnny's daughter. Tommy and I would co-host the daytime show and then guest with Johnny and June on the evening show. This would be six days and nights a week for ten months. Auditions would be set up in the next week. It was clear that I was going to be extremely busy, but I was used to that.

The auditions were quite the experience. Held over a three-day period in a venue downtown, the amount of talent that turned up was incredible. All ages showed up, and the youngsters were some of the best singers and musicians I'd ever heard. I was invited to be a part of the auditioning panel, but I declined, deciding instead to just sit in and listen. I felt that Tommy,

Jimmy and Jerry Purcell would know the American and Branson audience better. Besides, I wouldn't have had the heart to turn some of them down.

With the musicians chosen, the band were ready to start rehearsing. Lead guitar, bass guitar, drums, piano, pedal steel guitar, Dobro, fiddle and three backing vocalists, plus Tommy and me. This was one of the happiest times of my life. I was keen to share all the news with my family back home, but back then there were no mobile phones, no email, no FaceTime, just one or two calls a week on the landline. I felt really guilty about all the time I was spending away from home. Calling home, although exciting, was also really hard for us, especially Willie and Barbara. At the time, though, I really didn't have a choice. It has never been about bright lights and stardom for me, but always about getting the work, as it was for my family before me.

Rehearsals started and it was lovely meeting the members of the band and playing around with the songs. I'd just come from recording TV shows and working with a twenty-piece studio band and the RTÉ Concert Orchestra. This wasn't a question of better, but simply different. The style of playing and singing was different and, in turn, my style was different from theirs. After a few days, we had a terrific programme of songs. I can't describe how good this was beginning to sound. The harmonies were incredible and the songs fantastic. Jerry Purcell, of course, was in the middle of everything and had opinions that, really, he should have kept to himself at times. He was a loud, rude and domineering person, who had taken on the job of controlling every single thing I did: what I sang, how I sang it, what I wore, where I went, who I spoke to. I didn't know what a narcissist was back then, but I have since realised that Jerry Purcell was the epitome of one. I could hardly wait for him to go back to New York.

During this period my dad had his bypass surgery and was recovering. I hated not to be able to see him or talk to him, but I kept telling myself it was for the greater good. Geraldine and I were settling in well in the condo. There was a small bank just outside the main gate, so I said to Geraldine that we'd walk up and I could open a bank account, which I'd need for bills and so on. It was only a ten-minute walk. It had been a running joke since I arrived that I always wore high heels (I think until recently I'd had a complex about being short, but I've finally gotten over that), so with me decked out in my red heels and coat, we headed out to walk to the bank. We didn't see anyone else out walking, only the occasional car, which, oddly enough, slowed down to look at us as they drove by. This was Missouri in mid-February and after five minutes, we couldn't feel our hands or feet. By the time we reached the bank, we found it hard to even talk and we couldn't move our hands to open the door. Thankfully, one of the staff saw us and helped us in. The staff member brought us coffee to warm us up and we sat and waited until we thawed out. We were so embarrassed. It hadn't occurred to us why no one would even think about walking anywhere in Branson, Missouri at that time of year without proper clothing and certainly not wearing high heels.

Then we discovered Walmart, which we'd never heard of before. What a treasure trove! You could buy anything there, though of course we were on a tight budget. Geraldine and I had great craic looking at everything in the store and buying ridiculous things for the condo. It was going to be like the *Little House on the Prairie* when we finished. To top it all, at the checkout, the cashier looked at the basket and said, 'You're not from around here, are you?' I asked her if she knew where I could get a potted possum for my window. She went into fits of laughing and said a possum was an animal. I'd only ever heard Dame Edna on television addressing people as 'My little possum', so I'd assumed it was a flower. Branson was a beautiful place and a totally different way of living, straight out of all the movies I'd seen on TV: very rustic, very sweet, with wreaths and decorations everywhere. I also loved dropping by the post office to send home cards and little presents to the children, which helped me in some way.

I had foolishly agreed that my wages would be paid directly to Jerry Purcell. What the hell was I thinking? I should have known better by this stage. I was on really good money and made sure that Jerry's secretary in New York sent a good-sized cheque home every week to Mike and the children. I managed on a much smaller amount. Jerry kept his commission and was supposed to put the remainder into a savings account for me. I discovered later that never happened.

The rehearsals continued all day every day and our excitement was building. With the sound of builders and machinery in one end of the building and us blasting out the tunes the other end, everyone was under pressure. Then, as expected, a show producer arrived from Las Vegas to help put the show together to the highest standard. I'd been to see a few of the shows in Branson and they were indeed of a very high standard, sort of Las-Vegas-does-country type of thing. The producer was every inch glamour, with a Liberace hairstyle, very flamboyant, a consummate professional at his job and he really put us through our paces, over and over. I could hardly wait for opening night. We still hadn't officially heard when that would be, but I felt sure it couldn't be any longer than a few weeks, as the tickets were apparently selling fast.

There seemed to be a lot less building going on and there were only a handful of workers. News came that the Carter family were arriving: June's sisters, Helen and Anita, with Peggy Knight, a long-serving member of staff. Then soon after that, Johnny, June and John Carter Cash arrived. Helen and Anita were renting a beautiful house near me at Point Royale.

Much to my delight, they would always put my name in the pot when they were cooking. It felt like they'd adopted me and I loved that they chatted freely around the dinner table about most things. Everyone was excited to be starting the season in Branson.

A tour of the theatre was set up for Johnny and June, and I was invited to join them. Johnny arrived at the grand entrance of the theatre in his usual long black coat, shirt and trousers, June in her typical colourful, flowy bohemian style. We made our way around the theatre, chatting and laughing. You could honestly rarely be in their company without laughing a lot. June's funny jokes and John's stories made for a pleasant and very memorable afternoon. While visiting the dressing rooms backstage, I was shown mine. Still awaiting the finishing touches, it had yet to be plastered. Johnny suggested that I carve my name on a wall before it was plastered and that way, there would be a part of me there for ever. I did, as soon as I got the chance, so I'm still there in some small way.

The next evening, Johnny and June were to be interviewed by Larry King on *Larry King Live* to promote the opening of the theatre. There was a reception and we all gathered in the foyer and mingled while having finger food and soft drinks. Drinking alcohol was really frowned upon in Branson, especially for women. We were seated in a row, and then guests from some of the other theatres arrived, all taking turns to shake hands with each of us. The first person to shake my hand was Andy Williams. I was weak at the knees! I remember watching *The Andy Williams Show* on Granny Bee's black-and-white television in Ballintogher as a young girl and here he was shaking my hand!

The show was coming together well and we were kept extremely busy. With the musical end of things sorted, it was now time to promote, and

With Maureen O'Hara in Foynes in 1998, at a fund-raising concert for the Flying Boat Museum. (L–r): Me, Maureen O'Hara, my niece Sandie and my sister Barbara.

The main publicity shot for *Patsy – The Musical* in London's West End in 1994.

A press photo for *Patsy – The Musical* in the UK with George Hamilton IV.

*Below:* On stage in London's West End during *Patsy – The Musical* in 1994.

On stage with George Hamilton IV and cast while touring *Patsy Cline – The Musical* in 1993.

Singing on the Grand Ole Opry with George Hamilton IV (right) and his son George Hamilton V in 2007.

A celebration night was held for me in Sligo's Hawk's Well Theatre in 2015. *Above left:* (l–r): Mike, our son Willie, me and our daughter Barbara, backstage. Barbara is wearing some of her many Special Olympics medals. *Above right:* Willie, my grandson Frank Juhan and Kristiina Muru. *Below left:* Performing with my son Willie. *Below right:* Mike Kelly and Willie on stage. *Facing page:* Backstage with my niece Sandie Ellis, and (below) my last performance with my sister Barbara. *Photos © Colin Gillen*

*Above*: Laying down the vocals for my album *Leaving It All Behind* at Cash Cabin in 2019.

*Left*: On the steps of Cash Cabin with my son Willie in 2019.

*Below*: With some of the musicians at Cash Cabin in 2019: (l–r) Chris Leuzinger, Jamie Hartford and Matt Combs.

With John Carter Cash at the Cash Cabin studio in 2019, during a break in recording my album *Leaving It All Behind*.

With my grandson Frank Juhan and my daughter Barbara at Markree Castle in 2022. *(c)* RSVP *Magazine*

With my grandson Frank Juhan, filming the video for 'How Long Will I Love You' in May 2023.

promote we did. Tommy Cash, Jimmy Tittle and I, with members of the band, visited every hotel, restaurant and shop in Branson. For my part I would introduce myself, tell them about Cash Country and ask if I could leave some flyers for their customers. It was so funny for me because at that time back in Ireland, if I walked into any similar establishment to promote anything, I'd have been instantly recognised. But nobody knew me here and it was quite the awakening to be so anonymous. If I wanted to be recognised here I was going to have to work hard. I did have one great advantage though: my Irish accent. All over the world, people love the Irish. I believe I could have talked my way through that ten-month contract without singing a note. By1992, not many Irish artists had performed in Branson, maybe only Frank Patterson.

My favourite promotion was travelling out of the state to big bus conventions. Branson relied heavily on bus tours coming to town and everyone pulled out all the stops to try to make sure as many bus companies as possible would visit their theatre and show. As many of the major stars as possible attended these conventions and performed in one big concert. Tommy Cash and I represented Cash Country, as Johnny and June were away on tour. Tommy certainly had the Cash sense of humour and those journeys with him were a lot of fun. On another occasion, when I travelled with Mel Tillis and his band, I got to share a stage with Loretta Lynn, Andy Williams, Merle Haggard and Mel himself, among others. Loretta was always lovely to me, telling me great stories about Patsy Cline. This really seemed to be the perfect step forward for my career. At last, I began to believe my family would live a life without worry.

Back in Branson at the rehearsal room, our show was now ready and we couldn't wait for opening night. With Jerry Purcell back in New York, I was able to get to know the musicians properly. In fact, Brad the drummer and the Dobro/steel player, who were only in their early twenties, couldn't find accommodation and with Geraldine gone back to Ireland, I let them have the spare room at my condo for a few weeks. Looking back, I probably shouldn't have been seen to be doing that. But I found the young people in our show to be wonderful, polite and good living, very strong in their religious beliefs and prayer, all good Christians. At home, religion is a more personal thing and only discussed at certain times. I found this open and easy conversation about God a little strange at first.

On the other hand, I found the local people, especially the women, a little old-fashioned when it came to a woman living on her own. It dawned on me that if I wasn't very careful, I would become unpopular with the women and, as we all know, the women of the house usually have a big say in who joins the inner circle. In Ireland, from a very young age I was so used to hanging out with guys that I was comfortable in their company. Most of my friends were guys. Some of the women in Branson didn't appreciate my friendliness and outgoing ways. If I was seen getting a lift or drinking a cup of coffee with any of my male fellow musicians, it would immediately be construed that I was having an affair. This gossip filtered out here and there and, for a while, I didn't know. The main topic was Tommy and myself: we travelled together and attended other shows and receptions at the invitations of theatre owners. This was all by way of networking and promoting Cash Country and I saw it as normal and part of my job. But this rumour got back to Nashville and I got a call from my record producer and dear friend Harold Bradley to say that his wife, Eleanor, had met Tommy's wife (at that time) and she'd been upset to hear that Tommy and I were seen out together a lot. I said, 'Harold, of course we're out together a lot. We're leading a show and promoting it.' I picked up in the conversation that Harold wasn't personally happy either. I learned at an early age that the one thing you don't do in our business is mess around, especially with the married guys you work with, or that working relationship will be cut very short. That's one of the reasons I had a long and great working relationship with Johnny Cash. He was the ultimate gentleman and we had a strong friendship.

This nonsense was now really annoying me, so I picked up the phone and rang Johnny. I told him about the accusations regarding his brother and me, and that I was very hurt that these untruths were circulating when I was only trying to do my job. Johnny was furious that I was being treated this way and chatted to me at length. He knew that I was not that sort of person, and said, 'Leave this with me and I will sort it out.' I knew from working with Johnny and June that he rarely got mad, but when he did, and I only ever saw it once, everyone jumped to attention. I knew this would be the end of the rumour machine. However, Tommy's wife forbade him to travel with me or be seen out in my company. So that was that. It made things very inconvenient for me, workwise.

Johnny and June moved into a large log house out by Table Rock Lake at a resort called Big Cedar. Set in the woods, it was a stunningly beautiful, traditional rustic log house. Some of the major stars stayed there, like Waylon Jennings and Jessi Colter. It was also a popular resort for families, and still is. I was out there quite a few times, once to go fishing with Peggy Knight and one of Johnny's drivers. As we walked along the edge of the lake, Peggy said excitedly, 'Look, bear prints!' 'Christ,' I said, 'we'd better go back.' She laughed and said, 'The bears won't bother us none.' Well, I didn't have a mobile phone or Google back then, but if I had, I would have learned that at Table Rock Lake there were many dangers, including and not limited to: armed felons, venomous snakes, wasps, sudden weather changes, getting lost and, oh yes, large bears. Mother of the divine Jesus, I wouldn't have gone within a thousand miles of the place if I'd known. At their insistence, they went on to fish while I sat nearby nervously on a rock with my handbag sitting beside me, opened. Peggy shouted over to me, 'You'd better zip that baggy. You don't want to bring home a new companion with you.' I said, 'What do you mean?' She answered, 'This place is crawlin' with tarantulas.' I'm terrified of even a house spider. She continued, 'But don't worry. If they bite, it won't kill you, it'll just sting for a while. It's those black widow spiders and brown recluse that'll really get ya.' Very comforting, I thought, as I zipped up my bag.

John and June invited me out to their log home one day for a chat and a coffee. They were leaving that day for Dublin, for the start of a tour with The Highwaymen, the supergroup of Johnny, Willie Nelson, Waylon Jennings and Kris Kristofferson. They invited me over before they left. Seeing John and June together, you were immediately transported to some heavenly place. They were beautiful, charismatic, humble, Hollywood-like and rock stars all rolled up in down-home country. You were in the company of Liz Taylor and Richard Burton, John and Jackie Kennedy, Elvis and Priscilla. I was always sad to see them leave, but this time was worse because they were travelling to Ireland. They knew I missed my family and told me to ring home and invite Mike, my sister and my children to the concert in the Point Depot. I was delighted because I knew what a treat this would be for them. We said our goodbyes and I left trying desperately to hold back my tears. True to their promise, my family were invited to attend the show. They were asked to enter the venue through the artist entrance, where they were met by June, who brought them to meet and chat to everyone.

Back in Branson, things were starting to look not so jolly. Work on the theatre had really slowed down and there were rumours that the theatre developers were bankrupt. At least that made a change from rumours about me. At home in Sligo, Willie was due to make his confirmation and I was allowed two weeks off to travel home to be there for him. I bought myself a two-piece turquoise skirt suit, with the front of the jacket decorated in pearls, more a Branson look than a Sligo look at the time. I was really overjoyed to be going home to Carrowgobbadagh and to be seeing every-one. Seeing my children and being able to hug them was the best feeling! Willie's confirmation was a fantastic celebration with all the family, even Granny Bee. My dad, though, was still recovering from surgery. I found it very difficult to contemplate leaving my family again to return to Branson, knowing exactly how hard it would be. After chatting with Mike, I decided to bring Willie back with me. I couldn't bring Barbara because I wouldn't have the time to look after her needs and there was always the risk that she might need treatment of some kind. She was safer at home with Olivia, our nanny, who'd been with us for a number of years. Mike was still on the road with my sister Barbara and the band.

A few days prior to our departure, I received a lengthy fax from Jerry Purcell. To my absolute shock, the fax contained the worst possible news. Cash Country had stopped all plans to complete the building or to open. The company had gone bust because one of the major investors had pulled out. I could not believe what I was reading. Jerry told me not to return to my condo or Branson because my contractual monies were now stopped. He would instruct the realtor (estate agent) to have my belongings packed and stored. I read the fax over and over, trying to process what was hap-pening. I then tried to call Jerry but got no answer. I called Harold Bradley, who had also just heard the news and was equally shocked. I knew that the whole Cash Carter family would be upset so I decided not to add to their woes by calling them. I rang Tommy Cash and Lou Robin, who both confirmed what I'd just heard.

They both agreed that I should come back to see what was happening. I called the realtor to say that I was absolutely returning in the next few days and keeping my condo. Willie and I travelled to Branson. Having him with me certainly lifted my spirits, his excitement distracting me from the uncertain situation I was going back to. He loved the condo. The first thing he wanted to do was go up to the clubhouse pool and hang out with the other kids his age. He immediately became friendly with some of Merle Haggard's musicians' kids and two of Johnny's youngest grandkids, so he was in good company. He came back from the pool that first day declaring, 'Those goddam bugs are everywhere.'

As much as I could, I kept my anxiety and disappointment to myself. When Jerry Purcell heard that I had returned to my condo in Branson against his instructions and I was paying my own rent and other expenses, he screamed at me down the phone, ordering me back home. I told him straight that I had cancelled my TV series and all my other work at home and in the UK and that for the moment I didn't have anything to go home to, and I was staying. He went on to lay all kinds of threats on me. It was becoming clear that his dealings with me were all about control and, to a much lesser degree, work. Of course, it was only after I had signed his contract that I began hearing the dreadful stories about him and how dangerous he was. But you know what? I'd been through so much in my life already that he didn't either frighten or intimidate me. I think that's what infuriated him the most. He thought I was some little stupid Irish girl singer who would do anything to make it. Well, he got that wrong. I was Dusky Dan's granddaughter and I viewed show business and performing differently from a lot of people. I let him know that I would leave when I was ready.

I decided to downsize to a smaller one-bedroom condo nearby because it would be cheaper. Peggy Knight helped me pack and move. Willie was now a player on the local Little League baseball team, and Tommy Cash also spent a lot of time with Willie, so he was happy. All rehearsals had stopped and the theatre was a lonely-looking sight, all boarded up and fenced off. The Cash Carter family checked in with me on their way back to Nashville. Helen, Anita and Peggy had the huge task of moving everything back to Nashville, furniture and personal belongings. They had all thought they'd be living in Branson for several years, only leaving to go on tour when another headlining star would take the theatre for a term. They all felt really bad about my situation, but honestly, it wasn't a great time for them either. I can't help but think that if Cash Country had opened as planned, Johnny and June wouldn't have toured so much and they could have rested and focused on their health. They must have been devastated.

Word got out fast and I was offered opportunities to perform in a few of Branson's finest theatres. But these offers were quickly withdrawn when they heard they had to deal with Jerry Purcell. He also informed them that he would not allow me to perform. I brought Willie to Nashville for a few days and met with Harold Bradley, Eddie Arnold and Tommy Cash. While Willie enjoyed all the delights of Nashville, I had to make the difficult decision to return to Ireland. It was my only choice. Jerry Purcell would make sure that I was not going to work in America again anytime soon. On my return to Branson, I began the difficult task of packing, booking flights and saying my goodbyes. I was absolutely gutted at the outcome of my journey to Branson and furious at the callous treatment from Jerry Purcell, with no respect or regard for me or my family.

So just a month after we had got there, Willie and I were ready to go. Willie was sad to leave all his new friends and he never saw his mum perform in Branson, but I brought him to see some great shows, including Glen Campbell's, which he loved. A few days before we left, Tommy invited me to a show he was doing in a supper club nearby. It was a matinee, which was perfect. Tommy picked me up and brought me to the theatre. As we made our way through the door of the auditorium, I heard a loud 'Surprise!' with music and there were balloons. There, all together in a group waiting to greet me, were all the members of our Cash Country band. I burst into tears. One by one, they all hugged me. We were saying goodbye to each other. Each musician and singer took turns to either play or sing something for me and say a few words about our time working together. Tommy led the songs and tributes. I was an absolute mess by the end of it and then to finish, I joined everyone on stage and we all sang 'Love Can Build a Bridge' from our show. As if that wasn't enough, they presented me with a beautiful gold bracelet, which I still wear today. Nobody had ever done anything so sweet for me before and I was heartbroken to have to hug them one last time. A parting gift from the three backing female vocalists was a pair of white runners, because of the ongoing joke about my many pairs of high heels. I stored most of my things in Kathy Cash and Jimmy Tittle's house. They might still be there, as I never got back to collect them. A few days later, Willie and I left for home, sure of our welcome in Carrowgobbadagh, but, for me, very unsure of the future.

# 17

# PATSY

Stepping back in time a little, to 1989, due to the huge success of my record 'Crazy', with the help of Shay Hennessy, we picked enough songs that were popular and researched Patsy's story to put together a show of her music and the story of her life. I was already friendly with Patsy's widower, Charlie Dick, and her record producer, Owen Bradley, before I ever recorded any of her songs. As friends, we were able to chat about Patsy's life. I'd met Charlie through Harold Bradley at Fan Fair in Nashville in 1985 and, of course, Owen Bradley was Harold's brother. Owen was a music producer, Patsy's producer actually, and one of the pioneers of 'The Nashville Sound'.

Charlie Dick was a warm, funny, charismatic and generous man. We all loved him. When I returned to Nashville to record the Patsy backing tracks for my television series, both Charlie and Owen were helpful in every way possible. I couldn't have done it so well without them. Charlie collected me every day from my hotel and drove me around Nashville, showing me all the places that he and Patsy had been, where she recorded and sang throughout the years, allowing me to record every story he told me. This was so I could tell them on my TV show while also including them in the live touring show I was working on.

I will always remember when he brought me to the house that he and Patsy bought in May 1962, the year prior to her death: a beautiful bungalow in Goodlettsville, near Nashville. Charlie parked the car outside the house as he told me how happy he, Patsy and their children, Julie and Randy, were living there. It was Patsy's dream home, which they'd bought from the royalties from 'Walking After Midnight', 'Crazy' and 'I Fall to Pieces'. After all the years of hard work, Patsy could finally afford the home she wanted for her family. Sadly, she would only spend ten months there before she was tragically killed in a plane crash at the age of just thirty.

Charlie always kept the sunny side out, always laughing and making jokes, but on that occasion, a huge sadness was plain to see in him. I'm sure in the short time we sat there, a flood of memories came back to him. It was fascinating and helpful to hear all these things about Patsy directly from Charlie. I was grateful that he chose to share his memories with me. Over the years, he could have been plagued by people hanging out of him because of Patsy. He didn't suffer fools gladly and, from what I have been told, neither did Patsy. I'm sure Charlie knew, from the first time we met, that I was genuine and didn't much like bullshit myself.

We hit it off straight away and he also had a big liking for Mike. It was easy to see why Patsy and Charlie were attracted to each other. Both had the same sense of mischief and fun. Both were kind and very generous.

I know they had their problems but what couple doesn't? Charlie talked about Patsy's friendships with Loretta Lynn, Brenda Lee and June Carter, but I believe from what he said that Patsy had a special bond with Dottie West. He told me that, not long before Patsy died, she gave her scrapbook to Dottie to mind for her. Patsy had a premonition about dying young. Dottie returned it to him in 1990 when she got into trouble with the IRS (the US Internal Revenue Service), afraid that Patsy's scrapbook would get misplaced when they were going through her stuff.

On several occasions, Charlie kindly invited us to his home. In his study, he kept all of Patsy's music, memorabilia, photos and trophies. It was really wonderful and emotional and a little surreal to see them and to be able to hold some of the incredible awards that she had won. I could just sit in that room, looking around and taking in all its musical magic. In the sitting room, Charlie had a jukebox with a lot of Patsy's songs on it. Once, when Mike and I were at Charlie's house, he also invited their daughter, Julie, her husband, Richard, and their four children over to meet us. This meant a lot to me because I knew it wouldn't have happened if he didn't really like and trust us.

We had a beautiful and very memorable afternoon, chatting and laughing. Julie's two eldest children, Michelle and Virginia, were just the most adorable little girls. I'd say they were maybe eight and five years old. The three of us sat on the floor beside the jukebox and sang Patsy songs; of course they knew them all and sang very well. We had so much fun. Virginia and I brought the coffee mugs and some glasses out to the kitchen. Virginia, who was named after Patsy, seized her moment and, gazing up into my eyes, she asked, 'Is it really true that all the people in Ireland love Grandma Patsy?' Oh, my heart broke and I answered, 'Yes, they love her voice and songs!' Well, she beamed from ear to ear and went off so happy. I will forever cherish that day.

Owen Bradley produced all the hit records that Patsy sang on, and thankfully I was able to spend time with him too. He owned Bradley's Barn Studios. Owen was a lovely quiet man and I enjoyed his company. He had a small piano at the back of his office. I'd go in there, we would chat about Patsy and we'd do some of her songs together. It was such an experience! Then of course, between recording songs, Patsy's musicians and The Jordanaires also shared stories with me of their time working with her and with Elvis, who they all agreed was a perfect gentleman.

Harold one day brought me down to the Hall of Fame Museum in Nashville. He'd got permission to bring me downstairs to the private area where they kept all the photos and printed records about everything and everybody in country music. This included material on Patsy and the horrific air crash that had taken her life. For the longest time after that day, I wished I hadn't seen or read the articles about the crash. It was horrible.

On 3 March 1963, Patsy, along with other members of the Opry, including Cowboy Copas, Hawkshaw Hawkins and Dottie West, performed a benefit concert in Kansas City for the family of a well-known DJ, Jack 'Cactus' Call, who had died in a car crash earlier that year. Patsy, Cowboy Copas and Hawkshaw were travelling in a small plane piloted by Patsy's manager, Randy Hughes. It was very stormy and Dottie West, who had driven to the fund-raising concert, begged Patsy to travel back to Nashville with her in the car. Patsy considered it but decided to return with the others on the flight. She was suffering with flu and so was her son, Randy, and she was anxious to get home. The storm kept them grounded for a couple more days and they actually didn't leave Kansas until 5 March. It is believed the pilot (Randy Hughes) became completely disoriented in worsening weather, inevitably leading to the fateful crash. The plane came down in Camden, Tennessee, just 85 miles from Nashville. It was dark, very secluded and it took some time to find the wreckage. The next day, the devastation and extent of the damage was evident for those who came on the scene.

That will always be remembered as one of the darkest days in country music. How painful and awful for the families of those aboard the plane! Every one of Patsy's friends that I spoke to in Nashville all had the same kind words about her, giving glowing reports about her talent and her heart of gold. Brenda Lee also told me how Patsy had helped her when she started out in show business at an early age.

In 1989, Shay Hennessy, Kieran Cavanagh and Ian McGarry had all travelled to Nashville for the filming of *The Showman's Daughter* documentary, the same trip they filmed the recording of 'Woodcarver'. We filmed on Music Row, in the Western shops, the Hall of Fame and the Ryman. I interviewed Owen Bradley, Brenda Lee, Harold Bradley and Charlie Dick. So, with all of that and with the backing tracks recorded, we headed back to Ireland.

I spent hours and hours sitting at our dining table going over my notes and recalling all my conversations in Nashville, turning them into Patsy's story, right up until her death, and then picking and inserting the best songs for the show. It took quite some time. For one thing, I had to learn all twenty-one songs. My sister, Barbara, also sang some Loretta Lynn songs. *The Patsy Cline Story* was booked into the Braemor Rooms in Dublin, a supper club. It sold out instantly, the whole three-week run! It made a big difference in how the audience received the show that I had spent all that time in Nashville, getting to know Patsy by spending time with the people who really knew her, who loved her and had worked with her. I could tell her story from the heart. I could also deliver the songs in a similar way. Hers was a funny story in part but also tragic. I was exhausted every night after the show. Patsy Cline's story and music has been a thread weaving its way in and out of my career from 1989 up to the present day. After my recording of 'Crazy', all the opportunities I'd been hoping for over the years began to appear. I became very protective of Patsy's family and legacy and I presented her story and music the very best way that I could.

It was fun and beneficial that I could wear two hats, Sandy Kelly and Patsy Cline, and work under the banner of each one. I loved doing the Patsy show this side of the pond and was the first anywhere to do it. In America, however, I wanted to perform as myself and, of course, always include some of the popular songs of Patsy's that I had recorded. I was offered the part in three different shows on Patsy in America, but I turned them down. There were hundreds of Patsy clones trying to make a career out of it in America but, to me, it was never about that.

After the first *Sandy* series, we did a concert tour at home, about ten dates booked by Kieran in some of the best theatres and venues in the country. We brought over Harold Bradley as bandleader and The Jordanaires as guests, as well as a young twelve-year-old fiddle player, David Duffy. He was supremely talented and had appeared on my television show twice (the only other artist to do that was Charley Pride). We put together a great show, which included songs from the TV show, plus The Jordanaires with songs they had performed with Elvis and, of course, we had a segment with The Jordanaires doing Patsy Cline songs.

The show drew good crowds and I loved every minute of the tour, but by the time I paid wages, travel (including airfares), accommodation, theatre hire, promotion and management commission, I had lost a lot of money that I honestly could not afford to. It's just awful to slog for months and have nothing but bills to show for it. Although I was busy, successful and had a huge viewership for my series, I could not keep up with my management commissions and personal bills, which ultimately led to me going to Branson in February 1992. When I returned from Branson that July, the situation at home in Ireland had got really bad financially and the tension between Kieran and me was at its worst.

A promoter in the UK, Mervyn Conn, had, years earlier, approached me when I was playing the Irish ballrooms in London, asking me to allow him to manage my UK and European career. This was during the years when Kevin McCooey was taking my bookings, from 1983 to 1988. Conn, who had worked with the Beatles as well as Johnny Cash and Dolly Parton, set up a meeting with me at his London office, but oddly, it was after office hours. I found him sitting alone behind his desk in his very lavish office. He trotted out the usual list of what he could do to make me a big star. My grandfather had taught me very well and I had twigged that there would be more to this partnership than singing when Mervyn went on to tell me that he found me very attractive and that when we were working in Europe we could travel together. He went on to invite me to discuss this further on his Chesterfield couch, offering me a drink and, as soon as I sat on the couch, he made a lunge at me, but missed. I ran out of the office and down the stairs like a March hare, where Mike was waiting for me outside. I'd had a bad feeling about the meeting from the get-go and had asked him to come with me. I knew that I was walking out of the office of the biggest country music promoter in the UK, but I had made it this far by focusing on the music and that would never change.

Years later, in 1993, the same promoter rang Kieran to book my Patsy Cline show, to bring it to the UK on a national tour. I decided to go over and meet with Mervyn to talk about the show, and it was as if we'd never met, both of us totally ignoring what had happened before. He wanted to take my script and turn my show into a full stage production with a cast and band of around twenty to twenty-five people. After meeting with Kieran and Shay, I decided to do it. This would be a brand-new musical, the first of its kind. Slim Whitman was coming to the UK and Mervyn put me on Slim's concert tour so that we could promote the new Patsy musical.

George Hamilton IV would also be on that tour. He had appeared on my television show and we had met a few times in Branson. While Slim, his wife Jerry and their son Byron travelled by limousine, George and I travelled in the coach with Slim's musicians. We had many great conversations on those long journeys. He was really excited to hear about the upcoming musical, because he had known Patsy really well and had toured quite a bit with her. He shared some wonderful stories about her, which showed her great sense of humour. He was very complimentary about my interpretation of her songs and that really gave me a huge confidence boost.

As I got to know George better, I realised that he had a mild and gentle way about him and he had the most fabulous speaking voice. It's no wonder he was known as the 'International Ambassador of Country Music'. George was also an incredible historian, not just of country music; during our travels on this Slim Whitman tour, he would give us the history of every castle, king and queen, and their battles along our way through the British countryside. At one point, one of Slim's musicians sarcastically asked, 'Hey George, do you know how many fish are in the bay of Bristol?' But it didn't dampen George's enthusiasm.

Slim, his family and musicians were the nicest people to work with, and the following year, Slim and his son Byron came to see one of the Patsy shows. I loved that tour. At the start of it, I was almost completely broken.

I'd worked, recorded and rehearsed non-stop since 1989 and, more recently, I'd been under constant threats from Jerry Purcell in New York. I also had more business pressures at home, so it was a devastating time for my family and me. We couldn't afford oil for the central heating at home and yet I couldn't walk down the street without someone recognising me and asking for an autograph. Nobody in Ireland would have believed the way we had to live during that time.

To be in such lovely company on the Slim Whitman tour, especially alongside George, was a joy. I unburdened myself to him and told him all that had happened with my career in the last few years, how I'd lost communication with Kieran and that I planned to bury myself in the Patsy Cline musical to try to support my family and retain my sanity. When Slim's tour was nearly at an end, I suggested to Mervyn Conn and George that it would be a great idea for George to narrate the Patsy story on the UK stage production. He would talk about her life and career, a friend reminiscing about old times. George genuinely loved and respected Patsy and he would bring that emotion to the script and, in turn, to the audiences. George was thrilled when Mervyn agreed.

The Slim Whitman tour ended and George returned to Nashville, as we began preparations for the new Patsy Cline show in the UK. Yet again, I was leaving my family and home, but at least this time I was only going as far as England. In London, I met the director of the new musical, a man named Johnny Worthy, and we hit it off immediately. Johnny himself had a successful career as an actor, dancer and singer, and had been in some of the great West End productions, including *Hair*. He really didn't know anything about country music or Patsy Cline, so we spent several days talking about that before he began taking links from my script and turning them into scenes and songs for the musical. George as the narrator would tell Patsy's stories, while also singing songs from other artists and telling his own stories of artists whom both he and Patsy had worked with. Gradually, the awful cloud of defeat, tiredness and anxiety eased as I immersed myself in this new project.

When Mervyn Conn and Johnny Worthy held auditions to cast for the show, people turned up in the hundreds. Some months later, George and I met up in London to begin our full-on three-week rehearsals with the rest of the cast. We would rehearse six days a week from 9am until 6pm. Our hotel was walking distance from the rehearsal rooms. On the walk over that first morning, to my surprise, we passed the Hibernian Ballroom, a dance hall where all the major bands from Ireland had played over the years, myself included. It was a strange to think back on those times while on my way to rehearse a brand-new and exciting show.

George and I walked into a room full of young, vibrant and good-looking actors, all sitting around the large rehearsal room, with a piano off to one side. I was very aware that these young people had studied at and graduated from some of the best drama colleges in the UK and had been in some really successful shows. I'd acted on my family's show as a child, and that was about the height of my qualifications, but I did have a lot of confidence.

I arrived in a black leather jacket, fitted denim jeans and the black leather cowboy boots with silver-tipped toes that Harold Bradley had bought me in Nashville. The only thing I was missing was a horse. God only knows what their first impression of me was! After introducing George and me, Johnny Worthy handed out the scripts. We'd have three weeks to memorise our lines and do the scenes. I would play Patsy in character for the first time ever, with the American accent, costumes, wigs, boots, hats, the whole lot! I was a bit daunted by the task, but George spent time with me every evening, working on the accent and lines. Rehearsals were gruelling. I had already been through all that and more for the television series and in Branson. I brought some of the costumes myself and the production company had some more designed or bought for me. Beautiful wigs made from real hair were styled especially for me in the West End. A selection of publicity shots were done, some just of me and some with George IV, and selected for promotion.

Opening night was approaching fast. We would be on tour for six weeks, doing eight shows a week: six evening shows and two matinees – on Wednesdays and Saturdays – in each theatre. We were to have two days of dress rehearsals before opening night. At this point, there were twenty people in the show, including a musical director and the band, some of whom would double up as characters in the story. We also had a full stage set, which was really authentic and well designed.

On the opening night, there was great excitement backstage. Cards, flowers, nerves, everything that's associated with any opening night. We were all ready. George, with his laid-back manner, was the anchor of the ship. He knocked on my dressing-room door to wish me a great opening night and gave me a beautiful bouquet. That same knock would arrive on my dressing room door for many years to come.

We toured the musical all over England, Scotland and Wales. It was a huge success, selling out theatres everywhere, all eight shows each week. Then came the great news that we would open in London's West End, in the Whitehall Theatre. Mervyn Conn and Johnny Worthy decided to change most of the cast and had organised auditions in London. George and I attended some of the auditions. For one thing, I had to go look at my two new husbands, as the two I already had in the show were being replaced. Rehearsals started again soon after.

It was 1994 and one of the hottest summers ever recorded in London. George and I had apartments beside Regent's Park, so I walked to the theatre every day to keep fit for the shows, and then afterwards, George and I would get the Tube back. The show had come a long way and was really slick. There was a brand-new set, which at times could turn into the Grand Ole Opry, fantastic colourful Western costumes and even some line dancing. It was worth the ticket price just to see George line dancing!

While I was touring the UK with *Patsy – The Musical* in 1993, Lou Robin, who had always been a good friend, got in touch. Lou informed me that in April of that year there had been a bankruptcy hearing in Springfield, Missouri, against David Green, the developer of Cash Country Theater in Branson. Johnny Cash and all the others had been represented at the hearing. I'd known absolutely nothing about it taking place. You can imagine my shock when Lou told me that Jerry Purcell had represented me and, even worse, he'd been awarded over $100,000 on my behalf. I was very angry.

I could not let him get away with any more. Most people I'd met seemed to be afraid of him, but I wasn't. Lou recommended a lawyer from Nashville, Ralph Gordon, who represented a lot of big country artists. I hired Ralph to bring court proceedings against Jerry Purcell in New York to get my money back. Under the terms of my contract with Jerry, any court proceedings that might arise had to be heard by an arbitration court and had to be in New York. I knew that New York was very much Jerry's turf and, given the background I'd since learned about where he came from and his dubious connections, I knew this would not be in my favour, but I hoped that justice and truth would prevail.

When the court date was set, I took a break from the musical and booked a flight from Dublin to New York. I was travelling alone, which wasn't ideal and, in this instance, potentially dangerous. A few weeks previously, Mel Tillis (a huge country star) had brought me back to Branson to offer me a job in his show. My excitement dissolved on arrival at the airport when the driver who picked me up to bring me to my hotel said that Jerry had found out and threatened Mel if he hired me. Then he showed me a hand revolver he had under his seat and told me my reservation was under a different name and not to answer my door. It was like being in a movie. Mel brought me to sing at his theatre that night but, sadly, I had to return home the next day.

At Dublin Airport, unusually, I was asked to go to the immigration interview room to speak to a member of staff. I'd never had a problem before and it actually looked as though they were waiting for me. But as I approached the office I felt more relaxed, as I could see the head of immigration waiting for me, whom I knew really well from all my travels to and from Nashville.

This was a totally different conversation from what I'd had on previous trips, however. I was asked to sit down and he had a file with my name on it. I was confused, but not for long. He and a colleague, with very stern expressions, opened the files and took out videotapes, plus a contract. He said, 'There has been a complaint lodged against you to immigration for working illegally in the United States.' I was totally shocked. I had never worked or visited the US without the proper documents or visas. I said, 'This is absolutely a lie. You've known me for quite some time coming through and there has never been a problem.' He said, 'What have you to say about this?' and played videos of television shows in the US that I had appeared on, and produced a contract for a concert with Willie Nelson, for thousands of dollars, with what was supposed to be my signature.

By now, I was furious. I asked, 'By any chance, was this complaint and evidence sent to you by a Jerry Purcell from New York?' He replied, 'Yes.' I opened my briefcase, put the paperwork for the court case against Jerry on his desk and explained it all to him. I was also able to prove that I had never worked in the US illegally. I opened my passport and asked him to compare my signature there with the signature on the Willie Nelson show contract. They were completely different. I told him I'd done nothing wrong and asked that he let me continue my journey to New York to defend myself and retrieve my money. He was convinced and said that I could board my flight, which was leaving shortly. I thanked him and, as I was leaving, he said, 'Have you ever considered a different career?'

I was the last person to board the flight. It was one of those uncomfortable occasions when you're the person responsible for the flight being delayed. I sheepishly made my way to my seat. But when I sat down, the reality of what had just happened hit me like a thunderbolt. This man was evil and it was becoming more and more obvious that he was going to stop at nothing to try and ruin me, my family and my career. I'd have to be on top of my game and on full alert when I landed in JFK.

On arrival, I took a taxi to the city, where I'd booked a modest hotel for myself. It was all that I could afford because I'd had to book a top-class hotel for my lawyer. Once checked in, under a different name for safety, I went across to a small supermarket to buy some food and water so that I wouldn't have to leave my room other than to go to the hearing over the next three days. Next morning, I put on a smart dress and, with my Padre Pio relic in hand, walked the short distance to the court, meeting my lawyer, Ralph, on the way for a quick catch-up.

The court wasn't a big room. There was a long table in the middle. I sat on one side with Ralph and opposite us sat Jerry Purcell and his secretary, whom I'd gotten to know fairly well when I'd lived in Branson. The arbitrator sat at one end of the table, at a distance and on a higher level. As Jerry glared across the table at me trying to intimidate me, I stared right back, unafraid. He was just a bully with a ton of money and people to do his dirty work for him. I didn't need any notes, because when you're telling the truth you don't need reminding. The happenings of the last two years were all too vivid in my mind. Ralph opened by staking my claim, with supporting documents and information. Then Jerry's secretary brought in piles and piles of paperwork. I mean, what the hell? I hadn't known him long enough for there to be that many files.

So, in a nutshell, I was looking for my settlement of $100,000+, minus his commission. Simple, you'd think. Jerry had his secretary lay out invoices, expense sheets, airfares, car rentals, the list went on and on. In reality, I'd seen this man in person maybe ten times, so where had all these bills come from? Then he produced a list of monies that RTÉ had paid for my TV series, plus a summary of payments for *Patsy – The Musical* in the UK. If you added it all up, the way he was telling it, I would actually owe him money by the end of the proceedings. I had my lawyer explain to the arbitrator that I had had my solicitor at home put in an addendum to my contract with Jerry, saying that his management excluded Ireland and the UK. I had done this as a safety net in case anything went wrong in the US, so that I'd be free to work in these territories.

This attachment to the contract had mysteriously disappeared and Jerry denied the existence of any such document. Next day at court, I had my Irish solicitor give evidence under oath by phone to the hearing that the addendum existed and was included in the management contract with

Jerry Purcell. Jerry practically laughed at this evidence. I knew then I wasn't going to come out of this well. The hearings came to a conclusion and before leaving, I went to the bathroom. Jerry's secretary was already in there and she said to me, 'Sandy, I'm really sorry, but I can't say anything, I would have to fear for my life.'

As Ralph Gordon and I walked back to our hotels, we discussed the events of the last three days in court. I was finding it really difficult to understand how someone could come into a supposed court of justice, with falsified evidence, false testimony and have it so easily accepted. Ralph said, 'Sandy, this is New York, Jerry Purcell's patch. It was never going to be easy.' And then he said, 'Have you ever considered a different career?' It was the second time I'd heard this in the space of a week.

Next morning, I caught a flight home and went to work, awaiting the court's decision. When it came, Jerry was awarded all of my money, plus costs. I was completely devastated. I buried myself even deeper into the Patsy musical, so at least I'd be able to feed my family. But from then until the day he died in March 2002, I was not allowed to work in the US. He took everything I had worked so hard for from under my feet, destroying my career in America.

Opening night arrived and the excitement was building backstage in the Whitehall Theatre. It was an old theatre but had great character. All the top British theatre critics were in the audience, which was daunting, but by this point, we had done all the publicity and all the rehearsing, so we were as good as we were going to be. Thank God, the opening night was successful, with many curtain calls. I even had to come back out to sing 'Crazy' again, as an encore. Mervyn had a booked a VIP club for the after-reception, and our families came: Mike, Willie and my daughter, Barbara, all came to see me, and George's wife, Tinky, came with their son George V and his wife, Lillian. That night was definitely one of the highlights of my career.

The show had a good run in the West End and, because I had my own apartment, my family were able to visit more often. I even sneaked home one Sunday, flying to Knock Airport and having lunch with them all. During our run in London and after endless weeks of touring, halfway through a show I became very ill and couldn't sing. It was decided during the interval to put on my understudy and I was brought back to my apartment to rest. I was so upset: I could count on one hand the number of shows I have ever missed. I saw a specialist in Harley Street, who said I was simply exhausted. So I rested for two days and then was back in the show, much to the disappointment of my understudy.

The next Friday was payday. I was in early to get ready for the matinee and collected my envelope at stage-door box office, as did George. On the way to my dressing room, I opened it and saw that money had been deducted for the nights I had missed. Furious, I picked up the phone in my dressing room and rang Mervyn Conn's office to speak to the accountant. He said that because I had been unable to appear in those shows, I would not be paid for them. With steam coming out of my ears, I told him that the reason I had lost my voice was because I was exhausted and overworked from touring the show and had not been given a proper break before the West End. Then I said that they might be able to put my understudy back on and they might well manage without me, but they'd have great difficulty putting on the show without my costumes, hats and boots, and I hung up.

I went down to the changing area, where my dresser had all my costumes pressed and ready for the show. I gathered them all up and, armful by armful, brought them to the stage door, dropped them in a pile and asked the stage-door manager to call a taxi. The message got back to Mervyn's office pretty quickly. The stage-door manager told me there was a call waiting for me. It was Mervyn's accountant to say that there was a courier on the way to give me my cheque. I called for my dresser to help me rehang my costumes before the rest of the cast came in. They never tried again after that to deduct money from my fees.

The Patsy Cline story has changed in its presentation over the years and when we finished with Mervyn Conn's production, George and I continued to tour the show with my band from Ireland and my sister, Barbara, doing all the Loretta Lynn songs. I promoted the show myself and we used various agents in the UK. We did that on and off for a few years and then a promoter called Robert Pratt of Chimes International in Glasgow offered me a very big tour in England, Scotland and Wales. Still working with George, I had the best time travelling over the years with the show in its different formats.

One night in the UK, we were performing in one of the oldest theatres I'd ever been in. On the very top floor there was a small solitary room that housed a little chapel with a wooden chair and a bible. I took a quick look but didn't linger as it was creepy. On the last night of the show here, I was singing the encore, 'Crazy'. Everything was going along as normal until it came to the last line of the song, 'I'm crazy for crying...' I opened my mouth to sing the line but it was not me or my voice that delivered the line, it was Patsy! I took my bow, hurried off the stage and couldn't return. I rushed straight to my dressing room, got down on my knees and started praying, shaking with fear.

I didn't know what had just happened. George came to my dressing room, all flustered, to see what was wrong. I told him and he suggested that we go up to the little church together to pray. I'm not the sort of person who gets easily carried away with stuff like that, but honestly, this knocked me for six. Maybe it was Patsy playing one of the pranks she was well known for!

Another funny story was that I always had my quick-change area at the side of the stage because I had eighteen costume changes in every show. My dresser would be there waiting to help me in and out of my costumes. On one occasion, I had a bottle of Harvey's Bristol Cream in there as I'd been battling with a sore throat. I'd just left the stage for my quick change and George was passing me on his way back to the stage for his next song. I got out of my dress in a split second and lifted the bottle of sherry to take a sip, not realising that George had unknowingly caught the curtain on the neck of his guitar, slowly pulling it back and revealing to a full audience a side view of me in an all-in-one black corset, swigging out of a bottle of sherry. Chatting to some people after the show, I found out they thought it was part of the story!

In 2014, George and I were due to do another big tour for Robert Pratt. Three weeks prior to the start of the tour, we got the devastating news that George had suffered a heart attack and died. I was in total shock. We had been in constant contact with each other and had become very good friends. He'd been like a father to me, always looking out for me when we were on the road together. He was the ultimate gentleman. Heartbroken, I wanted to cancel the tour, but Robert had been speaking to George V in Nashville and they both agreed that three weeks' notice was too short a window to cancel. George V offered to take his father's place and, during the show, he could pay tribute to his father. I agreed reluctantly because it was going to be very difficult to watch George's son stand on his spot every night. However, hard as it was, we did the tour and a few more after that.

George V would have made his father so proud; he did a wonderful job.

I shared the stage on the Patsy Cline show with George Hamilton IV first in 1993 and for the last time in March 2013. Our working relationship had spanned over twenty years, we had sung together at the Grand Ole Opry several times and been to Patsy's hometown – Winchester, Virginia – where we performed at the Patsy Cline Memorial concert during Labor Day weekend.

The first time we went, Charlie Dick showed me around Winchester, driving me to all the various places that Patsy had frequented, in his vintage convertible Cadillac. I thought I was back in the 1950s. We went to the drive-in movies where he and Patsy would go, to WINC radio station, where as a young girl she sang every week.

These weekends were great, with Patsy's fans coming together to remember her and her music. There was a dinner one night, and a hayride, even a big open-air show in the middle of a field, with a barbecue and moonshine, all hosted by 'Joltin' Jim McCoy and The Melody Playboys, who were the first band Patsy ever sang with. Of course, Charlie and George IV were there too. At one point, I counted twelve steel guitarists on the stage, or, to be more precise, on the back of the long trailer. I went into the little makeshift bar and asked for a glass of white wine, which they all laughed at. One of them replied, 'We country folk up here don't drink wine. All we got is beer or moonshine.' Not wanting to be a wimp, I said I'd take the moonshine. They handed it to me in a plastic cup and I took the first sip; my God, it was so strong I could hardly swallow the gulp! I took my time and nursed it, and even at that I got tipsy and ended up singing with Charlie on the announcement microphone on the bus all the way back to the hotel. I never drank moonshine again!

George brought me to visit Gaunt's Drugstore the next day, where Patsy worked during the day on the soda fountain. Mr Gaunt, the son of the former owner, had one of the original booths that Patsy would bring the sodas to. So we sat in that very booth for some photos. He showed us the till that she used when she worked there, and said she'd come into work wearing her hair in curlers with a scarf covering them, to prepare for her singing engagements that night. Before I left the drugstore, he gave me three little antique pillboxes that were from the time Patsy worked there, which I've kept all these years.

On our last day in Winchester, there was a lovely graveyard service and we all sang some of Patsy's songs. It was quite an emotional thing for me as Patsy had done so much for my career, and she meant a great deal to me through all her friends and family whom I had come to know. I had huge respect and admiration for the powerhouse of a woman she was. I'd come a long way from the day Shay Hennessy dragged me into the studio to record 'Crazy'. Even that day in the recording booth, I remember laughing to myself, begging her to lend me the song for a little while. With all my heart, I firmly believed she answered my prayers. I will forever be thankful to her.

# 18

# MY SISTER BARBARA – THE LATER YEARS

At the time The Duskeys had the dreadful accident in 1983 and Barbara was in hospital with spinal injuries, she was engaged to David Duffy, the only child of Ruth and Tom Duffy, of Tom Duffy's Circus. She was only twenty-one and I felt that both she and David were far too young to be thinking of marriage. They met when they were eighteen or nineteen and immediately had a connection. David was Barbara's first boyfriend. She would visit the circus show when she could and David would come to see Barbara sing when he could. It wasn't your regular dating type of thing because of the careers they both had. Barbara got out of hospital several months after the accident, but still had a way to go before she was allowed to be completely out of the body cast. In December 1983, she and David were married in Sligo Cathedral. Several hundred fans and friends waited along the street to see the bride. It was a wintry day, they were cold and she was late, but still they waited. They were not disappointed: the bride looked stunning in her vintage cream Irish lace dress with a coat to match and a beautiful flowing veil. She was a vision!

We, the bridesmaids, all wore cream and burgundy, as did Willie, who was pageboy, and my daughter Barbara, who wore a gorgeous cream dress and burgundy sash. My sister told me afterwards that when she was standing at the altar, she felt surrounded by the scent of roses, which we found out later is a scent associated with Padre Pio.

The reception was in the Sligo Park Hotel. The wedding cake was a three-ring circus to honour David and his family. All in all, it was a fabulous day. My father was ten foot tall with pride. When it was time for Barbara and David to head off on honeymoon, I was sad to see her go. The Duskeys had disbanded by now and I played out the dates alone until I made the transition to country music. She was about to start a new chapter in her life, learning how to play her part in Duffy's Circus. They toured all over Ireland, and made a very striking couple in the ring, David with his daredevil Spiderman aerial acts and then showing his beautiful Appaloosa ponies. Barbara would do her part as ring mistress, dressed in a long sequined tailcoat and top hat. The show was fantastic. Our father, Frank, toured with them for a while as a clown and a mechanic.

My son, Willie, would also spend summer holidays on the show, joining Dad and David in the ring as a clown. They used to do a fantastic Ghostbusters piece, where David, Dad and Willie, all dressed as clown versions of the Ghostbusters, with hoovers on their backs, would come out looking for the ghost, which would be hiding in a large wooden box in the ring. As the audience shouted and screamed, the ghost would creep out to capture Willie and hide with him back in the box, with the inevitable antics of the search to follow. When David and Dad would eventually rescue him, all three would sit on the box to keep the ghost secure, Willie pressing down with every bit of strength he had, genuinely terrified. They were good times and we became close to the Duffy family.

About three years into their marriage, things were getting a little strained. Barbara had lost what would have been their first baby to an ectopic pregnancy and was extremely sick after her surgery. She was finding the continuous moving from town to town very hard. Whenever we visited, I could plainly see that something had changed. After four years of marriage, sadly they separated and Barbara came back home. She was devastated and I'm sure that David was too.

Even after all these years, I'm glad to be able to say that David and I are very close.

From an early age, my sister could be difficult at times, but I put that down to the fact that Mum was the way she was and that Barbara, from the age of six, did not have much of a home life. Once Mum became sick, she was very different and didn't treat us with any affection. At such a young age, Barbara went from getting all of our parents' attention to getting practically none. Dad and I were also working a lot, as well as looking after Mum.

During those first months when Barbara was back home after her marriage broke down, it was hugely difficult even to talk to her. She was angry about her life and if Barbara didn't want to talk about something, we didn't. I invited her into my new band, as I thought it might help her if she got back to work again. It was a country band, but Barbara was no stranger to country music. She was a really great singer of country songs and loved doing them. Once she was focused on what we were doing musically and being busy, she felt a lot better.

By 1989, we were so busy we barely had time to think. Barbara was with me on all the trips abroad, my TV series and a lot of my Patsy shows. One of our most memorable trips together was in 1990 when the band and I were invited to entertain the Irish peacekeeping forces in Lebanon, the 68th Irish Infantry Battalion. What an adventure that was! Before flying out, we went to Finner Camp near Bundoran in Donegal to meet with some of the soldiers' families. It was very close to Christmas and naturally some families wanted us to bring Christmas parcels, but we had already been told that this was not possible; when we reached the border crossing between Israel and Lebanon, we would have to walk across and go through security checks. It was hard to refuse, but we had to. We promised to pass on messages, though.

Soon it was time to go to Lebanon. We had Mick McCarney on guitar, Gerry Mooney on drums, Eugene McMullan on piano and, of course, my own Mike Kelly on bass. We brought 'Gibby', our engineer, and a journalist from the *Sunday World*, Paul Williams, to cover the trip. We met at Dublin Airport to make the long journey to Israel. Some army personnel picked us up at the airport and brought us in a peacekeeping coach to the hotel we would stay in that night, before making the onward journey to Lebanon. It was a quaint place; the reception area was like something out of an Agatha Christie novel and I loved it. The army press officer travelling with us informed us that, for this trip, the guys in the band would be staying in separate quarters from Barbara and me.

I went up to our room ahead of Barbara, escorted by an armed soldier, which made me feel quite important, actually. He left me at the door, I made my way in and proceeded with a sort of ritual I always do in hotels, which has served me well over the years. One of the first things I do is pull back the bedclothes. On a rare occasion, you'd find more in the bed than you'd like to share with, and more than once I've found a large spider relaxing under the duvet. I began this ritual after being bitten on the leg one night and having a nasty wound the next morning.

On pulling back the bedclothes, I saw the biggest cockroach I've ever seen, and I screamed like a banshee. The soldier burst in through the door, gun at the ready, closely followed by Barbara, who thought there was intruder in my room. By this time the cockroach was on the move but, fair play, my security managed to chase him down. I don't know what his fate was but I asked our detail to go through every inch of that room to make sure it was a lone 'roach, while Barbara and I took refuge in the corridor. I don't remember us having a good night's sleep – we talked until we couldn't fight the tiredness any longer.

Our hotel was somewhere near Jerusalem. The next morning on our drive towards the border, Barbara and I were both shocked at how weary the landscape looked. Battle-weary. We'd imagined it would be old, rustic stone buildings, palm trees and sand everywhere, but that was just a romantic notion. When we got to the border crossing, we got out of the coach, collected our luggage and walked across the border, making our way through the security hut to show our papers and have our bags searched. We'd heard how women were treated in these countries, but it was eye-opening and disturbing when you were actually there, being totally ignored because you were a woman.

On entering Lebanon, we boarded a different bus with a new driver. We had been well briefed before we left Ireland, but the army press officer advised that, other than chatting to our own army personnel, we should say as little as possible. That wasn't going to be easy for Barbara or me, as we both liked to talk. We arrived at Camp Naqoura some hours later. It was just like the TV series *M*A*S*H*. We were formally greeted and brought into the main dining area and, much to the delight of the whole band, we were served a full Christmas dinner. Afterwards, Barbara and I visited the commanding officer in his sitting room for a chat. Everyone was delighted to see us and we them. Then it was on to Camp Shamrock, where we would stay for the next four nights, only leaving each day to do our concerts and visit soldiers in other units. Once again, we were greeted in full military style and with impeccable manners. A sea of smiling faces welcomed us. I hadn't expected our visit to mean so much to the soldiers.

We went to Lebanon to do two concerts, but in the end we did six. Barbara and I had our accommodation at the camp hospital: bunk beds in a room that had been meticulously cleaned and tidied. Lying in my bed, I could see pictures pinned to the wall beside me of a soldier's family, his wife and children, and thought how sad it must be both for the families at home and the soldiers, especially at Christmas. It made me appreciate just how much is sacrificed to serve on these missions.

Most of the concerts were open air. Big, white UN tanks would be parked in a semicircle for the soldiers to sit on, and probably served as protection too. Then there were several rows of chairs in front of a stage. It was great fun and we would call some of the soldiers up to join us. One had a great repertoire of Christy Moore songs, another came down off a tank to do Elvis.

Between shows, Barbara and I visited some of the smaller, more remote outposts. We would travel out by jeep, with an escort and wearing bullet-proof vests. The jeep driver didn't ever hang around! The more I saw of what the Irish peacekeeping troops were doing for the local people, especially the children, the more I respected them. On one of those visits, Barbara met Corporal Ian Corcoran from Sligo, whom she had briefly met once at home. Barbara was a very attractive woman. With her beautiful blonde hair, almond eyes and radiant smile, she could charm anyone. She spent most of the time chatting to Ian and they seemed to really get along. Ian was stationed at his outpost and didn't have a pass to come into Camp Shamrock for the concert the next day, but we managed to get special permission for him to attend.

On our last day in Camp Shamrock, Barbara and I were taken by minibus to a jewellery shop. We were escorted by UN tanks, one in front and one behind. Two soldiers accompanied us into the shop to talk for us, because although it was OK to sell to us and take our money, it was not OK for us to speak to the locals or make any kind of communication. We were totally ignored and I was annoyed. On the way back, I asked our driver why we needed so much protection. He said that we were in an area with a high risk of kidnapping. Barbara and I just looked at each other, because you didn't get that sense of danger. But sure, what did we know? We'd been there only four days and the only frightening thing that had happened was when we had to stop one of our concerts and go to a shelter because there was some shelling happening somewhere relatively close. One of the officers told us afterwards that the noise from our concert might possibly have been the cause of that shelling. They obviously weren't country music fans!

We were given a cake and flowers, which were presented to us by a bomb disposal robot. That was different! We were sad to leave Lebanon. All the peacekeeping soldiers, not only the Irish, were so impressive, and their good manners, behaviour and kindness have stayed with me. When I returned home, letters arrived every week from soldiers from various different countries and we stayed in touch for the longest time. Barbara, on the other hand, was writing to Ian Corcoran and they had arranged to meet on his return to Sligo.

We were extremely busy when we got back, doing a lot of Christmas shows. Then in January 1991, my TV series started its first run. Barbara met up with Ian on his leave, as planned. Eventually she let me know that they planned to move in together. I was a bit hesitant about that because it had taken her so long to get over her marriage to David. But she was a grown woman and free to make her own choices. I just wanted her to be happy. They duly moved in together and even got a dog, a gorgeous boxer named Sam. We'd visit each other's homes for dinner (Ian is a great cook) and whenever possible, we all travelled together on the road and Ian would help out.

They got married in 1994 and had their wedding reception at Markree Castle. It was a Christmas wedding, which was really lovely. It was such a comfort for me to see Barbara happy once again. I knew that she was hoping for a baby, but it wasn't happening. She'd had an awful experience with the ectopic pregnancy and had then had major surgery. Now she felt it was time to try again. On her doctor's advice, she decided to try IVF but, before starting treatment, they went on holiday to the Bahamas. And about a week after they left, Barbara rang, all excited, telling me she was pregnant. It was just the most wonderful news and they were both over the moon. This would be a whole new chapter for Barbara and I encouraged her to rest and mind herself. She only had to work when she could. Our dad, Frank, was also thrilled with the news. He and Barbara had been especially close all her life; Dad always looked out for her and she for him.

Although Dad was back living with us in Carrowgobbadagh, Barbara suspected that he was seeing Hazell McCready, the daughter of a Mrs

McCready, who used to come out to Dad's garage in Ballintogher some years earlier. I took into consideration that, at one stage, Dad had three girl-friends at the same time and used three different cars so that he wouldn't be found out. So, although I found it hard to believe that Hazell was one of the three girlfriends – she was rather eccentric – it was very possible.

Hazell would often come to our house looking for Dad, bringing dif-ferent dishes she'd made for him. Dad, if he was there, would hide in the bedroom and instruct me to say he was away. Barbara insisted she was right about his girlfriends, even interrogating Dad to try and get him to admit that she was, but no joy. In the end he wasn't able for the three girlfriends. The crunch came when he had to eat four Christmas dinners, mine being the last, and even I could see he was struggling. So, he narrowed it down to one and informed Barbara and me that he was seeing Hazell. You could have knocked us down with a feather. Now, don't get me wrong, Hazell was nice, but she couldn't have been more different from Dad. She was from a very upper-class family and had led a life of holidaying with family in large country homes and she herself had been brought up in a big lavish home in Sligo town.

So Dad was living at home with me and seeing Hazell. I discovered that he'd told Hazell that Barbara and I didn't approve of them being together. Which was kind of true, but we didn't interfere. Our uncle Pat, Dad's youngest brother, was home to visit and they went out for the day and vis-ited Hazell. When Pat came back to our house, Barbara and I were getting ready to go do a show. As I was making a cup of tea for Uncle Pat, out of the blue he said, 'That's a lovely wedding album Frank got done up.' 'What?' I said, 'No, sure Mam and Dad eloped. There were only two witnesses at the church, who's in the album?' He said, 'No, not that wedding. Your dad and Hazell's wedding last year.' Barbara jumped up, 'I knew it, I knew it!' and turned to me, saying, 'I was right all along about Hazell.' Apparently, almost a year previously, Dad and Hazell were married in Portnoo in Donegal, in the Church of Ireland church there. 'Wait a minute,' I said to Pat, 'Sure Dad is Roman Catholic.' 'Not any more' said Uncle Pat, 'He changed to Church of Ireland to marry Hazell.' They had a wedding, around twenty guests and a reception in a hotel in Portnoo. For once, we were speechless, which didn't happen too often.

When Dad arrived home, Barbara said, 'Dad, are you and Hazell married?' 'We are,' he said. I then asked, 'Why did you not tell us about the wedding?' Calmly, he said, 'Well, you girls were busy.' Then off he went into his room. We followed him in and there he was with a bag, packing his clothes. I said, 'Dad, what are you doing?' He said, 'I'm going to move in with Hazell. Sure I might as well now that ye know we're married.' I mean, what could you say to that? It was impossible to be annoyed at Dad for very long, he was too laid-back about everything.

Barbara had other things to think about anyway, such as preparing for her new baby. Another new chapter in our lives. Dad and Hazell seemed happy. I was doing really well in my career and Barbara and Ian were excited for the new arrival. It had been a long, long time since we'd had something to celebrate on a personal level as a family and we could hardly wait for the baby to arrive. On 30 April 1997, Barbara went into Sligo General and gave birth to a beautiful baby girl, Sandie Ellis Corcoran. Ian and I were at the hospital and the first to see baby Sandie. Ian was able to hold her in his arms as soon as she was born. She didn't cry at all, just stretched and yawned – so adorable! When visiting was over, we went down the town on a shopping spree. I bought teddies, babygrows, dresses, as many as I possibly could. When we got back to the hospital, you could hardly see Barbara or the baby with all the flowers and balloons people had sent. Dad and Hazell were there too, Dad lit up like a Christmas tree. I couldn't wait to tell Willie and Barbara about their new cousin. Willie was eighteen years old and I wasn't sure he'd be that excited, but I couldn't have been more wrong, and Barbara was exactly the same. They immediately fell in love with Sandie, as did we all.

Our first Christmas with Sandie was special, because we sat her at the table in her high chair. An extra chair at the table is something to be treasured. I don't like the sadness of empty chairs at the table when you lose someone. In years to come there would be far too many empty chairs at my table.

Ian and Barbara bought a new house in Ransboro, County Sligo, to raise Sandie, and eased into parenthood well. Barbara was back singing in my band and then Ian, still in the army, would mind Sandie when Barbara was working. When we toured the UK, Ian, Sandie and my daughter Barbara came with us. The first thing to be unloaded out of the truck was a big cuddly toy, Barney the Friendly Dinosaur, and Sandie's pram. Those tours were pretty hectic. I'd gone from starring in the West End to touring with the Waltons and Barney!

It wasn't easy for Ian and Barbara looking after Sandie, both having such different careers. Sometimes Ian would be going to work when Barbara was getting back from a gig. So, once again, Barbara's marriage seemed strained.

By the time Sandie was six years old, her parents had separated and once again, Barbara was very angry. It was she who'd wanted the separation. She and Sandie moved to Strandhill to be near our dad, who was now living there. Barbara made new friends and Sandie new playmates. As always, they had animals: two dogs, and a cat called Blue. I had moved away from Sligo in this period because Mike and I, too, had separated. When in Sligo, I would sometimes stay with Barbara and Sandie and bring my daughter Barbara. We all loved Strandhill and the people there. Dad was now in his early eighties and his health was failing. He had dementia, although he still retained his great sense of humour.

Barbara was frustrated with the situation and her mood swings were getting worse and worse. We did not realise the number of different medications she was on because she never discussed it with us and, if you broached the subject, it was full-on war. In 2013, when our dad passed away, Barbara was crushed. Dad was the most incredible man and had always been there for us. He died aged eighty-four, having spent his last seven months in the luxury of Summerville nursing home in Strandhill with Hazell. Barbara and I sat together with Dad in his last hours and my son, Willie, was with him when he passed. We miss him hugely.

Sandie was now grown up and ready to go to university. It was a huge achievement for her. When she was accepted into University College Dublin, my sister was ten foot tall. Sandie would leave home and live on campus. By this time, I had also moved to Strandhill, not far from the family.

I'm not going to try to understand what went on in Barbara's mind during those difficult times. There is absolutely no question that I totally loved and adored her. Did she annoy and upset me sometimes? Definitely. And on occasion, she could bring me to tears. But I also have to take some responsibility for the way that I am. I was and still am difficult at times. I like everything to be in order and have little or no tolerance for people who don't work hard to achieve the best version of themselves. Of course Barbara achieved a lot in her life, but her approach was more laid-back. We were two totally different people. On the other hand, we could separately go shopping for fashion and come back with exactly the same thing. If I got an ache or pain, she got it. Once she declared she had the same toothache as me. The dentist X-rayed our teeth and said he'd never seen anything like it: we had identical abscesses. We were like twins, although eight years apart.

There had been a strain on our relationship since Dad died, which gradually became worse. In 2017, we had a disagreement that led to her requesting some distance, which I respected. Throughout all the years, we'd had disagreements, but we had always managed to resolve them, so I didn't think this time would be any different. Sandie and I were still very close, so at the very least I would know how Barbara was doing through speaking with Sandie.

Barbara decided to leave Strandhill, which, in hindsight, may have been a mistake because she had so many friends there whom she'd meet on her daily walks with her dogs in the village. When she moved to a little mid-terrace cottage in the village of Dromahair in County Leitrim, I thought she'd make friends easily. Barbara was very friendly, with a great personality. It was especially nice that her best friend from school in Ballintogher and once Granny Bee's neighbour, Maggie, was living nearby and also her dearest friend, Nuala Mulkeen, who visited often and had been a rock to my sister through all the years, and who today still helps me with her friendship and love. But Barbara was struggling and none of us realised how deep those struggles ran.

September 2018 was the last time I saw my sister. I was going to work on a cruise ship and had invited Sandie to join me. Mike and I were at the train station waiting for Sandie when we saw Barbara coming towards us. She looked drained and tired, but I hadn't really time to think anything of it. She put her arms around me and hugged me and something felt different. As she had her arms around me, she said in my ear, 'Mind my girl.' She hugged Mike and then, like a whirlwind, she was gone again. I just assumed she meant to mind Sandie on the cruise. When we got back from the cruise, everything went back to how it had been. I would hear the latest updates on my sister from Sandie, Maggie and Nuala.

Barbara's fifty-seventh birthday was on 8 October 2018, and I thought about her all that day. I resisted the want in me to reach out to her because we still hadn't reconnected since the brief meeting at the train station. That night I felt very uneasy, sitting up into the early hours of the morning.

The next morning, I got my daughter ready to go into respite when Sandie called me from Dublin, saying that she hadn't been able to reach her mother that morning or the night before. I tried calling my sister's phone and then called Willie to let him know something was wrong. After dropping Barbara off, I asked Mike to drive me to Dromahair. We had only set out when my mobile rang. It was Willie, who said, 'Mum, Barbara is gone.' I asked, 'Gone where? What do you mean she's gone?' and he replied, 'She passed away and has just been found by the gardaí.' Mike had pulled over the car by now. The only way I can describe my reaction was pure and total insanity. I completely broke down. I just wailed, saying 'No' over and over again. I could not let myself believe it.

My thoughts immediately turned to Sandie. How would I be able to tell her? I can't remember a lot of what happened over the next hours and days. Sandie came home but we didn't tell her the awful news until she arrived, although she too had a bad feeling. Part of me is glad that I don't remember all the details of the next few days, because it was a horrible, horrible nightmare. When I was told Barbara had taken her own life, it completely destroyed me. If only I had reached out, things might have been different. But that is something I will never have the answer to and I will have to live with forever.

Grief never leaves you; it walks alongside you. It has been painfully difficult to write this chapter. When I first began it, back in 2018, the chapter started, 'I have a sister ...' and three weeks later, she was gone. The pain of losing her rips deep into every part of my being and she rarely leaves my thoughts. Although Barbara was born eight years after me, and four years after my late brother Francis, we had a unique bond from the beginning. One of my main jobs became looking after her and then, in later years when Mum became sick and totally dependent on us, I became more of a mother figure in Barbara's life. At times, this was difficult and challenging, causing conflict on occasions. We had the very best of times and the hardest of times. My sister Barbara was beautiful, talented, kind to a fault, amazingly funny when she wanted to be and had a fantastic sense of humour. I will always remember her laugh. She could brighten up any room. Running alongside that, though, she was troubled and in pain. Like many, she struggled with mental illness. Suicide is not a word that you hear every day because it's not something people talk about. However, since my sister's tragic passing, many people have reached out to us to share their own experiences because we have the same pain in common. My heart goes out to any family who has lost someone to suicide. I will spend the rest of life missing Barbara every single day, and seeing her in Sandie. There is a large gaping hole that will never and can never be filled. As a family we hope she has found peace and, of course, we do our best to support and mind her girl, Sandie. We are blessed to have her in our lives and I will never be able to measure how much Sandie has helped me through these past few years.

# 19

# LEAVING IT ALL BEHIND

In August 2018, Willie arranged for me to reconnect with John Carter Cash at Cash Cabin studio, to make plans for recording my new album. Willie had already spent quite some time choosing the songs that we felt would suit me, and also wrote one song for the album. Just two months later, my sister Barbara passed away and I was in no way able to proceed with the project. It wasn't until August 2019 when I felt emotionally strong enough again, and we went back to Cash Cabin to start the album. I knew that recording this album wasn't going to be easy, as the songs reflect my stories and the place I'm at in my life now. Singing them would be very emotional but working with my son had helped me brace myself for the task and journey ahead.

We spent two weeks at Cash Cabin. Our mornings started at 7am (which is the middle of the night to me) and we'd be at the studio at 8.30am to begin the day's recording, not finishing until 6pm every day, except for lunch and a couple of coffee breaks. It was a complete luxury to have Willie organising everything, much as Shay Hennessy or Harold Bradley had done in my earlier career. This recording session at the cabin would be the first of two; we would lay down the tracks with the live band and then return in a couple of months to finish the vocals.

As we made our way to the studio, I was quite nervous, but once there, that nervousness left me because it is such a tranquil place. It's easy to see why Johnny Cash loved it and found so much peace there. He built the cabin in 1979 in a huge woodland across from his home, a place where he could be alone and write and sometimes spend time with his young son, John Carter.

The first morning we arrived before the musicians. While John Carter and Willie chatted about the songs, I went for a walk for a little while to gather my thoughts. It was a beautiful August morning, with birds chirping in the trees above and I could see wild deer in the woodland. I'd been here before, but this time it felt different. I was different. A lot of the people I loved and admired were gone, but I was still here. I felt very alone. I wondered if, when Johnny stayed out in these woods, he had felt lonely. Then I had a flashback. On one of my visits to Nashville back in the 1990s, Johnny had called me one night from the cabin. We chatted for the longest time and we laughed a lot. As usual, he was kidding around and took great pleasure in winding me up.

My loneliness left me as I stood looking at the old rustic wooden steps that led to the cabin door. I could imagine Johnny, June and John Carter sitting there on the porch in days gone by. I realised that his calling me that night from his quiet space meant he really had cared about me and had valued our unlikely but special friendship. I felt emotionally energised and not afraid. I would go into the studio and make the best album I could.

Inside the cabin, the walls breathe the Cashes and the Carters. They'd all spent time there and in 1999, when it became a studio, they recorded there. Johnny and June both did their last recordings in these very rooms. Private family pictures hang on the walls, instruments, Mother Maybelle's auto-harp, a Carter family handcrafted patchwork quilt on the wall, the wooden cross from one of Johnny's last videos – 'Delia's Gone' – and the very last picture of Johnny Cash, taken by Marty Stuart, hangs majestically with Johnny like a Native American warrior chief looking over the musicians. Though I had been uneasy about what the experience would unlock in my mind, now I felt cocooned by the sense of warmth around me. I was exactly where I should be and my heavenly choir would look after me.

Our day began and, one by one, the musicians arrived. They knew each other, of course, so there was instant chemistry in the room. I loved the way everyone sat together, listening to the songs in turn and, rather than be told what to play, they were given the freedom to share their own ideas and contribute their own choices to each song, working it out together as musicians. It worked perfectly, and why wouldn't it? John Carter and Willie had assembled some of Nashville's greatest musicians. These guys had played on multi-platinum worldwide hit albums: Chris Leuzinger on electric guitars, Robby Turner on steel guitar, Jamie Hartford on acoustic guitar, Dennis Crouch on bass, Tony Harrell on piano, Matt Combs on fiddle and man-dolin, and Sweepy Walker on harmonica. We had three different drummers across the sessions: Rick Lonow, Derrek Phillips and Jay Bellerose. Ana Christina Cash and Raina Murnak were on backing vocals. Plus, we had a special guest appearance from Marty Stuart, who played mandolin and added backing vocals on a couple of tracks. There was also Chuck Turner and Trey Call, both engineers on the record.

I was back to myself, relishing getting to sing with these musicians. I sang from the vocal booth and they played together out in the main room. It felt more like a live concert than a recording session. John Carter and Willie both knew what they wanted from the recordings, which made it all easier. The entire first two weeks moved along like that, with the guys sharing some great road stories and we had some wonderful laughs.

When we returned in November to do my vocals and the backing vocals, Shay Hennessy came with us. This would be his first time to hear the new songs. He had been on this journey with me for a little over thirty years, so I was delighted that he was with me on this very personal trip. He loved everything he heard, which meant a lot to me.

During the time I spent at the cabin, a lot of my lost family and friends came back to join me when I was singing, even making it difficult for me to sing at times. But at this cabin, nobody watches the clock; it's only about making truthful, honest music. On the first day, I noticed a rocking chair in the control room with the letters 'J.C.' carved into one of the armrests. John Carter said that his father had carved those initials and that it was the rocking chair from their kitchen. I'd seen it before: it was the chair Johnny Cash was sitting in when he asked me to record 'Woodcarver'. I sat in that chair every day I was at the cabin. Some months earlier, we had asked John Carter to store a box for us that Harold Bradley's daughter, Beverly, had sent on after Harold passed away early in 2019. As it was our last day in the studio, we opened it there in the cabin. Inside, Harold had stored tapes, song charts, photos, bios of everything we'd ever done together. It was as if he'd wanted it to happen like this, to join us in that room.

We took the original recording of Johnny and me out of the vault. John Carter and Willie had some ideas to change it a little. I wasn't quite sure how I'd feel about that, but having heard how new and fresh it sounds, I love it. When they played the original version back to us, it included Johnny and me chatting, and Johnny, of course, kidding around. It was like he was right there in the room with us.

After thanking John and Ana Christina Cash for their wonderful hospitality, John and Willie for their love and creativity, Trey Call and Chuck Turner for their workmanship, I left. I looked back in tears as Willie and I drove away. I had unshackled myself from the weight to which my heart was tethered for so long. By recording those songs and writing this book, I've allowed my ghosts to visit me and stay a while.

I've survived the sadness in my life by holding on to the good things, reminding myself every single day that, although there are some wounds that won't ever heal, I am truly blessed in so many ways. I've known some of the most interesting and wonderful people who ever lived, from all walks of life. I've travelled and worked with some of the most creative and talented people imaginable, including all the singers and musicians I've had the good fortune to share a stage with here in Ireland.

I feel very fortunate to have always had loyal and close friends throughout my life and, although I don't see them on a regular basis, I know that they are there if I need them. During the most difficult times for me, my friends John and Marie Mulligan, John Crosby, Robert Topliss, Neillie Keeney, Margaret Craig, Geraldine Brown Clark Andy Landis, Shay Hennessy and David Duffy have stood shoulder to shoulder with me, always helping me to come out the other side. I am eternally grateful to them.

One of my dearest and closest friends, Philomena Begley has always been supportive, but never holding back when I needed someone to pull in the reins. She's someone to whom I can always pick up the phone and talk about almost anything. Philomena and I have worked together a lot, especially in recent years. The amount of fun we have is unreal. I have great admiration for her as an artist and as a person. She's funny, caring and kind. I'm fortunate to have her as a friend.

My dear and loyal friend Nuala Mulkeen has supported me through some of my saddest times; in joining me out on the road, we've had some great laughs and memories. I will always have a special place in my heart for Nuala, as I will, for the same reasons, for John Crosby and Robert Topliss.

In the early 2000s, when my career had subsided somewhat, I didn't know how to turn it around. I approached a promoter in Dublin, Pat Egan, to work with me on bringing my profile back up. Pat agreed and did a fantastic job. From 2006 onwards, I was once again flying high. I was selling out the Ulster Hall in Belfast, the Helix and National Concert Hall in Dublin, the Opera House in Cork and the Limerick Concert Hall. I was interviewed by every magazine and newspaper and I was on every television show. Someone said to me jokingly at the time that the only thing I hadn't done on television was read the news. Pat was a fantastic manager and still today I count him amongst my dearest friends.

What matters to me most now is my family and my close friends, and spending more time at home. Covid forced us to stay at home and be more isolated. Initially, it was extremely challenging, but it made me step off the treadmill that I'd been on for most of my life. Time stood still, which gave me the opportunity to take a breath, reflect on life and think about my future and what I would like for the years that are left to me. I'd never done that before. I've always been driven, ever since those early years when, as a three-year-old, I was part of my grandfather's travelling show. I barely took time to have my children, and that is something I very much regret.

I'm now fortunate enough to live by the ocean, and it holds a huge healing power for me. As I lie in my bed at night, I listen to the Atlantic waves; it's a calming feeling that allows me to think and reflect about what truly makes me happy. It's very simple, really: the highlights of my life are now in seeing what my family has achieved.

My son, Willie, is a singer-songwriter, musician, record producer and a music industry professional. In previous years, he achieved great success with an amazing band he co-founded, Rackhouse Pilfer, a bluegrass rock band. In more recent years, I've had the wonderful experience of working on my book alongside the album with him. In fact, it was Willie's idea for me to record a new album and write this book. Willie has been a huge driving force and inspiration for me in recent years when going through my grieving. There were times I didn't want to be creative but Willie kept encouraging me to still dream.

In 2008, Willie met a very tall, beautiful girl from Estonia, Kristiina Muru, who'd recently moved to Sligo. They have been together ever since and she has become very much a big part of our family and has opened us up to a whole new and amazing culture, which I have grown to really love. I didn't know anything about Estonia, but the more I see and hear, the more I want to know. We've become very close to the Muru family, who come to Ireland to visit a lot, and recently we had the opportunity to visit their home, which was an amazing experience. On Christmas Eve in 2014, Willie brought Mike, Barbara and me for a drink in Hargadons, in Sligo. With our drinks in hand, we got the most amazing news. Mike and I were going to be grandparents and Barbara an aunt for the first time. Once Barbara processed this news, the baby could not come quickly enough for her.

When our new grandson was born, it was the week of the fleadh in Sligo. The town was buzzing, and so were we. Kristiina's mother and father, Merle and Mark, and her granny Elgi had all made the journey to Sligo to welcome the new baby. He is named Frank Juhan, after his Irish and Estonian granddads. I wish Dad had lived another little while to meet his great-grandson. Frank Juhan has brought so much joy into our family and I'm sometimes amazed at this little boy and the bond that has formed between him and his Aunty Barbara. They play games together and Frank does his very best to come up with ideas to entertain her and never tires of the challenges that can occur. On occasion he even gently reminds me that Barbara cannot help it if she kicks up a fuss, because she has special needs, which I find amazing.

Some of my favourite times are as a granny, when I collect Frank from whatever is in his daily routine – school, swimming or music – and listen to him relaying all the events that took place in his day. He'll FaceTime me to share some of his new ideas, whether it's for a design or an intro he's working on with his blue Fender guitar that Santa brought. It brightens my day to hear his infectious laugh and he has injected new excitement into every day for me.

I think of Granny Bee often and, while I've been honest about how strict she was, in all honesty she is partly responsible for my own strength. She showed us tough love, but that prepared us for our lives ahead. She herself had a very difficult life and that's why she found it so hard to show any soft emotions to us.

Granny Bee lived on her own until she was ninety-five years old, in her little house in Ballintogher, and I visited with her as often as I could. Bringing her to Sligo sometimes to buy groceries in Tesco. It was usually a Sunday as we rambled up and down the aisles, checking the prices advertised in the *Sligo Champion* against the prices on the shelves. Only so she could have it out with the person behind the till when she'd finished. I used to dread it, because this was at a time when everyone knew who I was. They'd see me every Sunday right after the nine o'clock news on RTÉ. As we'd pack Granny Bee's messages into the car, she'd say to me, 'You better get me home because you're on television above in RTÉ tonight.' She had no concept of pre-recording for television and thought that, on a Sunday right after she did her shopping, I was high-tailing it up to Dublin to do my TV show. It was hilarious. Though she'd never admit to watching my show.

Unfortunately, she had a fall and, after spending some time in Sligo General, she moved to Nazareth House to live out her days. She loved it there and the staff loved her, doting on her, saying how sweet and gentle she was. Which we all found funny, but she did find a gentleness in her remaining years. It was such a joy for us all to visit with her. She had a very loving bond with my son, Willie, and my dad even went to visit her on a regular basis.

On her birthdays, the staff in Nazareth House would have a party for her. My sister Barbara and I would bring in musicians, usually Willie and his friends, and we would sing for her. The last time we got to celebrate was her 106th birthday. We were all there, Mike, Willie, Barbara, my sister Barbara and Sandie. I sang my heart out to her.

The lovely nun in charge said, 'Now, Mrs Fallon, aren't you very lucky to have your granddaughter Sandy here to sing for you?' She said, 'Huh! She's singing the same auld songs this thirty years.'

I loved Granny Bee dearly and I miss her. I'm grateful that I was with her in the end. Thankfully, I was home. The sister in Nazareth House rang me and said I needed to come in because Granny Bee was very low. I asked if they could put her on life support, to which the nun replied very gently, 'Well, she is one hundred and six … It's a big age.' I arrived by Granny Bee's bed within fifteen minutes and it was just as though she were sleeping. I sat by her side and held her small, frail hand. I told her that I loved her and, not long after, she very peacefully took her last breath. I know it's a strange thing to say, but it was the beautiful passing of a great, strong, independent woman of her time and I was honoured to be there with her.

It is such a wonderful thing to have Kristiina in my life and in our family. Apart from making my son happy and being a great mum to Frank, she creates a beautiful sense of family in a warm, loving and caring way. The days we all come together as a small but committed family around her dinner table or mine, and have conversations over great food, led and enlivened by Frank, are the best.

I've been blessed to have my niece, Sandie, living with me since the day her mother passed away, sharing with me her love and strength. She's beautiful in every way, and has been a rock for me and encouraged me to believe in myself. She carried on with her education while dealing with her grief and graduated from UCD in English and drama. As I sat watching her graduation ceremony, I knew how proud her mother would have been and I wish more than anything that she could have been there to see it herself. Thankfully, Sandie's dad, Ian, was there. To say I'm proud of Sandie is an understatement. She is a strong, independent and caring young woman. Being her aunt is one of my greatest joys.

For all the challenges my daughter Barbara faces in her life, and I can't say that any of it has been easy for me either as a mother, she has brought so much understanding and an awareness to all of our lives that we would not have had if things had been different. As a family, we have a deep understanding about other people's needs and rights. Barbara herself is one of the most caring and loving people you'll ever meet and has greatly enriched the lives of those who know her.

Although Mike and I are divorced, we've known each other almost fifty years. We have a shared history and that's very important to us, and that's why to this day we are still so close and support each other.

I also have to thank my dear friend Shay Hennessy, for his encouragement and, of course, the late Michael O'Brien of The O'Brien Press, who would ring me over these few years on a regular basis, giving me advice and the confidence I needed to write this book. He had wanted to publish it without ever reading a chapter. He never got frustrated with me and his encouragement gave me the push I needed to keep writing.

To those who tried to silence my voice, I forgive you. I'm still singing; it's my safe place. I may not always want to do it, but I always feel better when I do. To those who always had my back and shared their love with me, I will always carry you in my heart. I've lived through the worst of times and the best of times and in doing so I can say that I have lived. The bad stuff, I'm now leaving it all behind.

Yes, I am blessed today. I live a very happy and simple life. I live in my favourite place in the whole world, Strandhill, County Sligo, a beautiful and historic place. I'm surrounded by great friends, both near and far, a family whom I love and am proud of. On any evening that I'm home, I can walk out my front door and visit one of my favourite pubs, listen to some great music, chat and have a nice glass of white wine or walk with the dogs on the beach. Not a bad life.

Many people have loyally followed me and my career. Whether I was singing on the back of a trailer or in a big concert hall, they would be there, and I have always been very grateful for that. Thank you all and I hope we can continue the journey together. Anything could happen, as I've found out.

*Love Always*
*Sandy*
*The Showman's Daughter*

# ACKNOWLEDGMENTS

My heartfelt gratitude to those who have helped and inspired me, particularly the following:

Shay, Alan and Ian Hennessy (Crashed Records) for your continued support and friendship.

Michael O'Brien, for his belief and inspiration; Paula Elmore and all the team at The O'Brien Press, for your dedicated work.

Mike Kelly, for your support.

Sandie (Ellis): I will always love you. I'm eternally grateful to you for the time you spent helping me with this book and encouraging me to once again to believe in myself.

Willie, I'm beyond proud of what we've created with the album and the book. Enduring some emotional challenges and dedicating a lot of time, we finally got there. Your creativity and passion are something to behold. Your belief in me has never waned. The journey so far has been beautiful and I'm looking forward to what the future brings us.

I love you all

# INDEX